Altruism

An

Communication

Beauty

Definition

Quiddities

Ideas

Euphemism

Free Will

Creation

Gender

Language Drift

Impredicativity

Knowledge

Marks

Necessity

Mathematosis

Truth

Negation

Paradoxes

Rhetoric

Semantic Switch

Tolerance

Universals

Quidditics

An Intermittently Philosophical Dictionary

W. V. QUINE

The Belknap Press of
Harvard University Press
Cambridge, Massachusetts

Copyright © 1987 by the President and Fellows of Harvard College
All rights reserved
Printed in the United States of America
10 9 8 7

Typeset in Linotron Bembo and designed by Marianne Perlak

Library of Congress Cataloging-in-Publication Data

Quine, W. V. (Willard Van Orman)
Quiddities : an intermittently philosophical dictionary.

Includes index.
1. Philosophy—Dictionaries. I. Title.
B945.Q53Q54 1987   103'.21   87-11974
ISBN 0-674-74351-2 (alk. paper) (cloth)
ISBN 0-674-74352-0 (paper)

To three stalwart Arthrites

Frederic Cassidy

Harold Cassidy

Edward Haskell

Preface

This is one of a loosely linked series of loose-knit books inspired by Voltaire's *Philosophical Dictionary*. As Voltaire remarked of the Holy Roman Empire, *mutatis mutandis,* his was neither philosophical nor a dictionary. Mine is philosophical in part, but lowlier themes occupy more than half the book and afforded me more than half the fun, philosophy being on the whole no laughing matter.

The one trait that the book shares with a true dictionary, namely alphabetical order in lieu of structure, brings grateful release from the constraint of linear exposition. Cross-references abound, but they refer forward and backward indiscriminately, there being no presumption that the reader will read the eighty-three pieces in one order rather than another.

My thanks to my wife and to Maud Wilcox and Camille Smith of Harvard University Press for helpful criticisms and suggestions.

W.V.Q.

Contents

Quiddities

Alphabet

Writing as we know it is an encoding of the spoken word. There is a conventional correlation, rough but vital, between the shapes and the sounds. This convenient arrangement is the result of a convergence of what at the dawn of history had been two distinct technologies, the immemorial technology of speech on the one hand and a crude technology of picture-writing on the other.

On the face of it, picture-writing is limited to the depiction of the visible. The limitation was transcended, to a degree, by happy metaphor; for example an early Egyptian hieroglyph for *bringing* depicts a bowl with feet. But the full power of writing awaited the convergence of writing with speech, and this reached its early stages five thousand years ago. Depictions of visible objects came to be pressed into phonetic duty on the rebus principle, as if in English we were to write *melancholy* by depicting a melon and a collie. This expedient was rendered more flexible and powerful, if less picturesque, by devoting the phonetic representations to brief sounds—single consonants or syllables. The sound was represented by a hieroglyph depicting something whose name merely began with that sound. The rebus principle thus gave way to an acrophonic one.

It was a notable step of abstraction. Finding a melon and a collie in melancholy is a matter of punning with familiar words; extracting a meaningless *me-*, on the other hand, and a mean-

ingless -*lan*-, and so on, calls for appreciating fugitive sounds
that are not words and name nothing.

How ever to divide smooth-flowing speech into short segments was less evident than we who were weaned on letters
are apt to think. You cannot even pronounce a lone *b, d, k, p,*
or *t* without appending at least the whispered ghost of a vowel.
The syllable was the more accessible unit in the early seg-
menting of the stream of speech. Syllabaries, not alphabets,
were the medium of writing in Mycenae, Cyprus, and perhaps
Crete in the second millennium B.C.

Egypt had already had its syllabary, of a sort, for a thousand
years. The hieroglyphs retained their ideographic use from
pictorial times, but doubled as syllabary. Egypt suffered an
embarrassment of riches, like modern Japan; for the Japanese
use their *kana* or syllabary in combination with Chinese ideo-
grams that could be spelled out in *kana* as well.

Egypt's syllabary was already a partial alphabet, in effect,
thanks to a pervasive trait of Egyptian and neighboring languages. The trait is internal inflection. We in English have a
bit of it in *give* and *gave, strive* and *strove, goose* and *geese, mouse*
and *mice.* Adequate written communication could be achieved
while leaving the inflection to the imagination. Ignoring it
meant letting a single character stand indifferently for *ba, be,
bi, bo,* and *bu,* and a single one for *da, de, di, do,* and *du,* and
so on. It was an ambiguous syllabary, one might say; or,
consonant-conscious as we now are, we might describe it as a
matter of writing the consonants and skipping the vowels. This
is how one does describe the writing of Hebrew and Arabic,
where the practice continues to this day. A name for this practice, suggested by considerations of symmetry, is *ebisceration.*
Evisceration being excision of the bowels, *ebisceration* connotes
similar treatment of the vowels.

The names of the letters in Hebrew and Arabic recall the
ancient acrophonic origins. *Aleph* means 'ox', and the letter
aleph presumably derives from a hieroglyph for the ox; *beth*
means 'house'; *gimel* means 'camel'.

Since vowels can be pronounced in isolation while many consonants cannot, it is ironical that it was the consonants that first got isolated. When vowels began at last to emerge in the alphabet, I suspect that it was due to a happy confusion. Aleph and ayin were frail consonants, glottal stops, that might disappear from a dialect or fail to register on a foreign ear. Given further that aleph was usually followed by the vowel *a*, the term 'aleph' might easily get misconstrued as denoting that vowel. Such perhaps was the course from aleph to alpha. That from ayin to *o*—omicron, omega—may have been similar. By the eighth century B.C., at any rate, a full complement of vowels was enjoying recognition on Greek soil, whither a Phoenician script had been imported by Cadmus if legend is to be believed.

Well after our Latin alphabet was established, the early Roman poet Ennius reverted imaginatively to picture-writing within the alphabetic medium. "*Saxo cere-comminuit-brum,*" he wrote, as much as to say "He split his brain with a stone"; and Ennius suited the word to the action by splitting the word *cerebrum*, 'brain', with his verb.

I am indebted to Peter Geach for the example, and for the word that describes it: *tmesis,* the sandwiching of one word in another. It happens also in Portuguese verbs; see INFLECTION. It happens at home, too, or just down the street: *a whole nother ball game.*

Altruism

Altruism is the main stem of morality and the primary concern of moral principles. The landlady says of her student lodgers that they are *good* boys, while knowing full well that they gamble, curse, drink, drive to endanger, and consort with loose women. What does she mean? Just that they are reasonably altruistic.

Altruism ranges from a passive respect for the interests of

others to an active indulgence of their interests to the detriment of one's own. It ranges from the barely erogatory on the one hand to the supererogatory on the other. What can be said for it?

Proponents of the moral order have long sought to heighten the persuasiveness of moral precepts by appealing to reason. A primitive but familiar argument invoked a myth of divine decrees enforced by sanctions, which consisted usually of reward or punishment after death. The myth itself was not sustained by any appeal to reason whose cogency we are apt to certify, but, granted the myth, the argument by appeal to it was indeed a rational argument to the effect that moral behavior is in one's own interest.

Another familiar argument from self-interest is that we are all better off if we all respect one another's interests. The fallacy is familiar too: any one of us may be even better off by infringing on another's interests, if the rest of society behaves properly. The weakening of the fabric occasioned by the one man's deviation is unlikely to harm him appreciably in his lifetime. Police and punishment are our way of redressing the balance by bringing further self-interest to bear.

Might we say then that self-interest does offer a rational warrant for altruism once we have instituted police and punishment? No, for two reasons. One, the penal code demands only erogatory altruism, leaving the supererogatory untouched. Second, self-interest condones even some unaltruistic cheating at the erogatory level, when the cheat sees his way to eluding police and punishment.

The enlightened moralist thus recognizes that self-interest, however enlightened, affords no general rational basis for altruism. Altruists are simply persons who prize the welfare of others outright and irreducibly, just as everyone prizes his own.

Some moralists feel that this lack of a rational justification on the basis of self-interest is a threat to morality. I say that such a justification would have been unworthy anyway, smacking of the venal and sordid. Let virtue be its own reward.

We must simply recognize that there are drives other than self-interest, and admirable ones. Ethologists represent some altruistic drives as innate in man and other animals, and they explain them by natural selection as ways of safeguarding the gene pool through the protection of kin. But man's altruism is not always as abundant as we could wish, nor are arguments from self-interest the way to increase it. The way rather is to play on whatever faint rudiments of fellow-feeling he may be capable of, fanning any little spark into a perceptible flame. Try the formative years for best results.

Nurturing altruism in our morally retarded fellows is one thing; widening its scope of application is another. Evolutionary theory accounts for innate altruism only toward kin. There is no mistaking the grading off of altruistic impulse as we move outward from kin; we are less protective of community than of family and still less of nation or race. But many of us have come to feel about as helpfully disposed toward Pygmies or Papuans as toward distant members of our own race. Philanthropy is girdling the globe and even reaching out to subhuman species. Dilemmas arise between human welfare and the welfare of other mammals. The human heart is distended until it is as big as all outdoors.

An easy precept by way of outer guidepost is the proscription of gratuitous killing, but short of that salient marker there are uncharted moral wastes over which only our dim consciences, briefed by a conscientious assessment of probable consequences, are our faltering guides.

Anomaly

Speaking of something as wonderful, or admirable, is in our vernacular an expression of approval. Historically these words connoted mere wonder, and left the question of value aside.

6 Anomaly

There has been a semantic drift, and it is one that bespeaks a general tendency to prize surprise. Some surprises are joyous and some are shattering, but there is evidently a premium on surprise as such, if in other respects the surprising event is neutral.

Our modern use of 'awful' could suggest the opposite conclusion: that awe, or wonder, is distasteful. Timid folk there indeed are, who recoil from surprise and puzzlement unless the surprise package is generously laden. Etymology puts the adventurers still in the majority, for the semantic shift of 'wonderful' and 'admirable' is observable equally in the Romance and German cognates. At any rate this eager group embraces all who have a lively intellectual curiosity, and hence in particular all of my readers—a statistically significant number, I like to think, and the more so if the statistics are qualitatively weighted.

"A difficulty is a light," Paul Valéry wrote. "An insurmountable difficulty is a sun." Any occult phenomenon—any clear case of telepathy, teleportation, or clairvoyance, a ghost, a flying saucer—any of these would delight the scientific mind. Scientists would withdraw in droves and glee to their drawing boards and linear accelerators. The mechanisms of the occult phenomena would cry out for investigation, and a basic revolution in physics would be on the way.

The thought of such glory has power to lend credence to anomalous happenings, through wishful thinking. And yet the more surprising a thing would be, if true, the less likely it is; this is what makes it surprising. So we witness here a certain tension in the scientific breast—the sort of thing some of my students used to call a dialectic.

Thus torn, what does the scientist do? Ideally he scrutinizes the purported anomaly with a sharp and skeptical eye, determined to detect fraud or illusion or some commonplace cause, while still hoping against hope that the phenomenon will withstand his scrutiny and turn out to be the world-shaking prodigy that it seems.

Time being in such short supply and the parascience buffs so prodigal with their purported prodigies, the scientist is bound to make short shrift of shoals of parascientific claims. None warrants examination unless it bears promise of unimpeachable documentation. The buffs accordingly charge bigotry, conspiracy, vested interests, and want of scientific objectivity, never dreaming that scientists would be overjoyed to see a real substantiation of any of the buffs' wild claims.

Scientists do not simply hold aloof. They are monitoring the radio spectrum for extraterrestrial signals, and well they may. Flying saucers were monitored for a time, and reports were sifted judiciously. Statistical studies of telepathy command less patient attention, because a mechanism for wordlessly encoding and transmitting the messages is so extravagantly remote from known processes and laws. One who has adjusted to the wonders of radio and television, but knows nothing of how they work, is all too ready to envisage telepathy without regard to how it could ever be.

Moving on to clairvoyance, we are faced with a challenge to our basic ways of thinking. Evidence of clairvoyance would have to be ironclad if it were to warrant a quest for the unimagined avenues through which clairvoyant information might pass.

The scientist must be left to apportion his finite time and effort prudently. It is a matter of cost accounting. Writing of miracles two hundred years and more ago, David Hume asked which is likelier: that the laws of nature that we have so well attested day in and day out should be violated now and then in miraculous ways, or that witnesses to the purported miracles have been deceiving themselves or us?

Seeing is believing, or is apt to be; but there is a place for skepticism even in seeing. The quickness of the hand oftentimes deceives the eye. I can hardly ever penetrate the professional magician's tricks, but I know they are tricks and he knows that I know it. The scientist is not in the dilemma of having either to think of a naturalistic explanation of an event or to recognize it as occult. He must allow also for a humdrum explanation that he just hasn't thought up.

There was a notorious case two generations ago of a Boston medium, Margery. She was investigated by a committee of Harvard scientists who were being properly open-minded about spiritualism. Her table-tippings and her purported tidings from beyond the grave half persuaded them. They should have had a professional magician in tow as consultant. Fraud did eventually transpire.

The scientist's position is peculiarly delicate when, as here, he must decide whether to accept the testimony of his own senses to a revolutionary phenomenon, challenging entrenched scientific theory, or to dismiss the phenomenon as a presumed effect of commonplace causes which he has merely not had the wit to think up. A too cavalier line in such dilemmas could block some momentous insight. Probabilities have to be estimated and weighed, not excluding such factors as the self-interest of a psychic medium.

Quite apart from all that is eerie and occult, the tension between law and anomaly is vital to the progress of science. The scientist goes out of his way to induce it. Sir Karl Popper well depicts him as inventing hypotheses and then making every effort to falsify them by cunningly devised experiments. It is the tension between the scientist's laws and his own attempted breaches of them that powers the engines of science and makes it forge ahead.

Artificial Languages

In the Middle Ages the Latin language was the international western medium of diplomacy and learning, such as learning was. By the thirteenth century the Dark Ages had paled; speculative thought was moving creditably, and there was a hint of science in the air. Latin bore the increasingly precious burden until early modern times, when science was full-fledged.

Meanwhile French, English, and other vernaculars had moved in on the embassies, and in the eighteenth century they invaded also the academies and the budding laboratories. Scientific Latin dwindled to the confines of doctoral and inaugural dissertations.

The consequent crippling of culture-wide intercourse was sensed and regretted, and late in the nineteenth century steps were taken. Instead of a Latin revival, however, more drastic and visionary projects were propounded: one or another artificial language, designed from scratch for simplicity of grammar and ease of acquisition.

There had been two prophetic efforts in that direction already in the seventeenth century, by the Scottish teacher George Dalgarno and the English bishop John Wilkins, warden of Wadham. These efforts were prompted rather by utopian visions of rational semantics and syntax than by any current crisis in international communication, for Latin still lingered as a fallback in scholarly and diplomatic circles. It was not until 1880 that the German priest J. M. Schleyer, impelled by social zeal to allay the Babel of tongues, launched his international auxiliary language, Volapük. Its lexicon was for the most part an unrecognizable derivative of English, and its grammar more nearly a streamlined simplification of German. In nine years Volapük spanned the civilized world, spawning 285 Volapük societies and boasting a million initiates. Then it began to splinter into rival dialects fashioned by devotees who had ideas or creative urges of their own. People who rise with enthusiasm to a language reform are apt to be just the ones with a taste for tinkering and innovating; and thus, ironically, an artificial international language approaches its intended universality only to crumble into a new Babel of its own.

Meanwhile the Russian physician L. L. Zamenhof was independently engaged in devising Esperanto. It appeared in

1887, and eventually inherited the major share of the vogue for international languages. In 1965 it claimed eight million users, despite having undergone the usual splintering at the hands of innovators.

The best-known of these splinters is Ido, introduced in 1907. It was largely the work of Louis Couturat, who is known also as one of the lesser Preprincipians. A Preprincipian, I should explain, is one who cultivated modern mathematical logic prior to the appearance in 1910 of the first volume of Whitehead and Russell's *Principia Mathematica*.

Ido was aggressively international, striving to maximize the internationality of each word in its vocabulary. Should the stem *man-* be used for hands, as in Latin and the Romance languages, or for people, as in the Germanic languages? Settle it by a head-count of Romance and Germanic speakers. And does this maximize the number of people who will guess the meaning of the word? Rather it leaves all too many of us undecided, speculating futilely on the Romance and Germanic population figures.

Tinkering with an artificial language appeals to some of the same tastes and impulses as does mathematical logic. It was another and greater Preprincipian, Giuseppe Peano, who produced in 1903 the least artificial and to my mind the most attractive of all the competing languages: Latino sine Flexione, later named Interlingua. Maximum internationality to the winds; every word of it is consecrated in the classical Latin corpus, except for concessions for pharmaceuticals and the like. What is simplified is the grammar: there is no declension except for the plural -*s*, and no conjugation. Grammatical structure is achieved by prepositions and compound tenses along Romance lines. A text in this language is utterly transparent to anyone conversant with a Romance language or semiliterate in Latin. Interlingua offered easy restitution, in reasonable facsimile, of the scientific Latin that had been incontinently abandoned two centuries before, and it did so at a level of powerful competition, I should have thought, with the more artificial proposals that had been enjoying some vogue. An Interlingua movement continues today, but, predictably, it was no match for its meddlesome enthusiasts. They have besmirched the classical purity of its lexicon and marred the transparency of the language with quirks that readers have to be instructed in, however easily.

This melancholy tale is not meant to incite to action. With the increasingly international use of English, especially in science, the need for an auxiliary international language abates apace. Such projects dwindle to more nearly the nature of a hobby, rather like their status in the days of Dalgarno and Wilkins when Latin still throve. But one's melancholy persists: sentimental regret of the lost Latin of three centuries ago and the limpid near-Latin that might have consoled us in the present century.

Artificial notation, stopping short of full-scale language, continues meanwhile to thrive in mathematics, as it has for centuries. It has been developed not for the purpose of bridging language boundaries, as the full-scale artificial languages were, but for the purpose of facilitating thought on special topics. The strides in mathematics down the centuries would have been psychologically impossible without the graphic and flexible schematism afforded by notations fashioned for the purpose. The splintering that so beset Volapük and the rest at the hands of meddlesome gadgeteers has spared mathematics, because the notation is not itself the apple of the mathematician's eye. The notation is the medium and very much the instrument, but the apple is something intangible out beyond. When variant notations intrude, no capital is made of them; the mathematician takes them in stride and looks beyond them to the message.

In recent years there has been a conspicuous outgrowth of mathematical notation, and more particularly of the notation of mathematical logic, that is somewhat nearer in spirit to the old full-scale artificial languages after all. I refer to Fortran, Loglan, and the other artificial languages that have been devised for the programming of computers. They have been proliferating much as the old artificial languages did, and the joy of tinkering is again no doubt a factor in the proliferation. But they are subject now to sharp and rigid criteria of selection, for their efficiency can be strictly measured in computer time. They are a new breed of artificial languages, media of artificial intelligence in an ever more artificial world.

Atoms

We are blessed, Leibniz assured us, with the best of all possible worlds. Best by what standard? A hint is provided by his concept of perfection: richness of ends and economy of means. Hence we might expect the infinite variety of our world to admit of a gratifyingly neat analysis into a few kinds of components acted upon by a few forces. The kinds of components and forces must be as few as could possibly achieve the observed luxuriance of our world, if it is the best world possible in Leibniz's sense of 'best'.

Scientists have acted accordingly, seeking the fewest and simplest mechanisms and the fewest sorts of ingredients capable of accounting for our observations. The resulting theories are more complex than one could wish, but the scientist's first duty after all is to his data, in all their stubbornness, and he does what he can.

Leibniz's concept of perfection was inspired by his own scientific endeavors; for the ideal of economy in scientific explanation is as old as science. "*Entia,*" William of Ockham had intoned, "*non multiplicanda sunt praeter necessitatem.*" Seventeen centuries before Ockham, the drive for economy prompted Leucippus and Democritus to propound an atomic theory of nature; and its economy was tight indeed. The atoms differed from one another only in shape and size, and some had little hooks with which to hang together. All the variety and turmoil of the world were held to be our blurred perception of the aggregate ballistic behavior of those subvisible pellets.

Science had a long way to go. Ancient atomism explained

none of the regularities that are observed in nature. It was purely metaphysical, or, to put it kindly, programmatic.

Programmatically it at length came through. In the seventeenth century, chemical reactions began to be accounted for in terms of the combining and recombining of unlike atoms in distinctive clusters, now called molecules. By the middle of the nineteenth century, it was conjectured further that gases consisted of molecules darting about at random, and that heat consisted in the movement of molecules; and this served to explain the pressure exerted by a heated gas.

By the end of the nineteenth century the atoms had ceased to be reckoned as atomic; they contained moving parts. These, the elementary particles, now figured as the true atoms etymologically speaking. They were not all of a kind; research has persisted in turning up new kinds, to the physicists' chagrin. The latter-day hypothesis of quarks as more utterly elementary particles was a move toward homogeneity, but these too betrayed heterogeneity ere long. Very well; there is no shaking the data. Even a motley world of heterogeneous particles promises a more economical explanation of physical processes than any visible alternative—save perhaps one.

That alternative is the abandonment of enduring particles in favor of point-events, or momentary local states. There are findings in physical theory that favor it. For one thing, theoretical difficulties have arisen in identifying a particle from one time to another. Even at a fixed time, moreover, two elementary particles alike in kind prove to be interchangeable in a subtly statistical way that challenges their individuality. But this contemplated abandonment of enduring particles still leaves us with an atomic theory, structurally speaking. Its atoms are the point-events.

Now that I have begun to generalize beyond atoms in the narrow sense—and I shall do more of it—we may do well to consider what key trait ought to qualify a theory as atomic. What key trait makes the atomic approach effective in organizing a science? I say it is this: there may be indefinitely or infinitely many atoms, but they must be partitioned into a manageably limited number of kinds such that atoms of the same kind play identical roles within the laws of the theory. This much, significantly, is just what is required in order that a theory lend itself to the measurement of INFORMATION.

The atoms of nineteenth-century chemistry were of ninety-two kinds, the elements. Our point-events are atoms whose kinds are the distinct states that a point can be in according to the physics of the day. In other words, the atoms here are minimal spatiotemporal localities and the kinds are the few things that can happen in such a place.

Linguistics thrives on an atomism in its theory of PHONEMES. What qualify as its atoms are not the phonemes themselves, but rather the countless almost momentary segments of oral activity that are classifiable under the phonemes. Each atom is the split-second event of someone's uttering a single letter, roughly speaking. It is of these atoms that all discourse in the language is composed. They are partitioned into a few dozen *kinds,* and these are the phonemes. Atoms falling under the same phoneme are equivalent for all purposes of the language in question, even if phonetically not quite alike.

A *sensory* atomism has figured prominently in the theory of knowledge. Rumblings of it were detectable in Locke's talk of "simple ideas," and more distinctly in Hume's talk of "simple impressions." Sensation came to be conceived as a mosaic of irreducible sensible bits, *minima sensibilia,* which came in wide but limited variety and could recur. Here the sensibilia should be seen not as the atoms but as the kinds of atoms. An atom, then, is any one occurrence of any of the sensibilia in the course of experience.

In the present century the Gestalt psychologists challenged sensory atomism, arguing that various gross forms are apprehended outright as wholes rather than constructed as mosaics from atomic components. If the Gestaltists' point is that there is commonly no conscious constructing of the gross forms from lesser elements, then we must grant their point but not find it worth making.

An atomistic approach is suggested, still, by the nature of the neural input. The atoms are the momentary triggerings of sensory receptors, we might say, and the kinds correspond to the receptors themselves: all the triggerings of one receptor count as atoms of one kind. No, this is unpromising. Contrary to my proposal of what to count as an atomic theory, the number of kinds here is unmanageable; any one person has an unknown and uninterestingly large number of sensory receptors. No illumination of theory is to be hoped for on this basis, nor any way of measuring input of INFORMATION.

One dreams of a meaningful perceptual atomism: a repertoire of basic features, noticed or not, in terms of which every neurologically possible human perception and perceptual distinction can be specified. In such an atomism the features would count as kinds; their individual occurrences would be the atoms. Only future developments in neurology and psychology can determine how such an inventory of features might look. Scientists are discovering what a bewildering lot of reorganizing and digesting of stimulatory input takes place in the split second before we begin to be aware of what hit us. Edwin H. Land has shown that the color we ascribe to a position in the scene is not determined by the wavelength of the light from that position; it depends rather on how that wavelength compares with the rest of the wavelengths emanating from the whole scene. If it exceeds all the rest of the wavelengths, the place will probably look red; if it is exceeded by all the rest, the place will look blue. David Hubel and Torsten Wiesel have been finding further, to the gratification of the Gestalt contingent, that some banks of brain cells are specialized to register only one or another broad feature of overall design. Some of these cells respond only when conspicuous diagonals happen to lie across the scene from upper right to lower left; other cells are devoted to other such broad features.

Writings by Paul and Patricia Churchland, philosophical neu-
robiologists, suggest that the dream of a perceptual atomism
may not be vain. The features would be ranged in minute
gradations along many dimensions and would be activated in
bundles, much as separately variable pitches are blended in
chords.

Atomism figures prominently in technology. A prime example is the halftone. The dots and blanks are its atoms, individually invisible to the myopic or distant viewer, who sees
only their aggregate as a picture. In the black and white halftone
the kinds of atoms are two in number; in the colored halftone
there are more. The television screen operates on the same
principle, I gather, in a subtler way.

One thinks also of the movie reel, which simulates smooth
movement by a rapid succession of photographs. The frames
would be the atoms, but then the trouble is that there is no
limitation on kinds. The movie reel resembles the halftone only
in illustrating DISCRETENESS, and it may be relegated to that bin.

B

Beauty

Contrary to John Keats's First and Second Laws of Aesthetics ("Beauty is truth, truth beauty"), truth and beauty are poles apart. Keats's ode itself, while denying this by precept, bears it out by example. Truth preoccupies the alethic pole of the intellectual sphere and beauty the aesthetic pole. Each is admirable in its way.

The alethic pole exerts the main pull on science, in the broad sense: *Wissenschaft*, comprising mathematics, history, and all the hard and soft sciences in between. The aesthetic pole is the focus of *belles lettres*, music, art for art's sake. But it is a matter of emphasis, not boundaries. Scientists in pursuing truth also seek beauty of an austere kind in the elegance of a theory, and happily some of them seek literary grace in their expository writing. The alethic and aesthetic poles can thus join forces up to a point, but beyond that point they conflict. If in expounding some theoretical matter a scientist hits upon a literary conceit that delights him, and subsequently finds that the theoretical point ought strictly to be hedged about in a way that spoils the joke, he faces a quandary between the alethic and the aesthetic poles. His decision to bite the bullet and scrap the wisecrack confirms his affiliation with the scientists.

To what degree, conversely, may the artist's, writer's, or musician's pursuit of beauty involve him in pursuing truth? Experimental painting on the part of some of the Impressionists was aimed at insights into truths about visual perception, as was the struggle with perspective in earlier centuries. Research in auditory perception, however inarticulate, may perhaps be ascribed to experimental music.

A novel can be designed to induce a true sense of some aspect of society. It is then even said to be *true* in some higher sense, but this is double-talk. Anyway what such a novel involves is not the quest for truth, as experimental painting and music perhaps do, but rather the indirect communication of it. A better literary analogue of experimental painting and music is avant-garde poetry, or *Finnegans Wake*.

Truth and beauty are not the only goals. Painting and fiction can also aim at social action, as witness Diego Rivera's depiction of the billionaires or Dickens's of the charity schools and debtors' prisons. If poles were less stubbornly binary, more than two would be called for. The alethic and aesthetic poles need a third, the ethical, to round out the immemorial TRINITY: the true, the good, and the beautiful. Still further ones clamor at the gates. (Block that metaphor. These are poles, not Poles.) There is one in particular, the *rhetorical* pole, that bears notice because of tensions between it and the alethic pole; see RHET-ORIC.

Belief

To believe is to think, in one very limited sense of the latter versatile verb. To believe that beauty is truth is to think that beauty is truth. To believe so is to think so. The two verbs are thus interchangeable before *that* and *so*, but they diverge elsewhere. We can think hard, but we cannot believe hard. We can believe something, but we cannot think something. Grammar forbids.

Believing is a disposition. Thinking, apart from the contexts *that* and *so*, is an activity, however sedentary. We could tire ourselves out thinking, if we put our minds to it, but believing takes no toll. We sit and think, but do we sit and believe? The White Queen, indeed, professed to do so: "When I was your age, I always did it for half-an-hour a day. Why, sometimes I've believed as many as six impossible things before breakfast." But it will be agreed that the White Queen was atypical.

She represented beliefs, some of them anyway, as voluntary activities rather than dispositions. She was wrong about their being activities; they are dispositions. But we may still ask whether they are ever voluntary, for some dispositions are. We are voluntarily acquiring a disposition, or trying to, when we memorize "Il Penseroso" or the multiplication table or make a New Year's resolution. Belief, however, is not that kind of a disposition. To speak of simply deciding to believe something, independently of any evidence real or imagined, is to stretch the term 'belief' beyond belief.

An enamored young man has his reasons for subscribing to the tenets of his fiancée's church, and a heretic threatened by the Inquisition had his reasons for a similar move; but these are cases of feigning belief, of paying lip or pen service, and not of believing. Pascal's notorious wager, on the other hand, and Tertullian's *credo quia impossibile est,* and William James's *Will to Believe,* strike me as strange distortions of the notion of belief. Hoping or wishing can conduce to believing, but only by seducing the subject into overestimating his fancied evidence.

Now that we have agreed that a belief is a disposition, as I trust we have, it is time we went on to consider what it is that the believer is disposed to do. One who believes that beauty is truth, or that his Redeemer liveth, is disposed presumably to respond in the affirmative when asked whether beauty is truth or whether his Redeemer liveth; but lip service, again, is subject to discount. Actions, behaviorism teaches, speak louder than words.

One way of testing belief, powerful where applicable, is by calling upon the professed believer to put his money where his mouth is. Acceptance of a wager evinces sincerity, and the odds accepted conveniently measure the strength of the belief. But this method is applicable only in cases where the believed proposition is one that can eventually be decided to the satisfaction of both parties, so that the bet can be settled. It is not applicable to the one about beauty, or about one's Redeemer. One wonders whether Keats really believed that one about beauty or whether he was merely bent on creating a bit of beauty on his own, like Christian Morgenstern's weasel who sat on a *Kiesel* in a *Bachgeriesel* only for the sake of the rhyme. Or Poe's Lenore, Yaanek, and Guy De Vere. Or Al Smith's Mamie O'Rourke. There are those who would commit mayhem—not murder, perhaps, but mayhem—for the sake of a rhyme. I recall a line from a song: "Fair Naples sleeping, a vigil keeping." Cognitive content to the winds.

A belief, in the best and clearest case, is a bundle of dispositions. It may include a disposition to lip service, a disposition to accept a wager, and various dispositions to take precautions, or to book passage, or to tidy up the front room, or the like, depending on what particular belief it may be. It is remarkable that we can apply this single familiar noun or verb effortlessly to such a heterogeneous domain; for, apart from the lip service and perhaps the wager, the dispositions that constitute one belief differ extravagantly from the dispositions that constitute another.

Beliefs do sometimes make good behavioral sense without admitting of wagers. This is true of very theoretical beliefs, having to do, say, with the expanding universe or elementary particles or the dawn of language. The turn that one gives to one's research, and the supporting evidence that one marshals or the corollaries that one derives, are substantial indications that one holds the belief, though it be a belief on which a bet could never be settled.

But beliefs grade off, as my first two examples illustrate, to where their dispositional content apart from lip service becomes tenuous to the vanishing point. What shared trait can have grouped all these extravagantly diverse states of mind, real or professed, under a single serviceable term, *belief*? None, I submit. They are grouped rather by a linguistic quirk, the adapter *that,* which can be prefixed thoughtlessly to any and every declarative sentence to produce a grammatically impeccable and hence presumably meaningful direct object for the verb *believes.* The many useful and behaviorally significant sentences of the form '*x* believes that *p*' seduce us into supposing that the rest of the sentences of that form make sense too. Sense dwindles from case to case, and we are at a loss to draw a line.

Loath though one is to kick a concept when it is down, it would be wasteful to pass over a curious and well-known paradox in which the concept of belief is enmeshed. To believe something is to believe that it is true; therefore a reasonable person believes each of his beliefs to be true; yet experience has taught him to expect that some of his beliefs, he knows not which, will turn out to be false. A reasonable person believes, in short, that each of his beliefs is true and that some of them are false. I, for one, had expected better of reasonable persons.

C

Classes versus Properties

Whatever is said about a thing is seen as ascribing a property to it, or an attribute. In earlier usage an attribute of a thing or species was called a property of it only if it was peculiar to that thing or species; but this nicety has lapsed, and the two terms have become interchangeable. I shall use 'property' and drop 'attribute'.

If it makes clear sense to speak of properties, it should make clear sense to speak of sameness and difference of properties; but it does not. If a thing has this property and not that, then certainly this property and that are different properties. But what if everything that has this property has that one as well, and vice versa? Should we then say that they are the same property? If so, well and good; no problem. But people do not take that line. I am told that every creature with a heart has kidneys, and vice versa; but who will say that the property of having a heart is the same as that of having kidneys?

In short, coextensiveness of properties is not seen as sufficient for their identity. What then is? If an answer is given, it is apt to be that they are identical if they do not just happen to be coextensive, but are necessarily coextensive. But NECESSITY, q.v., is too hazy a notion to rest with.

We have been able to go on blithely all these years without making sense of identity between properties, simply because the utility of the notion of property does not hinge on identifying or distinguishing them. That being the case, why not clean up our act by just declaring coextensive properties identical? Only because it would be a disturbing breach of usage, as seen in the case of the heart and kidneys. To ease that shock, we change the word: we speak no longer of properties, but of *classes*.

The accommodation is persistently misunderstood. Classes are felt to differ from properties in more than their extensionality, that is, the identity of coextensives. The identity of coextensives is expressed by saying, correctly enough but imprudently, that the class is determined by its members; and this is imprudent in that it suggests that the members are somehow the cause of the class, in a way in which things are not felt to cause their properties. Classes are thought of ideally as specified by listing their members—a method that is almost never feasible for any class worth talking about. Classes are described as "collections" or "aggregates", in an unwarranted metaphor of the sorting and gathering of objects by bodily displacement. All this is pernicious metaphor. A class may be said in more suitably neutral terms to be any *multiplicity* of objects—except that this neglects the singletons, or one-member classes, and the empty class. A class in the useful sense of the word is simply a property in the everyday sense of the word, minus any discrimination between coextensive ones.

The word 'class' in these logical contexts, with or without pernicious metaphor, is not old. The Latin *classis* in its earliest attested use, according to Meillet, applied to the various classifications of draftees in the call to arms. The word may have been borrowed, he suggests, from the Etruscan. The word came, still in Roman times, to be applied more generally to social classes; current Marxist usage is thus strictly conservative. In the eighteenth century the word entered taxonomy, but only for one specific taxon, or level of classification; thus the class Mammalia, the class Crustacea.

Thenceforward it proliferated, taking on all the suppleness and versatility of 'property' and 'attribute', except, again, for the extensionality constraint. By the nineteenth century it could go without saying that every membership condition determines a class, just as whatever is said about a thing ascribes a property. It is at that point that classes obtain the status of properties minus discrimination of coextensives—a status which, as I have been complaining, is still insufficiently appreciated.

And then came Russell's bombshell, shattering the platitude that every membership condition determines a class. See PARADOXES; also IMPREDICATIVITY. But this does nothing to contravene the view of classes as properties minus discrimination of coextensives. The reasoning behind Russell's Paradox applies to properties precisely as to classes, and shatters likewise the platitude that whatever is said about a thing ascribes a property. Whatever set-theoretic restraints may be imposed on the existence of classes, in order to preserve consistency, would need to be imposed *pari passu* on properties if we were so perverse as to continue to recognize properties in lieu of or in addition to classes.

We must acquiesce in ordinary language for ordinary purposes, and the word 'property' is of a piece with it. But also the notion of property or its reasonable facsimile is needed for technical purposes in scientific theory, especially mathematics, and in these contexts classes are the reasonable facsimile that takes over, since these contexts never hinge on distinguishing coextensive properties. One instance among many of the use of classes in mathematics is seen under DEFINITION, in the definition of number. For science it is classes *si*, properties *no*.

Classes versus Sets

Man is a practical and even a penurious animal, and as such he has little patience with multiple labels. Some say 'furze' and some say 'gorse', but none, in a state of nature, will say both. Faced with two terms for the same thing, one tends to cast about for a distinction. Faced with the two words 'ape' and 'monkey' for what is indiscriminately called *Affe* in German and *singe* in French, we evidently found an easy out: sort them by size. I suspect that the situation was similar, but less easily resolved, when the invading Danes introduced the word 'ale' into our language in competition with the already current 'beer'. Encyclopedias are inconclusive and a bit frantic in their effort to state ways in which ale, properly so called, may generally or frequently be said to differ from beer, properly so called. I sense an effort to sustain a preconceived maxim: "Two words, two senses."

This has been the way with 'set' and 'class'. They were interchangeable, and accordingly invited a factitious distinction of meaning. So we find some logicians or mathematicians treating of sets and classes side by side. They think of classes as something on the order of properties (for which I applaud them; see above), and they think of sets as somehow more robust, though abstract still. The contrast is an insubstantial metaphor, but they implement it by adopting a strong or impredicative theory of sets (see IMPREDICATIVITY) and then superimposing classes, which are construed as admitting sets as members but not admitting themselves or one another. Some membership conditions must fail to determine any sets, as we know, on pain of PARADOX, but they can still with impunity determine classes; for instance, there can be no set of all sets that are not members of themselves, but there can still be a class of all such sets.

John von Neumann, in 1925, was the first to set forth such a scheme explicitly. It greatly simplifies proofs in set theory and also strengthens the system, though in a way that runs no increased risk of paradox. But it involves wasteful duplication and fanciful distinctions; for, besides providing supplementary classes like the one just noted, the theory assumes for every set a coextensive class.

We can quite well dispense with this exorbitant duplication and still enjoy all the benefits. We can simply identify the sets with the coextensive classes, as has been my line since 1940.

We can still make capital of the double nomenclature 'set' and 'class', for the sets become classes only of a special sort. A class is a set if it is a member of a class. A class is an *ultimate* class if it is a member of none.

Some have thought, by their separation of sets from classes, to represent Russell's Paradox and its kin as mere confusions rather than true antinomies. No paradox issues from the platitude that every membership condition determines a class, they say, because classes themselves are not substantial objects such as might figure as candidates for membership under a membership condition. Sets *are* such objects, but, they tell us, sets never were thought to be determined by all membership conditions. Sets emerged only in Cantor's work a hundred years ago, they tell us, and were regarded from the outset as existing only as determined by principles of the sort that soon became explicit in Zermelo's set theory.

It is pernicious reasoning. In their utility, in their *raison d'être*, and in the very origin of the notion, by whatever name, sets were classes. Any vagueness in the one word was vagueness in the other. Granted, what Cantor first dealt with under the name of 'sets' (*Mengen*) were sets of points, but that is hardly indicative. Such restraints of the domain of sets as can be read into Cantor's mature set theory are ascribable to shrewd premonitions, on his part, of antinomy. There are passages in Cantor that may or may not be read as foreshadowing the distinction that von Neumann eventually exploited so fruitfully, but these passages, if so read, are likewise ascribable to those sophisticated premonitions. The myth that sets were conceived independently of classes, and were afterward conflated with classes by Russell and others, reflects the disposition again to see a difference in things behind a difference in words.

The benefits conferred by von Neumann's expedient are independent of that myth. They can be enjoyed, as we saw, while recognizing only classes; in other words, only sets and ultimate classes. Here the double nomenclature is explicitly exploited but not rationalized by fancied history.

Communication

What are commonly said to be communicated, apart from diseases, are ideas. An idea that has been occupying one mind gets duplicated, it would seem, in another mind. "Peering into the darkness of another's mind," in Santayana's phrase, we cannot easily say how faithful the duplication is. Such is the vagueness of the very idea of IDEAS, *q.v.*, indeed, that it is anybody's guess what the form, content, and limits even of one of our own ideas might be said to be. Anybody's guess including our own.

The nature and limits of communication can be somewhat clarified if we put the vaporous idea of ideas aside and address ourselves to tangible, visible, and audible reality. Simple sentences about this robust subject matter are apt to be unfailing vehicles of communication, especially if the objects concerned are of kinds that both we and our communicants continue to encounter from time to time. The words and phrases used in such cases are ones that both we and our communicants originally acquired in the presence of these same objects or ones like them. Our use of these words and phrases has been refreshed, checked, and kept in line by interim communication with those same communicants, or ones like them, in the very presence of those same objects or ones like them. Successful communication at this level is no wonder, let ideas fall where they may.

The ground of communication is less simple and obvious when what I communicate is that someone stole an old sword toward which I felt a sentimental attachment because it had been wielded by my mother's stepfather in the battle of Gettysburg. My communicant, bored with museums, has never seen a sword, and he has never knowingly laid eyes on anyone's stepfather. Neither he nor I has ever witnessed a theft nor a battle nor, we may suppose, viewed Gettysburg. As for sentimental attachments, one scarcely knows where to begin. Unquestionably, still, the communication is successful.

One can see why. My communicant knows the word 'sword' from hearing and seeing the word in various contexts and hearing or seeing it explained in words or pictures. I know the word from hearing and seeing it in *other* contexts and hearing and seeing it explained in other ways, including presentations of the real thing. These multifarious ways of getting at the word all link up across society in a coherent network. The coherence is no coincidence, for the network is self-corrective. When communication is seen to falter through misuse of the word, the misuser is set right, shunted back into line. The shared understanding of all the words in our example, even 'sentimental attachment', may be similarly accounted for.

Examples taper off to where communication is less firmly assured, as when Hegel writes "Truth is in league with reality against consciousness," or I write "Logic chases truth up the tree of grammar." I am confident that I grasp and appreciate this message of Hegel's, and that there are philosophers of logic who grasp mine. But mere acknowledgment, however sincere—"I dig you," or "I read you. Roger and over"—is not conclusive evidence of successful communication. The Latin pupil gets low marks who says "Oh, I know what it means, but I can't quite put it into words." Stage comics have dramatized failure of communication by protracted cross-purpose dialogue in which the audience is privy to the misunderstanding while the performers ostensibly are not.

There are objective checkpoints. We are content that we have communicated if our interlocutor reacts appropriately, perhaps by stepping briskly up onto the curb, or by looking up at a particular quarter of the night sky, or by continuing the dialogue in so penetrating a way as to render cross purposes unthinkable. Checkpoints also expose failure of communication; these are the rebuffs that improve our grasp of the language and close the ranks of communicant society.

The farther we venture from simple discourse about familiar concrete things, however, the farther apart the checkpoints tend to be spaced and the less decisive each checkpoint tends to be. We discourse blithely to patiently receptive ears and pick up only an occasional inconclusive indication, if any, that we have communicated our idea (excuse the expression) or perhaps engendered some unintended one. No news is good news. We read the listener's mind by what Neil Wilson called the principle of charity. We get an exaggerated idea of how well we have been understood, simply for want of checkpoints to the contrary. The miracle of communication, in its outer reaches, is a little like the miracle of transubstantiation: what transubstantiation?

Complex Numbers

We all know that the square of any number, positive or negative, is positive. No wonder then that $\sqrt{-1}$, or briefly i, and its multiples are called *imaginary numbers*. Still, for all the invidious contrast with what are celebrated as real numbers, these are in point of fact rather more of the same. To begin with, it is scarcely more reasonable to think of 2 as having a square root than to think of -1 as having one. There is merely the difference that the irrational reals were thought up and drawn into computation long before the imaginary numbers. In both cases it was a matter of extending the scope of the arithmetical operation of extracting roots: extending it first to all positive numbers by dint of the irrationals, and then to all negative numbers by dint of the imaginaries. The two extensions afford every algebraic equation a solution, and indeed n solutions where n is the highest power occurring in the equation; and they afford untold numerical wealth also over and above that. In both cases the extension was simply by fiat; until toward the end of the nineteenth century there was no account of what objects these supplementary numbers might be taken to be. But then that was true also of the good old NATURAL NUMBERS themselves.

REAL NUMBERS, as examined in later pages under that head, are only positive and 0. Preparatory to coming to grips with imaginary roots of negative real numbers, then, we must provide for negative real numbers. In developing the REAL NUMBERS from the ratios we found it convenient to develop a new brand of ratios along with the irrationals, all under the head of real numbers. It is convenient similarly in developing *signed* real numbers, positive and negative, to develop a new brand of positive reals along with the negative ones. This development is simpler than the other, however, to the point of triviality. Where x is any real number in the prior sense, the corresponding positive and negative *signed* reals can be arbitrarily construed as *ordered pairs* $\langle 0, x \rangle$ and $\langle x, 0 \rangle$.

This puts it to us to come to grips with the general notion of ordered pair, and high time too. It is a widely useful notion, wanted not just for numbers but for objects of any sort. A relation, for instance, is a class of ordered pairs; thus the uncle relation is the class of all pairs $\langle x, y \rangle$ such that x is uncle of y.

And just what, in general, is an ordered pair? We want $\langle x, y \rangle$ to be determined by x and y, and we want it to differ from $\langle y, x \rangle$ unless y is x. This is all we care about. What sort of thing $\langle x, y \rangle$ might be is indifferent to us so long as we are able to recover x and y uniquely given $\langle x, y \rangle$. One artificial way of construing $\langle x, y \rangle$, adequate to that purpose, is to define it as the class $\{\{x, y\}, \{x\}\}$ of two members one of which is the class $\{x, y\}$ of x and y and the other of which is the class $\{x\}$ of x alone. Given the ordered pair in this sense, we can recover x uniquely from it by this trait: it is a member of both members. Afterward we can easily recover y.

Back at last to $\sqrt{-1}$ or i, the imaginary unit. An imaginary number is any product yi, where y is a signed real number. A *complex* number is any sum $x + yi$ where x and y are signed reals. Unlike 5, which can be broken down both as $3 + 2$ and as $4 + 1$, the complex number $x + yi$ can be broken down in only the one way because of the indigestibility of i. Consequently complex numbers are sometimes pressed into service to represent the points in a plane; $x + yi$ is x paces over and y paces out.

When philosophically minded mathematicians began toward

the end of the nineteenth century to wonder what they were talking about, an easy way of making sense of a complex number $x + yi$ was suggested by the foregoing consideration; namely, just identify it with the ordered pair $\langle x, y \rangle$ of the two signed reals.

We note under REAL NUMBERS that ratios come through in two senses and positive integers in three. The same effect recurs here. There is the real number, $\sqrt{2}$ say, as originally construed; there is its counterpart the positive signed real $\sqrt{2}$, or $+\sqrt{2}$; and finally, again distinct under the present constructions, there is the complex number $\sqrt{2}$, *sive* $\sqrt{2} + 0i$, *sive* $\langle \sqrt{2}, 0 \rangle$. Correspondingly the ratios get pushed now to four senses, and the positive integers to five. But, as remarked under REAL NUMBERS, such reduplications play no role in practice, nor do these philosophically motivated constructions themselves.

Without much increase in complexity, these constructions can in fact be reworked in such a way as to eliminate the reduplications almost entirely.★ Real complex numbers $x + 0i$ become identical with the signed reals x after all, and these become identical with the basic unsigned reals, as in unphilosophical mathematics. Rational reals, likewise, become identical with ratios in their basic sense. All these numbers, moreover, become mere classes of NATURAL NUMBERS. Only the latter get reduplicated, and they only once, from natural number n to ratio $n/1$. The plan is gratifying for its elegance and its near conformity to the mathematical vernacular, but it is no more instructive in other respects than the more readily communicated constructions that I settle for in these pages.

Consonant Clusters

There are those among us who find it inconvenient to say *tmesis*. (See ALPHABET.) Many might likewise have been incon-

---

★Such is the way of my *Set Theory and Its Logic* (Harvard, 1969), §§ 18–19.

venienced by *mnemonic* had they not been emboldened by the
wide currency of the word to neglect the first letter. Similarly
for *pneumonia, pterodactyl, psychology.* There is little currency to
reassure us in the case of *ctenoid,* but outright despair of artic-
ulation suffices in this desperate case to carry the day. These
many cases conspire to impress us with the articulatory agility
of the Greeks, who could evidently bark out these initial double
stumble stops without turning a hair.

Latter-day insights into the phonetics of ancient Greece tell
us something about *phthisis.* It was not *f* as in *fin* followed by
th as in *thin.* The Greek phi, represented by our *ph,* was pronounced in those days simply as *p* followed by an aspirated *h,*
as in our *pin* (see PRONUNCIATION), and theta was simply *t*
followed by aspiration as in our *tin.* So *phth* was just *pt,* as in
pterodactyl, followed by aspiration. But that is bad enough.

As a household word in England and America, in any event,
phthisis was bound to erode; and household word it was, for
phthisis was the scourge of the nineteenth century. The word
shrank to *tisic* and gave way in higher circles to a semi-Latinate
tuberculosis and, less pretentiously, *consumption.*

The glossolaryngeal virtuosity of the old Greeks is further
attested by their readiness to begin a word with *skl,* which
gives us pause, and even with *skn,* which stumps us utterly.
Yet, strangely, they began no words with *sl or sn.* Without a *k*
to reinforce them, these were evidently too flimsy to get a grip
on. Yet they began words with *sm.*

The Spaniards, Portuguese, French, and Turks have all been
reluctant to begin words with *sc, sp,* or *st.* The Spaniards and
Portuguese prefixed an *e* to create a further syllable; thus *estado*
for 'state'. So did the French at first, but then they went on to
drop the *s* itself, while keeping the *e* that was meant to accommodate the *s;* so we have *état.* The Turks coped by prefixing
not *e* but *i,* as in *Isparta.*

Italians, unlike other Romance speakers, are almost as tolerant of initial *sc, sp,* and *st* as we. I say "almost" because they
do balk at pronouncing the article *il* before such a beginning;

they change the article to *lo*. Given this accommodation, however, they are more tolerant of initial *s* clusters even than we; they begin words with *sb*, *sd*, *sf*, *sg*, and *sv*. This is the more striking when we consider how sonorously unreceptive Italian is elsewhere to consonant clusters. It is proverbially *cantabile*.

Hostility to consonant clusters reaches its extreme in Polynesia. Those islanders have only nine consonants to work with altogether, yet they never join them; vowels always intervene. One gets a similar impression of Japanese from our transliterations, but this is wrong; the *u* in the transliterations is often just a silent by-product of a Japanese syllabic notation. When we hear a diner in our neighborhood Japanese restaurant ask for chicken *skyaki*, for *sukiyaki*, he is not being careless; he has been around.

Slavic orthography, conversely, can give us exaggerated notions of Slavic consonant clusters. The Polish prefix *prze-* looks impossible, but phonetically it is just *pje-* where the *j* is as in French. Bad still, but not very. The ubiquitous Polish *cz* is just our *ch*. The syllabic *r* in Czech and Croat is startling, as witness *Srb* and *Krk*; but these are pronounced substantially as we Americans pronounce *Serb* and *Kirk*. It is we, really, who write in an idle additional vowel.

For impressive clustering of consonants, indeed, we English speakers need not look beyond ourselves. Who is to rival *sixth string*? The cluster *xthstr* here consists of six consecutive consonantal PHONEMES, but they do not correspond exactly to the six letters; *x* represents two, *ks*, and *th* represents one.

Another sturdy specimen is *fringed gentian*. Spelled out in phonemes, the middle cluster *ngedg* becomes *ndjdj*, using again the French *j*.

Constructivism

The use of this term in mathematics is not wholly pinned down, but it may be roughly defined as the practice, project, or policy of mathematizing with one's hands tied. There have been heterodox mathematicians, of a somewhat nominalist cast (see UNIVERSALS), who resolutely eschewed freer ways. But others also, who would happily tread any path however luxurious that leads to the truth, have still found it of methodological and philosophical interest to distinguish between constructively demonstrable theorems and others, and to seek constructive proofs before settling for others.

If an example of a constructive theory might be helpful, predicative set theory is one; see IMPREDICATIVITY. As there noted, predicative set theory is too weak to prove that there must be unspecifiable classes and unspecifiable real numbers. Indeed one precise meaning that might be assigned to constructivism is that every abstract object is specifiable.

There is a variant version of VARIABLES and quantification that becomes available when the domain of objects over which the variable ranges is such that each object is specifiable. (The NATURAL NUMBERS are one such domain; each has its Arabic numeral.) In its classical or *objectual* reading, the universal quantifier '$\forall x$' of PREDICATE LOGIC means 'everything x is such that', and it produces a true sentence if and only if the formula to which it is prefixed is fulfilled by every object x in the chosen domain. In the variant version, called *substitutional*, the requirement is rather that the formula to which the quantifier is prefixed come out true under every grammatically admissible substitution for the letter 'x'.

Where the domain is the natural numbers, clearly the two versions come to the same thing. If on the other hand some of the objects are not individually specifiable by any singular terms of the language, the two versions diverge. The formula appended to the quantifier may happen to be fulfilled by all of the specifiable objects but not by some of the others, and in that case the substitutional reading comes out true and the objectual one false.

Existential quantification is parallel. In its objectual reading '$\exists x$' means 'something x is such that', and yields truth if and only if the adjoined formula is fulfilled by some object in the domain of quantification. Substitutionally the requirement is rather that the formula come out true under some substitution for 'x'. The two readings conflict when the formula is fulfilled by some unspecifiable objects but by no specifiable ones.

Substitutional quantification is unrealistic for concrete objects. Is each concrete object individually specifiable—each past and future bird and bee, each atom and electron? In principle, yes; we could subject the whole of space-time to a system of numerical coordinates, using just rational numbers. But unfettered objectual quantification is far more natural here.

For predicative set theory, on the other hand, substitutional quantification is both feasible and attractive. It is attractive because abstract objects seem to be parasitical on language in a way, however dim, that concrete ones are not. This is a point that has been urged by Charles Parsons. It is not to say that substitutional quantification over abstract objects simply eliminates them from the ontological inventory. Expressions themselves are abstract, as noted under TYPE VERSUS TOKEN, but they are less wildly so than the denizens of higher set theory. Substitutional quantification may be viewed as according the values of its variables a tenuous grade of existence distinct from the robust existence imputed to concrete objects by objectual quantification. It is a compromise with militant nominalism.

This seductive scene is predicated on a combination of objectual quantification over concrete objects and substitutional quantification over abstract ones, these being classes as of predicative set theory. Parsons has shown how the two modes of quantification, using distinctive styles of variables, can be made to work smoothly side by side and intertwined.

But the trouble with the picture, as Parsons appreciates, is the proverbial inadequacy of predicative set theory to the classical mathematics of real numbers; see again IMPREDICATIVITY. Russell, as we there noted, gave up predicative set theory and settled for the full-strength affair because of the presumed inadequacy of the former to a mathematics adequate to the needs of natural science. And the full-strength affair, with its excess of unspecifiable real numbers and other unspecifiable classes, does not lend itself to substitutional quantification.

Sanguine souls there have been and are, however, who envisioned and envision a constructive mathematics adequate to all scientific applications after all. L. E. J. Brouwer was at it two generations ago, but his approach involved unattractive deviations from standard logic. Hermann Weyl worked at it with standard logic, as have Paul Lorenzen, Erret Bishop, Hao Wang, and Sol Feferman in later years. It becomes a matter of making do with predicative set theory through ingeniously circuitous constructions. One obstacle to a knock-down proof of adequacy is the problem of determining just how much mathematics is wanted for natural science. But the hope is there—not of an out-and-out nominalism, as we saw, but of an attractive approximation.

Copula

Logic-minded philosophers have cautioned us from time to time over the past century or so that the *is* of IDENTITY is one thing, the *is* of predication another. The latter may best be viewed simply as a grammatical adapter for making an adjective play the grammatical role of an intransitive verb. We sing "Thou art green in winter" apostrophizing the *Tannenbaum,* where the Germans directly conjugate the color adjective as a verb: *Du grünst in Winter,* "Thou greenest in winter". The Japanese are more extreme: their color words are verbs to begin with, across the board.

It is good methodology to ask what this last remark really means. It means that the Japanese color words agree in form and grammatical behavior with the multitude of Japanese words that do go over into what we call verbs when Japanese is translated along the most natural and convenient lines.

And how do adjectives differ from intransitive verbs even in

English? Not at all, essentially, as predicates; but we use them also attributively, as in *green tree*. Still, might the adjective in its predicative use not simply be allowed to stand as a verb without the help of the copula—thus 'You green in winter'? The Semitic languages thrive without a copula.

Perhaps its principal utility for us is in marking the grouping of phrases. I was told of a telegram sent by journalist to check on the age of Cary Grant: HOW OLD CARY GRANT. Came the reply: OLD CARY GRANT QUITE WELL STOP HOW YOU. The copula would have distinguished 'How old is' from 'How is old'. The adjective is predicative in the one and attributive in the other. In some languages such an ambiguity might be averted rather by a distinction in form between attributive and predicative, or by some convention of word order.

The copula of predication has a converse, *-ing*. Just as the one is an adapter for turning adjectives into verbs, so the other is an adapter for turning verbs into adjectives. They thus cancel out: 'You are reading' reduces to 'You read'. Granted, we have utilized the excess to register a shade of meaning: the progressive *aspect,* so called, as over against the habitual.

Creation

Creation out of nothing was evidently the biblical idea: "In the beginning God created the heaven and the earth." The Greeks, scholars tell us, had a different idea: creation began in what they called *chaos*. This was not a void, but just an awful mess—awful in the strictest sense. Creation was a matter of whipping it into shape. The German words *schaffen* and *schöpfen,* for 'create', retain a trace of this view; for they are cognate with English *shape*.

Persius wrote in the early years of the present or Christian era that *de nihilo nihil, in nihilum nil posse reverti*. Here, and in Lucretius and Epicurus before him, we have the law of conservation of matter backwards and forwards: no decrease and no increase. By Galileo's day a parallel law of energy was recognized. In the fullness of the time Einstein succinctly repudiated both laws, writing that $E = mc^2$. Physicists now convert matter into energy and vice versa, increasing either domain at the expense of the other. Conservation endures, however, in a higher form: at last reports there is no decrease or increase in matter and energy taken collectively.

Both the biblical line and the Big Bang would seem to violate backward conservation, in affirming the generation of something from nothing. Actually there is a reconciliation, in the case anyway of the Bang. It was not preceded by a void, or nothingness, for it was not preceded at all. Time began only with the Bang, for time is only an abstraction from happening; time makes sense only when there is something going on by which to tick it off. It can thus be said that the universe "always" existed, even though it began only finitely long ago. Time began with a cosmic quota of concentrated energy detonating at a point.

Can the Bible be reconciled with backward conservation by this same appeal to a beginning of time? Not on a naive reading, since the biblical account posits something prior to the creation, namely God. Theologians have perhaps accommodated this difficulty by their sophisticated notion of the eternal as timeless rather than everlasting. Anyway, conservation would be the least of one's worries if one were bent on sustaining Genesis 1:1.

Applied to artifacts, the idea of creation is rather the Greek one: a rearranging of antecedently available materials. The weaver creates his tapestry by rearranging his threads, and the painter his painting by rearranging his pigments. The sculptor of stone is still more conservative: he chips away bits to expose a shape that was inside the stone all along. The big neolithic painting of a bison in the cave at Altamira was clearly inspired by a bulge in the rock wall that provided an evident bas-relief. E. H. Gombrich cites approvingly the theory of Leone Battista Alberti, five centuries back, that sculpture had its origin in the touching up and elaborating of a chance resemblance to man or animal that the artist encountered in a stone or a piece of driftwood. Creation and discovery, here as in theoretical science, are all of a piece.

If the fantasy of the UNIVERSAL LIBRARY were realized, literary creativity would likewise reduce to discovery: the author's book would await him on the shelf. In actuality the author, like the weaver and the painter, rearranges antecedently available elements: his vocabulary, with freedom of repetition.

At this point my flatfootedness is perhaps getting out of hand. It is in his ideas and plans, and not in the rearranging of his threads or pigments or vocabulary, that the artist's creativity lies. Looking then rather to ideas, we might ask whether new ideas are just recombinations of simple components that have been handed down; and we might conclude that they cannot *always* be just that, since the generations of man and his prehuman ancestors do not extend back forever. The idea of IDEAS, *q.v.*, is too fragile an idea to sustain intensive analysis, but at any rate there is no conservation law here to contend with; creation *ex nihilo* may be allowed free rein.

D

Decimals and Dimidials

In our language and other familiar languages, modern and ancient, the integers are named in cycles of ten. Our Arabic numeration follows the same plan, and so did the Roman numerals in their clumsy way. We have all been told, perhaps rightly, that numbering by tens goes back to counting on our fingers. *Digit*, anyway, is from the Latin for fingers.

There are traces, even so, of other archaic systems. It takes a dozen inches to make a foot. Groceries are purveyed retail by the dozen, and *en gros* by the gross, or dozen dozens. Years are dozens of months. The years themselves, on the other hand, are sometimes reckoned by the score. Was the dozen based on fingers and elbows? and the score on fingers and toes? The score, if so, evidently antedates the shoe.

The ten digits that we use in our so-called Arabic numeration do not look like those used by the Arabs, but what is important is the positional system. This we acquired through the Arabs from the Hindus. Multiply each digit of your numeral by 10 raised to a power equal to the number of subsequent digits, and add the results; what you get is the number named by your numeral. For instance

$$365 = 3 \cdot 10^2 + 6 \cdot 10^1 + 5 \cdot 10^0.$$

Why is $n^0 = 1$ and not 0? Because we want n^{m+1} always to be $n^m \cdot n$. Take m as 0 and you get $n^1 = n^0 \cdot n$, or $n = n^0 \cdot n$; so n^0 must be 1.

The positional notation is a built-in abacus. It cuts through a maze of complex computation that plagued the Romans and the Egyptians. A later boon is the decimal point, inspired by the sophistication of negative exponents. Thus

$$3.1416 = 3 \cdot 10^0 + 1 \cdot 10^{-1} + 4 \cdot 10^{-2} + 1 \cdot 10^{-3} + 6 \cdot 10^{-4}.$$

Before that breakthrough, counting and dividing had little in common. Though counting in tens from time immemorial, we persisted in dividing successively by 2. This custom still survives in our folk measures: we divide our inches into halves, quarters, and down to thirty-seconds, our gallons into four quarts, eight pints, and thirty-two gills, and our bushels into four pecks. It survives also in fractions on the stock market.

All REAL NUMBERS, rational and irrational, are represented by decimals, some of which terminate and others not. The real number ½, a ratio, can be expressed as .5. The real number ⅓, another ratio, is .333 . . . without end. The correspondence of real numbers to decimals is not quite one to one, because each terminating decimal is equivalent to an endless decimal; .5 = .4999. . . . But we can perfect the correspondence by insisting on unending decimals; forget '.5' and cleave to '.4999 . . .'.

Readers unreceptive to nonsense may wonder at the idea of an unending decimal expansion. Let them then think of all decimal expansions, ending and unending, not as written expressions but outright as numbers. An expansion to six decimal places, say 4.237251, is the ratio of 4,237,251 to a million. An unending decimal expansion is likewise then simply a number, namely, the number that is approached as a limit by the series of ratios represented by longer and longer segments of that unending decimal. This limit may be a ratio in turn, as in the case of .333 . . . or .14281428 . . . , or it may be irrational, as in the case of 3.14159. . . .

Readers will see, under INFINITE NUMBERS, that the real numbers outrun all means of expression. Yet we saw just now that they can be rendered as unending decimals. So we are warned anew not to view unending decimals as expressions.

Any base from 2 upward would have served numeration nicely in place of 10, some more nicely than others. In calculation, 12 and 20 would have advantages over 10, because they have more factors. The larger the base, the more compact the notation will be and the larger the multiplication table. The system with 2 as base is thus the longest-winded of the lot, but it enjoys the slightest of multiplication tables and striking economies of a higher kind. Its only digits are '0' and '1'. It is called the *dual* or, more frequently, *binary* notation, but a better parallel of 'decimal' would have been 'dimidial'. The decimal system breaks numbers down by tenths (*partes decimae*), and the dimidial breaks them down by halves (*partes dimidiae*). However, I shall not persist. Let it be 'binary'.

In binary notation 365 becomes 101101101, which is to say, in powers of 2,

$$2^8 + 2^6 + 2^5 + 2^3 + 2^2 + 2^0.$$

This expression illustrates a remarkable law: every positive integer is a sum of *distinct* powers of 2. The same cannot be said of any other base than 2. We saw that in 365 the power 10^2 figures not once but three times; the power 10^1 six times; the power 10^0 five times.

In binary notation the decimal point becomes rather a dimidial point. Places to the right of it mark negative powers of 2, and bring our folk dichotomies of yore back into their own. Thus .0001 inches is a sixteenth of an inch.

Computers can take long-windedness in their stride, and happily accept it as the price of higher simplicities. Thus it is that 2, as base of numeration, has dominated computer design. It meshes neatly with wiring, for the vacillation between 1 and 0 in binary notation becomes a simple matter of on and off. This technical convenience is extended to nonnumerical texts by more arbitrary measures; for, as the Morse Code reminds us, texts generally can be got down to two characters when brevity is no object.

We can appreciate a neat consequence of the binary notation if we limit our attention to the real numbers from 0 to 1 (excluding 0, including 1). We find that there is a one-to-one correspondence between those real numbers and the infinite classes of positive integers. The reasoning is as follows. Each such real number, represented now in binary expansion rather than decimal, is identified with a binary expansion that is un-ending in the sense of there being no last recurrence of '1'. Take as the corresponding class of integers, then, the integers that count off the places where '1' occurs. If the binary expansion of the real number in question begins with '.001011001', the corresponding class of integers will begin with 3, 5, 6, and 9; for '1' occurs in the third, fifth, sixth, and ninth places of the binary expansion. The class of integers thus determined will be infinite, since the binary expansion has no end of occurrences of '1'; and conversely each infinite class of positive integers will determine one of the real numbers, by indicating all the places where '1' rather than '0' occurs in its binary expansion.

Definition

Definition, define thyself. Dictionary entries are a far cry from what philosophers and mathematicians call definition. Dictionaries are for facilitating our negotiations in the language, and for that purpose it proves efficacious to resort only here and there to definition in the philosophers' and mathematicians' sense. Definition in the philosophers' and mathematicians' sense remains an important matter, however, deserving of a name. Such will be my sense of the word and the topic of these pages.

To define an expression is, paradoxically speaking, to explain how to get along without it. To define is to eliminate. We define an expression, the *definiendum,* by presenting another, the *definiens,* to the same effect. Availability of the definiens renders the definiendum dispensable, save perhaps as a convenient abbreviation.

The conveniently brief expression 'man', for example, might be defined by equating it to 'rational animal'. Such was the line taken by the old Spaniard Seneca. It has also been equated, subject to protest, to 'featherless biped'. But a word does not have to be defined by equating it to a phrase thus directly. What matters is unique eliminability, and a definition to the purpose commonly involves excursions into the context. Thus we might define the connective 'or' by the instruction to paraphrase each context 'p or q' as 'not both not p and not q'.

People speak thus of defining an expression, but they speak also of defining objects. What is man, they ask, that Thou art mindful of him? What is number, that man is mindful of it? The one way of talking of definition reduces to the other, since we define men by defining 'man', and we define numbers by defining 'number' and the numerals. Definition of expressions is the broader idea, since it applies equally to expressions such as 'or' that do not refer to any object. But one tends to speak of definition in the object-directed sense when puzzled less about use of the expression than about the nature of its objects.

It is especially helpful to think of definition as elimination when we contemplate the multiplicity of ways of defining NATURAL NUMBERS, *q.v.*; for each way is separately acceptable but no two are compatible. All that is really afoot, we there observe, is a multiplicity of effective progressions.

An even neater case to the same effect is the ordered pair $\langle x, y \rangle$, defined under COMPLEX NUMBERS; for, as there noted, the one and only demand upon the definition is unique recoverability of x and of y from $\langle x, y \rangle$. Any number of divergent definitions of $\langle x, y \rangle$ can be devised to meet that requirement.

Definition can have various purposes. Sometimes it serves as instruction in some detail of the established language. Sometimes it prepares the reader for the author's special use of some technical term. Sometimes, as in the two last examples, it resolves a philosophical quandary regarding the nature of some partially understood objects. Sometimes, finally, it serves merely to show that a notation at hand is adequate to treating of some ulterior topic. In all these cases, definition can be regarded as an instruction for translating one language into another: a more verbose language into a more economical sublanguage with the same coverage. (See RECURSION, however, regarding recursive definition.)

In philosophy, logic, and mathematics it commonly happens that the more verbose language and the sublanguage are both prized for their unlike virtues: the one for the convenient brevity and flexibility of its notation and the other for the simplicity of its underlying structure. The definitions that afford translation of each into the other are then likewise prized, as enabling us to oscillate and enjoy the best of both worlds; see SINGULAR TERMS.

Discreteness

An ordering of numbers or other objects is *discrete* if each object has an immediate successor or predecessor or both. The whole numbers are discrete. The ratios, in contrast, are *dense*: between any two there are more. The *real* numbers, comprising the ratios and irrationals together, are accounted not merely dense but *continuous,* owing to an added trait that need not detain us (see REAL NUMBERS). The vernacular shuns mathematical niceties and settles for just the binary opposition, as shall I for now: discrete and continuous.

Discreteness affords us our first grip on the number system. We learn the natural numbers by learning to count. Afterward we fill in the ratios by describing them in terms of whole numerators and denominators. The first irrationals emerge likewise by description in terms of whole numbers, as square roots, cube roots, and the like. Further irrational numbers eventually get picked out by independent methods, but we know from a theorem of Georg Cantor's that most of them must forever elude us (see INFINITE NUMBERS).

A discrete ordering has, on the face of it, the charm of simplicity. A little reflection on arithmetic, however, reveals another side to the picture. Addition and multiplication of whole numbers are indeed a breeze, but division can prove frustrating: some of them are not divisible by others. The invention or discovery of ratios then eases matters: division becomes feasible across the board, apart from a small matter of zero. Extraction of roots continues to be spotty, until the further invention or discovery of the irrational numbers takes care of that. The resulting continuum of real numbers affords a smooth and simple domain for computation, as the discrete series of whole numbers did not. Discreteness opened the way to arithmetic, but continuity streamlines the work.

This contrast carries over into mathematical research. The mathematics of real numbers and of functions of real numbers is a massive and powerful apparatus, exploited by the exact and approximate sciences at every turn. The mathematics of whole numbers, called number theory, is a stubborn and halting affair, as FERMAT'S LAST THEOREM bears abundant witness. It is a domain in which the exercise of much mathematical ingenuity has tended to issue in sporadic theorems, poor in respect of the broad and systematic connections that are the joy of mathematics.

The contrast is drawn in precise terms by a pair of theorems. GÖDEL'S THEOREM shows that no proof procedure can encompass all the truths of elementary number theory. On the other hand Tarski has shown that truth in the exactly parallel theory of real numbers can be routinely checked. A computer could be programmed to do it. Yet the two systems are identical in notation. Their difference lies solely in what the variables are interpreted as ranging over: the positive whole numbers and zero in the one system, and the positive real numbers and zero in the other. This difference in interpretation entails a difference in the truth of formulas. The formulas that are true under the real-number interpretation turn out to be a manageable lot. The ones that are true under the natural-number interpretation do not.

The interplay of discreteness and continuity is not limited to numbers. Phonemes impose discreteness on a phonetic continuum, and not just for the convenience of linguists. We note under PHONEMES that the recognition of phonemes at an unconscious level is indispensable to the acquisition and the handing down of language.

Discreteness of the written alphabet, moreover, has been crucial to the relaying of literature and learning down the literate millennia. Manuscripts deteriorate, but have been persistently copied afresh. The copies would suffer from accumulated inaccuracies in the imitating of the fading ink marks, were it not for the discreteness of the alphabet.

Pictures, in contrast, are a continuous medium; there are no discrete standards to which to rectify a decaying original or an unfaithful copy. In a 1954 *Bulletin* of the American Academy of Arts and Sciences we read as follows of the Academy's seal:

> With the passage of time, when various new line cuts had been made from poorly inked impressions of earlier ones, the seal that had been so imaginative in its original concept deteriorated into . . . muddy and disreputable condition. As no impression suitable for making a new cut could be located, the Committee . . . asked Rudolph Ruzicka . . . to make a fresh drawing.

Ruzicka's reconstruction was then adopted by amendment of the Statutes.

Interplay between the discrete and the continuous dominates much of technology. Traditional clocks and watches depend on a pendulum or oscillator for their timing, and thus are discrete in their mechanism, but the resulting time-telling is meant to seem continuous and usually does. Computers are divided on the point: discrete and continuous, digital and analog. A computer that is discrete in its input may be so fashioned as to yield a discrete or a continuous output, and one that is continuous in its input may be so fashioned as to do likewise.

In cinematography we encounter an elaborate interplay of the discrete and the continuous. The actors' antics on the movie lot are continuous, between the director's interruptions. The continuous film records the antics in a discrete sequence of frames, which in due course are discretely projected for our delectation. Thanks to the rapidity of the discrete projection, however, and the sluggishness of our perception, what we experience as viewers has all the original continuity of the antics on the movie lot, to the exclusion even of the director's interruptions.

Continuity, then, in the movies as in clockwork, is our blurred perception of the discrete. So likewise in nature, according to the theories of ATOMS ancient and modern. Whereas the atoms are separated from one another in space, the discreteness in movies and clockwork is a temporal discreteness of events. But quantum physicists have determined to their satisfaction that temporal continuity in nature as well, even to the actual antics of the actors on the movie set, is only the effect of our blurred perception. Nature's nearest approach to continuity of events is a succession of fits and starts at intervals which, though unimaginably brief, are no briefer than Planck's constant.

E

Etymology

The Indo-European family of languages embraces the majority of the languages that most of us are prepared to put a name to. They span Eurasia from Hindi and Bengali in the southeast to Gaelic and Icelandic in the northwest. English and the other Germanic languages are among them, as well as the Slavic languages, Latin and its descendants, and Greek. Outriders whose membership credentials have been recognized only in the present century are Albanian, Armenian, and ancient Hittite. All these evolved from an ancestral language that was spoken perhaps six thousand years ago.

The American Indian languages, in contrast, are sorted into dozens of families between which no adequate evidence of common ancestry is forthcoming. This circumstance is attributed primarily to the lack of ancient documentation of these languages. Our records of past stages of Indo-European languages have revealed patterns of change which linguists could extrapolate backward toward common origins. American Indian languages give the linguist little more to reason from than current similarities.

There is a wealth, certainly, of these. Arresting similarity is noted from time to time even between an American Indian word and a word to the same purpose in Hebrew, perhaps, or Polynesian; and such observations have been known to prompt bold conjectures. The trouble comes in distinguishing between significant correspondences and mere coincidences, in the absence of a grasp of pertinent laws of development such as we enjoy in the Indo-European family.

We can steel ourselves against unwarranted conjectures of linguistic kinship by reflecting on the wealth of homonyms in our own language, where documentation attests to convergence from unlike antecedent forms; thus 'sound' from *sonus*, 'sound' from *sanus*, and 'sound' for Long Island Sound from an Anglo-Saxon *sund*. But what are more instructive are cases where both form and meaning would attest conclusively to sameness of origin in the absence of documentation to the contrary. See KINSHIP OF WORDS. What with all the anomalies there noted, it is not to be wondered that false etymologies have been scarely less frequent than true ones, at least in unscholarly circles. Thus one is more than ready to derive *outrage* from *out + rage*, but the true origin is rather the French *outre*, or *ultra*, plus the suffix *-age*, as if to say *ultrage*, 'beyondage', 'excess'. *Nugget*, again, might plausibly be traced to *nougat*, which represents a late Latin *nucatum*, 'nut-laden'; but the truth is otherwise. One might even be tempted to derive *offend* from *off + end*, as if to say out of line; but that would be out of line indeed.

Responsible authorities occasionally diverge. One case in point is *glamour*; see SYNTAX. Another is *orchard*. The preferred account is Latin *hort(us)* plus English *yard*. *Hortus* means 'garden' or 'yard', and in fact all three words are the same in Indo-European origin; so orchard is yardyard. But by the competing account it is rather *wortyard*, 'herb garden'. It is a long pull from an herb garden to an apple grove, but it seems that there was a custom of devoting part of one's garden to herbs and fruit trees.

There is a more puzzling divergence over *corporal*, 'squad leader'; French *caporal*, Italian *caporale*. The Latin echoes are *corpus*, 'body', and *caput*, 'head'. Two of my dictionaries represent the English form as a corruption of the French and

Italian, but Skeat argues that the corruption went the other way, since the middle syllable -por- is integral to *corpus, corporis*, and alien to *caput, capitis*.

Authorities have diverged also over *element*. Some derived it from the letters *el-em-en*, L–M–N, as if to say "as simple as A–B–C." But why L–M–N in particular? Skeat and Meillet reject the account and leave the etymology unsolved. Meillet thinks the origin may be Etruscan.

A far-fetched etymology that flaunts its absurdity to the least discerning eye is the derivation of the verb *atone* from *at + one*. But the crowning irony is that this one is the God's truth.

Faltering etymologists of an in some ways less favored century than our own based a number of etymological conjectures on a desperate hypothesis to the effect that some things were named for what they lacked. This explanatory principle is denominated by one of its own irresponsible instances: *lucus a non lucendo*—'A grove is called a *lucus* because there is no shining there.' My own untenable example of *lucus a non lucendo* is *dastard*: so called because he dastn't.

Hills offer tempting cases of the same. The word *hill* itself and the word *low* are the same in origin: Anglo-Saxon *hlaw*. Or I should say *a* word *low*; for I must spoil the story by adding that it has nothing to do with the adjective *low*. The *low* from *hlaw* is an obsolete noun that survives only in *Ludlow* and other place-names.

There is a companion piece in another word for hills: *down*, as in the Berkshire Downs. This word, which is cognate with *dune*, does bring us a step nearer to the perilous *lucus non lucens*, for it is indeed related to the adverb *down*. The adverb is traced to the Anglo-Saxon *of-dune*, 'off hill'.

A distant kin of *lucus a non lucendo* is occasionally encountered today in an owlish allusion to "identity of opposites." The two examples about hills would be pat illustrations, but we have seen that each of them is accounted for without appealing to any mystical principle. A case for identity of opposites that is invariably cited is *altus*, Latin for both 'high' and 'deep'. What we actually have here, however, is a case rather of parochial outlook on our own part. What is objective about height and depth is distance from top to bottom. We call it height or depth according to our point of view; Latin simply tells how it is, with no thought of opposites.

Another tempting case for the identity of opposites is *cleave*: 1. adhere, 2. sever. However, Skeat argues that this is a convergence of two words, independent in origin. A rather weak case is *dispose* in two senses: 1. get rid of, 2. have at one's disposal. Another is *sanction*: 1. approval, 2. penalty. Another is *enjoin*: 1. order, 2. forbid. Another, perhaps, is *unqualified*: my support of a proposal may be unqualified either because it is whole-hearted or because I lack the requisite qualifications. A further example, it would seem, is *fast*: static as in holding fast and dynamic as in moving fast. This dialectic can be *aufgehoben*, however, as Hegel would have had it, on a par with *altus* above: *fast* in both cases connotes a quality of intensity.

May identity of opposites be manifested not only by sameness of word for opposite senses, but also by sameness of sense for opposite words? Well, there is *fast*, again, and its opposite *loose*: there are fast women, I am told, and loose women, and no clear distinction between them. *A little* and *a lot* are opposites, but quite a little is quite a lot. Again goals and targets come to much the same thing in figurative speech, though we like our goals and shoot our targets. But I stray progressively from my declared topic, etymology.

Word origins are delicately laced with poetry here and there. To be *recalcitrant* is to dig the heels in. A *scruple* is an uncomfortable pebble in the shoe. An *outcast* is at once an outsider of the caste system and one who has been cast out. To *impede* was to put one's foot in someone's way, and to *expedite* was to take the foot away and let him pass. *Scrutiny* is pawing through the trash. *Succor* is a running under, perhaps to break someone's fall. To *escape* is to slip out of one's cape, leaving it perhaps in a captor's clutch. Another natural is *retaliate* for a clawing back, when we think of *talon*; however, this connection cannot be sustained.

Errand offers strange counsel when we examine it: *errandum est,* 'one ought to err'. Actually the word is unrelated.

Euphemism

There was a day when even the mildest of oaths, *My God!*, wanted tempering for tender ears. Escape into another language was felt to help: *Dio mio!* A subsequent step, whether by way of further tempering or through mere phonetic confusion, reduced *Dio mio!* to *Dear me!* Another period piece of high Victorian Baroque, understandably short-lived, served to soften the edges of swearing to God: *Well, I swan to man!*

Euphemism, perversely, has power to render mild words harsh. Thus *ugly*, said of a person, was softened to *homely*, in the neutral sense of 'ordinary' or 'nothing fancy'. By now *homely* has taken on all the harshness of *ugly*, at least in vernacular use. The plain word *plain* was moved into the breach and by now it is not much softer than *homely*. *Naughty* began at naught, plainer than plain, as if to say 'nothingly'.

The word *vile* for bad or ill-natured people was originally a euphemism; it had meant 'common' or 'ordinary'. Turning harsh through its euphemistic use, it gave way to *mean*, which meant, again, 'average' or 'ordinary', but in due course lost its euphemistic value in turn. 'Ordinary' itself was at last invoked in some quarters, in the dialect form *ornery*, which has likewise become a term of harsh reproach.

Vulgar and *lewd* are more of the same. *Vulgus* is the people, and *vulgar* simply meant 'of the people', hence again 'common', 'ordinary'. *Lewd* in the Middle Ages meant 'laymanly', hence 'unlettered', hence 'common'; and in the fullness of time it plumbed the depths of *vulgar* and below.

The unsavory air of *hussy* arose likewise from euphemism; *hussif* originally stood for 'housewife', and quite innocently of any insinuations about icemen or traveling salesmen. *Idiot* had a similar career; see IDIOTISMS.

Euphemism, we see, renders neutral terms pejorative. In rare cases, through other forces, a neutral or humble epithet becomes honorific. Examples are *lord, lady,* and *knight. Lord* comes from *hlaf-weard,* 'loaf guard', denoting the man in charge of the bread. *Lady* is thought to have come from a term for the kneader of bread. *Knight* is thought to have begun as a term merely for a fellow tribesman. These three examples are evidently inflationary effects of the rise of a ruler's power and prestige. Dignity accrues to his menials *pari passu.* There is a curious further honorific, however, whose rise from lowly or even scurrilous beginnings cannot be thus explained, namely *prestige* itself, which originally meant 'trickery', from *praestringere.* I wonder if it could have been influenced by an unrecorded *praestitium,* which would mean 'a standing forth'.

Homely, plain, ornery, hussy, and the rest emerged as euphemisms for admittedly undesirable traits. They did not reflect approval of the traits, but merely softened the reference. To cast about for a euphemism for such a trait is itself to evince disapproval of it. A devious way of expressing contempt for something, say sociology, would be to ask, "What would be a good euphemism for 'sociology'?" The natural rejoinder would be "What's wrong with sociology?"

But there is also an opposite use of euphemism. Some terms, racial ones notably, owe their harshness not to objectionable denotations but to objectionable attitudes in which they have commonly been bandied; and here the point of the euphemism is rather to disavow the attitude. One curious racial term in poor standing is *Chinaman,* which came to be felt as derogatory. Ironically, it departs from the usual patterns of the English language precisely in order to conform to the way in which the Chinese refer to themselves: *djung-kuo run,* 'China man'.

Excluded Middle

The venerable law of excluded middle, or *tertium non datur*, says that every statement is true or false. There is much to be said for it, and much against.

The mathematician L. E. J. Brouwer lashed out against it two generations ago with his doctrine of "intuitionism," according to which a mathematical statement qualifies as neither true nor false unless its truth or falsity can be shown to hinge on considerations that are *constructive*, in some sense; see CONSTRUCTIVISM. Thus FERMAT'S LAST THEOREM still qualifies as true or false, even though nobody knows which, because we could mechanically check a counter-instance of it if one were presented. On the other hand much of set theory fails to meet intuitionist standards, and is reckoned neither true nor false. Classical logic with its law of excluded middle is accordingly rejected in favor of a more complex intuitionist logic.

In recent writings Michael Dummett extends the intuitionist constraints beyond mathematics to science in general. Statements do not qualify as true or false unless observations are describable that might reasonably be reckoned as direct evidence for or against them.

Such doctrines are sparked by congenial empiricist sentiments, but they obstruct the no less congenial clarity and simplicity at which science aims. Intuitionist standards are obscure, especially when projected beyond mathematics. The deviant logic aggravates matters, complicating and muddying up the crystalline simplicity of classical PREDICATE LOGIC. Two is the smallest and simplest number that gets off the ground, and two-valued logic, embodiment of the law of excluded middle, is minimal, streamlined logic stripped for action.

We who are unpersuaded of intuitionism accordingly remain unmoved, protesting that warranted assertability is one thing, TRUTH another. Insofar as a statement deserves a place in scientific language at all, calling it true deserves one too; for, to quote Tarski, 'Snow is white' is true if and only if snow is white. Dissociating truth from warrant, we become free to recognize that some truths are discoverable and some not; and we become free to call the rest of the statements false. Sweet simplicity is our reward.

The law of excluded middle came under fire also from another quarter, motivated less by empiricism than by theology. It was argued that contingent predictions are neither true nor false. See FUTURE for argument and response.

A third challenge to the law of excluded middle is leveled by names such as 'Pegasus', which enjoy a respected place in the language but fail to designate anything. Sentences containing such names are reasonably regarded for the most part as neither true nor false. Here I acquiesce in a double standard: the law of excluded middle lapses for everyday discourse where empty names are concerned, but we can sustain it for purposes of logical analysis when we are prepared to regiment scientific language along economical lines; see SINGULAR TERMS.

A fourth challenge to the law of excluded middle is presented by the vagueness of terms. Language has evolved in use, and it plays fast and loose with needless distinctions. Thus no need has been felt to settle how much residual hair is compatible with baldness, nor how to demarcate the base of a mountain. So, if a sentence hinges for its truth or falsity on whether to regard some sketchily thatched old man as bald, or whether to regard some cabin a little way up the trail as on the mountain, it is reasonable to waive the law of excluded middle and reckon the sentence as neither true nor false.

But I would again invoke the double standard. We can retain the luxury of the law of excluded middle in logical analysis simply by proceeding as if all terms concerned were precise. We can even introduce genuine precision by a supplementary convention whenever it matters, and so indeed we do, in legislation and in science.

Vagueness has long irked the logical mind, as witness the ancient paradox of the *sorites*, or heap: removal of a grain from a heap leaves a heap, and yet if we persist, grain by grain, we are left with little or nothing. If removal of a grain *always* leaves a heap, it follows by mathematical induction (see RECURSION) that a heap can consist of a single grain or even none. Here we have dramatic evidence of the dependence of logical analysis upon the fact or fiction of sharp distinctions. We save mathematical induction by positing a precise lower limit of heaphood, though not bothering to specify it. Removal of a grain from such a minimal heap leaves no heap.

We have now encountered reservations over the excluded middle from four fairly independent quarters. Pretty devastating, one might have felt, were it not for the overwhelming virtues of the law of excluded middle in respect of logical clarity and simplicity. I have argued for overruling the first two of the four objections, and appeasing the other two with a double standard.

Philosophers have been known to maintain the law of excluded middle across the board by representing it as applying not to sentences but to propositions, these being abstract objects posited in the partial image of sentences. Whatever failures the law may be seen to suffer as applied to sentences, then, is put down to failure of those sentences to correspond to propositions. This resort is reminiscent of one noted in connection with the correspondence theory of TRUTH, *q.v.*, and it is an equally empty verbalism.

Let us just recognize rather that the law of excluded middle is not a fact of life, but a norm governing efficient logical regimentation.

Extravagance

Etymologically it is a wandering outside; thus a straying off the beam. The immediate connotation is excessive spending, but what I now have in mind is cheap extravagance: mere extravagance of asseveration. "You're a million miles from nowhere," an understandably not very popular song ran, "when you're one little mile from home."

Most of us have been told, and insistently, that it is more tiring to walk down a mountain than to walk up. Some of us have been told that the glowing coals are hotter than the flame. I have heard it said that it is a poor idea to eat ice cream on a hot day, because the body heats up in combatting the inner chill. Many of us have heard that a hot beverage is a good thing on a hot day because it induces sweat, which, evaporating, cools us off. I may even have heard that it is well to wrap up warmly on a hot day, so as to sweat the more. Why don't people like to tell the truth?

I think I know the answer: it is because truth is less strange than fiction, and there is a charm in strangeness, or surprise (see ANOMALY). This conjecture, by the way, reminds me of a sixth absurdity to add to the above five. Truth, we are told, is stranger than fiction.

A persistent, ubiquitous form of extravagance is exaggeration. "She *hates* to be called Winnie. It makes her *furious*." The fact is that when asked whether she preferred to be called Winifred or Winnie, she merely replied with some hesitation that she really preferred the former. I have heard it said that when GÖDEL'S THEOREM first appeared, John von Neumann was drawn into the reflexive subtleties of its proof and contemplated exploiting them for possible further results, but that he dropped the matter because he found it was threatening his sanity. I suspect that all it really came down to was that von Neumann once remarked in casual vernacular that the convolutions of Gödel's proof made his head swim. And I wonder whether Dr. Johnson, in his celebrated rebuttal of Berkeley, really kicked the stone with as painful violence as Boswell would have had us believe.

I think a frequent cause of overstatement is diffidence: wondering whether what one is about to say is worth hearing. So one embellishes it a bit, not quite deliberately. If the message is relayed, embellishment is subject to iteration; and the message becomes the more worth relaying as the embellishment proceeds. A tacit, tentative reservation of full belief is the part of the prudent listener.

It is the part most emphatically of the prudent listener to broadcasts and reader of newspapers, where embellishment of news can be a deliberate element of enlightened merchandising. 'Embellishment' indeed is the wrong word; ugliness prevails over beauty. By considerations of symmetry, playing up good news would serve the journalists' purpose of astonishment fully as well as playing up the bad; but the trouble is that good news is harder to come by. This circumstance may be seen as a sad commentary on contemporary life, but it can also be seen in quite the opposite light. Perhaps the level of contemporary life is so high that there is more scope for novelty downward than upward.

Fermat's Last Theorem

Let me begin, in the words of W. S. Gilbert, with a lot of news about the square on the hypotenuse.

Euclid was doubtless not the first to observe that a straight line is the shortest path between two points. If in flat and unobstructed country you have walked three miles out and four miles over, you could have saved two miles by walking the diagonal. For, as Pythagoras reputedly *was* the first to observe, you square the three and the four, add the results, and take the square root, getting five for the diagonal.

The Pythagorean Theorem holds for right triangles of all shapes and sizes, but the nice thing about this example is that all three lengths are whole numbers, thanks to the arithmetical circumstance that $3^2 + 4^2 = 5^2$.

3, 4, and 5 are not the only triad of whole numbers that satisfies the Pythagorean equation '$x^2 + y^2 = z^2$'. The triad $n^2 - 1$, $2n$, and $n^2 + 1$ satisfies it for any n, by elementary algebra:

(1) $$(n^2 - 1)^2 + (2n)^2 = (n^2 + 1)^2.$$

Take n as 2 here and you get $3^2 + 4^2 + 5^2$ again. Take it as 4 and you get $15^2 + 8^2 = 17^2$. Take it as 5 and you get $24^2 + 10^2 = 26^2$.

If three numbers x, y, and z satisfy '$x^2 + y^2 = z^2$', clearly any other three proportional to them will satisfy it too. Besides all the cases of '$x^2 + y^2 = z^2$' that are covered by (1), therefore, there are all further cases that are proportional to cases covered by (1). Thus from the above three examples we have further that $9^2 + 12^2 = 15^2$, $30^2 + 16^2 = 34^2$, and $12^2 + 5^2 = 13^2$. In this last case we exploit the proportionality downward.

Having noted such facts about the equation '$x^2 + y^2 = z^2$' that was Pythagoras' stock in trade, a mathematician next looked inquiringly at '$x^3 + y^3 = z^3$', linking fancy unto fancy as was his wont. He found—and it was no small feat—that there are no positive whole numbers x, y, and z whatever such that $x^3 + y^3 = z^3$. What then of higher powers, higher exponents? A third of a millennium ago Pierre de Fermat claimed to have proved in full generality that where w exceeds 2 there are never any positive whole numbers x, y, and z such that $x^w + y^w = z^w$. He left us the claim but not the proof.

Such is Fermat's notorious Last Theorem. Mathematicians have tried for a third of a millennium to prove it. The effort has been fruitful of by-products, I am told, advancing the theory of numbers on several fronts; but no proof of Fermat's Last Theorem has emerged. Mathematicians have also tried in vain to disprove it: to find positive integers x, y, z, and w (> 2) such that $x^w + y^w = z^w$. It has been painfully proved, case by case, that any such exception will require a pretty big w. The lower bound on such a w has been raised by leaps and bounds by enlisting computers for the control of complex combinations.

Fermat's Last Theorem is briefly stated, we see, and stated in the utterly elementary vocabulary of arithmetic. It is startling that so simple and lucid a conjecture should resist proof and disproof for all these centuries. Is it perhaps true but incapable in principle of proof by any recognized proof procedures? We know from GÖDEL'S THEOREM that some truths are indeed in that predicament, even though stated purely in the notation of elementary number theory. But it would be strange for any of them to be so simple as this one.

Fermat's Last Theorem is simple in an important respect over and above its brevity and lucidity. Namely, if in fact it is false then it does admit of disproof by known methods, indeed by a very rudimentary method. The disproof, once discovered, would consist simply in writing down the four exceptional numerals x, y, z, and w, where $w > 2$, and inviting the reader to verify by computation that $x^w + y^w = z^w$. Fermat's Last Theorem simply denies an infinite lot of numerical formulas any of which can be checked by computation.

This particular brand of simplicity should not, however, encourage us to expect that Fermat's Last Theorem is demonstrable if true. Gödel's own complicated example of an indemonstrable truth, which he produces in proof of his theorem, actually shares the same disarming trait: it likewise merely denies an infinitude of formulas any of which can be checked by computation.

Fermat's Last Theorem can be vividly stated in terms of sorting various objects into a row of bins some of which are red, some blue, and the rest unpainted. The theorem amounts to saying that when there are more than two objects it can never happen that

(2)   the ways of sorting them that shun both colors are
       equal in number to the ways that shun neither.

To show that this is equivalent to Fermat's Last Theorem, I shall show that (2) boils down to the Fermat equation '$x^w + y^w = z^w$' when w is how many objects there are, z is how many bins there are, x is how many bins are not red, and y is how many are not blue.

There are z choices of bins in which to deposit the first object, and for each such choice there are again z choices of where to deposit the second object, and so on; so altogether there are z^w ways of sorting the w objects into bins. The ways that shun red are x^w in number by similar reasoning, and those that shun blue are y^w in number. So where A is the number of ways that shun both colors, B is the number of ways that shun red but not blue, C is the number of ways that shun blue but not red, and D is the number of ways that shun neither, we have

$$x^w = A + B, \qquad y^w = A + C, \qquad z^w = A + B + C + D.$$

These equations give '$x^w + y^w = z^w$' if and only if $A = D$, which is to say (2).

The version (2) of '$x^w + y^w = z^w$' enables us to see why that equation is so readily satisfiable when $w < 3$ and not, to our knowledge, otherwise. When there are fewer than three objects, the ways of sorting them that shun neither color must shun the unpainted bins. The number of such ways, namely D, will be 0 in the case of a single object, and for two objects it will be the number of red bins times the number of blue bins times 2. In the one case we can fulfill (2) by taking the number of unpainted bins as 0, and in the other case by taking it as the square root of D if D happens to be square. When on the other hand there are three or more objects, computation of D becomes a complicated affair—partly because of the intrusion of unpainted bins and partly because the combinations and permutations of three or more things so vastly and complexly outnumber those of two. Whether (2) can ever be fulfilled when there are more than two objects becomes anybody's guess, and so it has remained.

I might remark as one final curiosity that Fermat's Last Theorem can be stated in terms purely of power, rather than plus and power. It says that for all positive integers x, y, z, and w,

$$\text{if } (w^{w^{xw}})^{w^{yw}} = w^{w^{zw}}, \text{ then } (w^w)^w = w^{w^w}.$$

Formalism

Deduction has its utility where the truth of some statement has been in doubt. We may establish a moot statement by deducing it from recognized truths, or refute it by deducing an absurdity from it. We may try a hypothesis out by seeing what can be deduced from it. By the time of Euclid, however, utility was ceding place, in part, to the playfulness of theory. Euclid was at pains to prove theorems some of which were no more in doubt to begin with than the postulates from which he proved them. He was out to minimize his postulates, seeking elegance independently of the demands of utility.

This pursuit engenders a predicament. When we take to deducing conclusions that we know in advance to be true, how are we to prevent that prior knowledge from creeping into the proof and begging the question? One tries to feign ignorance, but ignorance of how much? How to draw a *cordon sanitaire* between the acknowledged knowledge of the premises and the unacknowledged knowledge of the thesis? Rigorous modern methods have revealed that Euclid, for one, muffed this delicate discrimination at a point or two.

Traditionally the usual way of coping with this predicament, often unconsciously, was disinterpretation. Such logical particles as 'not', 'and', 'unless', 'all', 'some', 'is', and 'equals' would be permitted to retain their full force in order to implement the logical steps of deduction involved in proving the theorem, but the terms peculiar to the subject in hand would be treated as gibberish, both in the theorem to be proved and in the theorems or postulates from which it was being deduced. These terms would be conceded only the barest syntactic recognition, as in Carnap's "Pirotes carulate elatically." Such was the way of assuring that the theorem was a purely logical consequence of its premises.

This precautionary practice led many mathematicians to look upon their subject as intrinsically uninterpreted; when interpreted it ceases to be pure mathematics, and becomes applied. Thus Russell's *mot* of the turn of the century: that in pure mathematics "we never know what we are talking about nor whether what we are saying is true." It is to Russell's credit that he soon dropped this idea; but many mathematicians have not.

The straightforward view of pure mathematics puts it more

on a par with the rest of science. Pure arithmetic is indeed the pure science of pure number, but pure numbers participate in the subject matter of physics and economics on a par with bodies, electrons, and petroleum. Variables in physics and economics range over numbers as well as over other things. The 'some' and 'all' of quantification, along with their associated pronouns or variables, apply in physics and economics to numbers as well as to anything else. When light is said to travel 300,000 kilometers a second, a relation is affirmed between the pure number 300,000 and the light waves; the unit of velocity does not sully the number, but merely specifies the relation. When crude is pegged at $35 a barrel, the pure number 35 is sullied by neither the dollars nor the barrels; dollars-per-barrel is the relation, rather, between the pure number and the crude oil. The purity of pure arithmetic resides not in disinterpretation, nor yet in some difference between pure numbers and the numbers of natural science and commerce. It resides merely in a restriction of subject matter: arithmetic is occupied purely with those truths which concern numbers and make no specific reference to bodies, electrons, light rays, or petroleum.

Granted, there is abstract algebra. It may even have been stimulated by bad philosophy of mathematics, and for that we can be grateful, however ill the wind. But abstract algebra is best seen as part of the mathematics of classes and relations, and this is best seen still as a theory of classes and relations in general, classes and relations of all sorts of things, ordinary and otherwise.

Disinterpretation is not the only way of assuring that theorems be purely logical consequences of their premises. Another way is by codifying logic and then monitoring proofs to see that they do not exceed the rules. The codified logic that had come down through the Middle Ages, largely from Aristotle, fell far short of the uncodified logical reasoning that went on in mathematics and elsewhere. But by 1850 efforts toward an adequate and explicit logic were mounting. In Gottlob Frege's little *Begriffsschrift* of 1879 they flowered, albeit to waste their fragrance for an inconscionable period on the desert air.

The codification of logic posed a predicament too, analogous to the old mathematical one. The old problem was how to inactivate our prior knowledge of the truth of a theorem so as to put full burden on the proof. The new problem was how to inactivate our prior flair for logical implication so as to put full burden on the codified logical moves. The solution again was disinterpretation, but disinterpretation this time of the logical particles themselves. The codification must consist strictly of instructions for the manipulation of marks: instructions for concatenating, inserting, substituting, deleting. Such a formulation, as innocent of semantics as the driven snow, is called a formalism. Frege was its pioneer, though history sagged between.

Ironically, though formalism is the ultimate in disinterpretation, it spares us the need of disinterpreting. Once the allowable moves in a deduction are stipulated in aseptically typographic terms, we are free to luxuriate in the full meaning of the logical and mathematical expressions that we are manipulating; there is no longer a danger that the meanings will affect the deduction.

I suppose there were practical-minded mathematicians in Euclid's day who scoffed at Euclid's pedantic proofs of things that anyone could already see were true. Certainly Frege's pursuit of ultimate rigor, in the explicit formalization of logic, went long unappreciated. It was thirty-odd years after the *Begriffsschrift* that Whitehead and Russell brought out their *Principia Mathematica*, in which mathematical logic, set theory, and the foundations of arithmetic and mathematical analysis were rigorously developed in three formidable volumes of formulas. Many mathematicians scoffed at this, at least *viva voce*, as pedantic and unproductive. But even *Principia Mathematica* was a long step backward from the *Begriffsschrift* in respect of formalistic rigor.

In the 1920s, thanks largely to David Hilbert, formalistic rigor came increasingly to be prized in some circles. In 1931 it proved instrumental to the philosophico-mathematical sensation of the age: GÖDEL'S THEOREM. Gödel's proof hinged on modeling the formalism of logic and arithmetic in arithmetic. The theorem could not even be conceived and conjectured, in its latter-day generality, without the clarification of the idea of a proof procedure that formalism affords.

The nit-picking pedantry of formalist logicians, likened by old-guard mathematicians and down-to-earth technologists to the esoterica of stamp collecting, was thus vindicated in the eyes of all whose breadth of vision could accommodate the magnitude of Gödel's discovery. A second vindication was soon to follow, and this time at the heart of high technology. Through insights of Alan Turing and Emil Post, formalism joined forces with the abstract theory of computing machines, with the effect of illuminating both domains. Today formalism is the stock in trade of the thousands of no-nonsense technicians who make their living programming computers. A computer requires blow-by-blow instruction, strictly in terms of what to do to strings of marks or digits, and eked out by no arm-waving or appeals to common sense and imagination; and such, precisely, is formalism.

There is an analogy in the splitting of the atom. Whether it could be done was an academic question for our abstract brethren in their ivory tower, and funds for trying to do it were at first an indulgent if not grudging concession on the part of the level-headed men of the world who make funds possible. Here again, in a trite phrase, a bombshell was in store. Nuclear fission and its redoubtable offspring, nuclear fusion, transcended the ivory tower with a vengeance.

Freedom

Herman Fetzer, affectionately known as Jake Falstaff, regaled Akron readers daily with a breezy column of bright observations and reflections in prose and verse under the title "Pippins and Cheese." J. P. McEvoy contributed another witty column on random topics of the time and place, conceived in the spirit of Pepys: "Up betimes and to the office . . ." Both writers might be said to have enjoyed an enviable freedom from constraint, unlike our strictly political columnists Avi Nelson and Peter Lucas; but this would be a grave misuse of 'enjoy' and 'enviable'. Nelson and Lucas are the more enviable ones. No day is without its political issues, nor any issue without its clear and nevertheless controversial merits. The political columnist reads the press dispatches, consults relevant archives as needed, and brings his literary craftsmanship to bear. Fetzer and McEvoy suffered, on the other hand, under an unenviable freedom. They were responsible for sheer virtuosity with no constraints to guide them—no constraints but the deadly daily deadline.

Constraint is restful in countless smaller ways. The constraint of the naval uniform is restful in sparing one the trouble of choosing each day's costume. 'Freedom from constraint' strikes the ear as pleonastic, but constraint, even so, is itself a freedom of second order: freedom from decision.

Consider the free spirits who throw off the trammels of social convention. The cast-off necktie is indeed good riddance, if the tieless minority is not too conspicuously small for comfort or if conspicuity is not distasteful. More to the point: what to do in the way of a creative, unconventional marriage ceremony? Or, scratching that, how to mention or introduce one's cohabitant? How to be nice to people without retreating into the conventional niceties? Decisions, decisions. Freedom from the trammels of an age outworn can mean quandaries at every turn, for want of a rule, a precedent, a role model, even a vivid self-image.

A humdrum example from logic instructively illustrates the dialectic of freedom and constraint. There is a technique in PREDICATE LOGIC of proving the invalidity of a formula by substituting for its variables in certain systematic ways.* The

---

*It is Skolem's method of functional normal forms in my *Methods of Logic,* third

constraint is imposed that the substituted expressions be chosen from a certain specified class. The constraint is not imperative; substitutes could be freely chosen from outside that class, issuing equally in proof of invalidity. Yet the constraint is more than welcome, for it limits our search; it assures us that if the proof can be achieved at all it can be achieved without searching beyond those bounds. What this example brings out more sharply or flatly than the others is that freedom, which sounds jolly, and constraint, which sounds irksome, grade off respectively into groping, which is irksome, and helpful hints.

Freedom to remodel society, gained by revolution, can be a delicate affair. Society up to that point, if stable at all, was stable in consequence of the gradual combining and canceling of forces and counter-forces, some planned and some not. The new and untested plan shares all the fallibility of the planner, this young newcomer in a complex world. Maybe the new order bids fair to overprivilege a hitherto underprivileged group; maybe it will presently prove to underprivilege all. It is delicate, and delicacy is seldom the revolutionary's forte. The constraint imposed by social tradition is the gyroscope that helps to keep the ship of state on an even keel.

None of which is to underrate freedom from the constraints imposed by a despot upon our voice in the government, or imposed on our movements and transactions by a paralyzing bureaucracy. If "Freedom" as a battle-cry fosters such freedoms, shout it.

Free Will

For hundreds of years it has been thought by some philosophers, and not by others, that determinism in the natural

---

and fourth editions, New York, 1972, and Cambridge: Harvard University Press, 1982.

world is incompatible with freedom of the will. If everything that happens in the world is causally determined by what went on before, then one's actions, in particular, being events in the world, are causally determined from time immemorial, and there is no scope for freedom of action.

I count myself among the others. One is free, in the ordinary sense of the term, when one does as one likes or sees fit; and this is not altered by the fact, if fact it be, that what one likes or sees fit has had its causes.

The notion that determinism precludes freedom is easily accounted for. If one's choices are determined by prior events, and ultimately by forces outside oneself, then how can one choose otherwise? Very well, one cannot. But freedom to choose to do otherwise than one likes or sees fit would be a sordid boon.

In reconciling freedom and determinism I do not affirm determinism. That is a separate question. What does determinism claim? Not just that what will be will be; that would be insufficiently controversial. Nor that a scientist could predict all of tomorrow's events on the strength of a full account of today's. That is excluded on two counts: the data would be unmanageably numerous, and furthermore the laws concerned would probably exceed, in part, the present stage of science. Or perhaps the claim is just that there *are* laws, some still undiscovered, which, taken in conjunction with a full account of today's events, mostly unknown to us, do logically imply tomorrow's events. But here the trouble is with 'law'. If any and every truth counts as a law, or even any and every general truth, then this version of determinism can be shown to boil down to the empty 'What will be will be'. If on the other hand some distinctive concept of law is intended, failure has long attended the efforts to define it. See NECESSITY.

A robust sense might be made of determinism in terms of cause, where cause is construed simple-mindedly in terms of the flow of energy from cause to effect. Determinism in this sense says that all events have causes and are determined by them. Determinism in this causal sense is thrown into question by quantum mechanics.

Causal determinism applies widely, surely, even if not universally; and in particular it may very well hold for human behavior. But, as I have just argued, the will is free for all that.

The earnest and enduring concern with the issue of free will is due to the question of praise and blame. I agree that praise and blame should be reserved to free acts; a man is not to blame for bruising someone into whom he was pushed. But I hold that heroes, geniuses, and criminals deserve praise and blame, reward and punishment, for their acts ('free act' is really redundant) despite any causal chains in the way of brilliant tutelage, early training, Vietnam traumata, child abuse, or genes. We admire or deprecate a work of art or technology for its qualities, fully aware that they have extraneous causes; and I claim the same for the hero, genius, and criminal. We may admire or deprecate the creator of the work of art or technology too, and just so we may admire or deprecate also the parent or mentor of the hero, genius, or criminal.

A penal code serves society by so adjusting the individual's cost accounting as to offset his gain from antisocial acts. Correspondingly, in an inverse way, for a system of wages and rewards. The social efficacy of these institutions does not hinge on freedom of will as *opposed* to causal determinism; on the contrary, we weave reward and punishment into the causal network in order to help to cause the desired behavior.

Punishment deters by setting an example to lend credence to threat. This, and not the sweetness of revenge, is its utility. Still, let outrage and vengefulness not be deplored; they have had survival value in social evolution by sustaining the institution of punishment. It might otherwise languish under pressure of fellow feeling, which is also a lively social force, valuable in its place.

The rightly but insufficiently maligned insanity plea, as a defense in criminal courts, is predicated on ill health of the offender's decision–making faculties. The theory would seem to be that healthy faculties make decisions spontaneously and hence with full responsibility, while diseased ones are the pawns of outside forces. It is a hard line to draw, and the more so when one appreciates that all our actions subtend causal chains from far away and long ago. The plea has no evident place in the rationale of punishment as we have been picturing it, and a persuasive justification of it is not easy to conceive.

Functions

The word is awkward in its ambiguity. We often need it in its mathematical sense even in other than mathematical contexts, and we often need it in its other sense of 'use' or 'purpose' even in fairly mathematical contexts; and thus we are put now and again to groping for paraphrases. I shall be concerned with the mathematical sense.

The impatient mathematician tells us that x^2, $x + 5$, etc. are functions of x, and that this means that for each value of x there is a unique value of x^2, $x + 5$, etc. Wrong; x^2, $x + 5$, etc. are not functions but numbers, if anything; they would be numbers if we were told what number x is supposed to be. Well, they are variable numbers, varying with x. Wrong, there are no variable numbers. Well, they are expressions. Wrong again; 'x^2' and '$x + 5$' are expressions. See USE VERSUS MENTION.

Frege was clear on the matter, all unheeded, in 1879. The incompletely specified number x^2 or $x + 5$ is one thing; the function $\lambda_x(x^2)$ or $\lambda_x(x + 5)$ is another. (The lambda notation is Alonzo Church's modification of Frege's.) The function is an operator or operation which, applied to a number (or other object), yields a number (or other object). Thus $\lambda_x(x^2)$, applied to 5, yields 25. Applied to any number x it yields x^2. This much by way of clarification could have allayed the bewilderment of countless bright students at their introduction to the differential calculus down the decades.

So a function is an operator, or operation. Intent on further clarity, one may still reasonably ask what sort of thing *that* is. Giuseppe Peano recorded the inevitable answer only in 1911, but it is one to which I think Frege might have responded *"Natürlich!"* already in 1879. The function, Peano explained, is a *relation*. It is the relation of its values to its arguments, to revert to mathematical jargon. The "values" are the results of applying the function; the "arguments" are the things to which it is applied; and the function is the relation of the former to the latter. So $\lambda_x(x^2)$ is the relation that 25 bears to 5, and 4 to 2, and, in general, x^2 to x. (But see MATHEMATOSIS.)

And what is a relation? It is a class of ordered pairs; see COMPLEX NUMBERS.

In $\lambda_x(x^2)$ and $\lambda_x(x + 5)$ we have one-place functions, or, as mathematicians have long since put it, functions of one variable. Addition is a two-place function, $\lambda_{xy}(x + y)$; multiplication is another, $\lambda_{xy}(xy)$. Just as one-place functions are dyadic relations, or classes of ordered pairs, so two-place functions can be construed as triadic relations, or classes of ordered triples; and so on up to three-place functions and higher. An ordered triple $\langle x, y, z \rangle$ can be explained as a pair $\langle x, \langle y, z \rangle \rangle$, a quadruple as $\langle x, y, \langle z, w \rangle \rangle$, and so on.

But Frege had a neat alternative way of accommodating many-place functions, and it has fitted nicely into some offbeat logics (combinatory logic, term-functor logic). He construed a two-place function f as a one-place function whose values are one-place functions in turn. He explained $\lambda_{xy}(x + y)$ as $\lambda_x(\lambda_y(x + y))$: the function which, when applied to a number x, yields as value the function which, when applied to a number y, yields the number $x + y$. Thus $f(x, y)$ is explained as $(f(x))(y)$. Similarly for three places and more.

Future

The question whether the past determines the future, in some sense or other, has long been debated (see FREE WILL). Among those who take the negative position, and thus hold that the future is in part contingent as of now rather than determined, there are some who go on to maintain that a sentence predicting any such contingent event is not yet either true or false. It becomes true or false only when the event ceases to be contingent and becomes clinched or precluded.

This position has enjoyed Aristotle's prestigious support, and it finds some current support among theologians. The theological angle is that if sentences about the future were true now, God in his omniscience would know them now, and so they would be determined now, by God's knowledge, rather than contingent. (Here then is a further sense for determinism, not mentioned under FREE WILL.) But human actions, the argument continues, have to be contingent in order to be free (a point that I contest under FREE WILL). And freedom, finally, is a prerequisite of praise and blame, sin and grace.

I trust that the reader has not been convinced by my rendering of this argument. Rather than undertake a point-by-point rebuttal, then, I shall proceed directly to urge the superiority of the usual view, that predictions are true or false when uttered, no matter how ill-founded and capricious. A major virtue of this view is that it is indispensable to treating time on a par with space, as a fourth dimension (see SPACE-TIME).

We began by noting how some religious preconceptions made for withholding truth and falsity from predictions of contingent events. We may end, symmetrically, by noting how the full acceptance of futures, through spatialization of time, can be welcome on moral grounds too. Thus consider the following dilemma. Conservation of the environment is called for by the interests of people as yet unborn, and birth control is called for by the menace of overpopulation. On the one hand, thus, we are respecting the interests of people as yet unborn, and on the other hand we are denying them the very right to be born. Observe, then how the four-dimensional view resolves the dilemma. On that view, people and other things of the past and future are as real as those of today, where 'are' is taken tenselessly as in 'Two and two are four'. People who will be born *are* real people, tenselessly speaking, and their interests are to be respected now and always. People who, thanks to birth control, will not be born, are a figment; there are no such people, not even tenselessly, and so nobody's right to life has been infringed. The four-dimensional view affords a place in the sun to all future actualities, however unpredictable, but offers no aid nor comfort to mere possibilities that are never due to be actualized. To put it less perspicuously, the rights of an unactualized possible are contingent upon his actualization.

G

Gambling

Gambling and gamboling are etymologically unrelated, but their affinity is more than phonetic. There is gamboling on the green and there is gambling on the green baize tabletop. Gamboling can break one's *gamba*, or leg, and gambling can break one's bankroll. Both activities are called playing, but they differ as horseplay differs from playing the horses.

Peter Geach told me of a trust officer who had a run of bad luck on the horses and persisted in playing them in the vain hope of recouping. At length he was driven to embezzling from the trust. His juggling of the accounts was an exacting task. He kept on anxiously betting and craftily falsifying for two years, never daring to leave his accounts for the space of a vacation. At last his tireless industry, which could have earned him a fortune in legitimate channels, ended in exposure and suicide. From speculation to peculation is but a step, and taken at one's peril.

Gambling can have its playful side, but its playfulness is a fragile affair. The prospect of winning or losing money adds spice to a friendly game as long as the stakes are high enough to be felt but not high enough for serious concern. Above that narrow margin, play gives way to business and spice to stronger stuff. The pain of losing, moreover, is not fully offset by the pleasure of winning a friendly game when the stakes are high, for there are twinges of regret over impoverishing one's friends.

Operation of a gambling house or hell is a notoriously profitable business even if the house is honest and even if the house waives the modicum, the dead spot on the roulette wheel, that is its recognized due. The reason is that the addicted gambler, in his greed or desperation, will persist in playing until he has lost everything; and this will happen before the house has exhausted its ample reserves. It is a profitable business and a heartless one.

Eager gamblers are capable, many of them, of complex and patient cerebration. They compute probabilities—such indeed were the roots of the mathematics of probability. They compile statistics on the behavior of a particular roulette wheel in hopes of detecting a bias. Wishful thinking, even so, persists. The gambler's fallacy is said to be endemic among them: the notion that the likelihood of a good turn of luck is somehow proportional to the length of the run of bad luck that precedes it. Wishful thinking tends also to encourage statistically unwarranted conclusions from the gambler's reams of data regarding the roulette wheel.

Anyone who plays state lotteries for more than casual amusement is imprudent, except in cases where a pot is known to have appreciated through failure to be hit. Otherwise the statistical expectation of gain is a fraction of the price of the ticket. First there are the profits for which the state runs the lottery, as much as 40 percent, and then there is the income tax on any winnings; and this is not offset by any tax deduction for failures. We can applaud the state lottery as a public subsidy of intelligence, for it yields public income that is calculated to lighten the tax burden of us prudent abstainers at the expense of the benighted masses of wishful thinkers. It differs morally from the private casino or underground numbers game in that its beneficiaries are all of us in the prudent sector of the general public, rather than a greedy few private operators on or over the edge of the law.

Gender

Social change has linguistic repercussions; see LANGUAGE DRIFT. The latter-day upheaval in sexual mores has increased the frequency of occasions for referring politely to copulation, and has thus created a demand for a short but equally polite word for the practice. The word *sex* has been pressed into that service, and thus rendered less convenient as a means of referring to the sexes. The resulting need has been met in turn by calling the sexes *genders*. For the space of the ensuing remarks, however, I shall continue to refer to the sexes as sexes, and shall reserve the word *gender* for genders.

In the original meaning a gender is simply a kind, irrespective of sex. The word comes from the ablative *genere* of the Latin *genus* via the French *genre*. Nouns and adjectives in our familiar languages divide into kinds, or genders. We do indeed associate genders with sexes by calling them masculine and feminine, and for a good reason: nouns for males are mostly masculine, and nouns for females mostly feminine. At the time of the original Indo-European language, our ancestors were perhaps much preoccupied with sex differences, and projected them, in an animistic spirit, all across nature.

Such, perhaps, was the irrational origin of gender as we know it. But its survival value is an independent matter, and resides in the utility of gender in sorting out anaphora, or cross-references. In complex sentences there is a continual threat of ambiguity as to which of two nouns is meant to be the antecedent of a given pronoun. We are told that

> He removed the manuscript from the briefcase and cast it into the sea

and are left wondering whether he cast the manuscript or the briefcase. In French, all is clear:

> Il retira le manuscrit de la serviette et le (la) jeta dans la mer.

Manuscript, *le*; briefcase, *la*. As luck would have it, the two nouns differ in gender. And luck does have it thus, often enough to matter.

If there are three genders as in German, Latin, and Greek, and if in respect of frequency of occurrence the nouns of the language are equally distributed over the three genders, then it is the work of a moment to compute that there are two chances out of three that ambiguities of the sort just noted will be averted by difference of gender. If the genders are two, as in the Romance languages, then the chances are even. Writers in those languages are thus spared half or two-thirds of the fumbling that we writers of English are put to in recasting our sentences to keep the cross-references clear.

Gender disappeared from English except in the personal pronouns. Good riddance, say the students who chafe at learning French and German genders. In our struggles with cross-reference, on the other hand, we have paid a price, and it may or may not have been a bargain. Certainly there is much in gender to chafe at. The sexual clues to gender extend only to words for people and a few other animals, and even here they occasionally betray us, as witness *das Weib* and *das Mädchen*. Over the rest of the vast lexicon we grasp at formal regularities where we can; thus *-chen*, in German, is always neuter and *-ée*, in French, is usually feminine, as indeed is a mere final mute *-e* more often than not. In French *-al, -el, -et, -eau, -eur* are usually masculine. But who would guess *le musée, le beurre, la nef, la peau, la fleur, la peur, la vertu, la forêt*? Mostly they can be explained to the extent of pushing them back to Latin or Greek, but etymologies are no easier to learn than the genders themselves. More fun, but no easier.

Even the adjective *élysées* is masculine, as in *Champs Elysées*. If it were ever called for in a feminine context, it would be a museum piece; thus *vallées élyséees*. The explanation of *élysée* and *musée* is that the *-é-* is not participial here, but represents rather a Greek *ai*. Very well, but why then add an *e* to the *é*?

I was once bemused by a sentence in which the feminine

pronoun *elle* referred back to the masculine subject *le Docteur Françoise Lebrun.* The writer is torn; *docteur* is masculine, but the doctor is female. Cross-reference is a matter of words; has the writer confused sign and object? Or might he justify himself by pleading that the grammatical antecedent is not *docteur* but *Françoise?* Cutting thus into a compound subject is cutting things pretty fine. We see here something of the burden not of grammatical gender as such, but of the unholy alliance of gender with sex.

An ironical etymological point wants noting regarding that unholy alliance, on the heels of my etymological dissociation of the two. The parent word *genus* itself, for all its semantical irrelevance to sex, stems from the Indo-European root *gen,* 'beget', along with *genesis, generate, genital.* But this, I protest, has nothing to do with the case.

Gender is sometimes remarkably tenacious. *La mano* is glaringly at odds with Spanish and Italian patterns, but there it stands, a firm monument to the Latin *manus, -ūs,* f., hand. Yet there are cases where, for no such good reason, gender slips. Thus whereas the French *dent,* 'tooth', keeps its Latin femininity, the Italian *dente* is masculine.

Image in French is an odd feminine among a host of masculine *-ages.* It is from the Latin feminine *imago,* accusative *imaginem,* whereas the usual source of *-age* is a late Latin *-aticum.* We might compliment the French on preserving the distinction in gender, but they muffed it in *cartilage* and *mucilage,* which went masculine from the feminine *-aginem.* The endings *-aginem* and *-aticum* did not converge in Italian, so gender held its own there. In Portuguese the whole lot were swept into the *-aginem* pattern, Portuguese *-agem,* feminine. In Spanish the matter is fussier; but enough of that.

Latin neuters regularly go masculine in the Romance languages, but a funny thing happened to twenty or so of them in Italian. An example is *uovo,* 'egg'. The masculine singular *l'uovo,* from the Latin neuter *ovum,* presages a masculine plural *gli uovi,* but we are startled to get instead a feminine plural *uova*. Its *-a* is that of the Latin neuter plural *ova,* but *-a* suggests to an Italian a feminine singular. The confused and confusing resultant of these forces is this singular-looking feminine plural of a masculine singular. Similarly an arm, a knee, a lip, a bone, and a wall are masculine, but arms, knees, lips, bones, and walls are feminine. But let me not confuse words with things, nor sex with gender.

The Greek and Latin neuter singular *problema* and its ilk posed a different problem, for here it is the singular that sports the misleadingly effeminate *-a*. The Italian laudably recognizes the word as neuter, which goes into the Italian masculine: *il problema*. But what of the plural? Singular *-a* in Italian normally gives plural *-e*, but normally it is feminine. What we find is *i problemi,* as if the singular had been *problemo* or *probleme.* Granted, *i problemata* is too much to ask.

Travelers abroad can be grateful for gender in distinguishing between turning right and going straight ahead: *droite* and *droit.* The words are alike except in gender, and stem from the Latin accusatives *directam* and *directum*; evidently *directam* got confused with *dextram* somewhere along the line. This created an ambiguity that was fortuitously resolved by the femininity of the word for 'hand'; *droite* is for *la main droite.* The story is the same for Spanish and Portuguese.

Outside of Cefalù in Sicily there is a hostelry named *le Calette.* It is common enough in Anglophone lands, if not in Italy, to give an establishment a French name *pour le chic.* Thus in Oberlin in the twenties there was a beauty parlor named Bon en Chant. Accents adorned the name in all three styles to lend an air of authenticity: Bón ên Chànt. *Calette,* however unfamiliar, is French at a glance, as French as Maurice Chevalier, but *le Calette* is naggingly indigestible; *-ette* is always feminine. Can the management, in their elegantly executed sign and leaflet, have committed a Bon en Chant? Comes, then, the dawn: *le* here is not a French singular masculine article, but an Italian plural feminine article. *Calette* is not a French feminine singular, but the plural of an Italian feminine singular *Caletta,* again however unfamiliar. That little point of an article's gender made all the difference between singular and plural, between two syllables and three, and between French and Italian.

Gödel's Theorem

Mathematics, proverbially, is where proof is. Natural science goes forward by trial and error, and a good job too. But mathematics, one felt, proceeds inexorably from self-evident truths by infallible steps of inference. Euclid's *Elements* set the style.

Self-evidence turned out to be too much to ask. Euclid's postulate of parallels, for one, resisted that requirement. Set theory, again, shaken by PARADOXES, settles pragmatically for a serviceable set of postulates without further aspiration to self-evidence.

But self-evidence could still reasonably be expected in the foundations of pure arithmetic, or elementary number theory. Self-evidence indeed already prevailed in the little set of axioms for number theory that is customarily credited to Dedekind and customarily named for Peano. There remained a question of adequacy: perhaps there were valid laws, expressible wholly within the notation of elementary number theory, that could not be derived from the Peano axioms. There were. But presumably the axioms could be completed by further additions, self-evident or not. The same was presumed, as a matter of course, for any other branch of mathematics.

No such luck. In his ground-breaking, bond-breaking, road-breaking, epoch-making theorem of 1931 Kurt Gödel proved that a complete deductive system was impossible for even so modest a fragment of mathematics as elementary number theory.

Several points cry out for clarification. First, the scope of elementary number theory. The numerals and the notations for plus, times, power, and equality are there, along with the sentence operators 'not', 'and', and 'or' and the *quantifiers* 'every number x is such that . . .' and 'there is a number x such that . . .'. The numbers concerned are just the positive integers and zero. This formal language is adequate for expressing such homely truths as

For all numbers x and z there is a number y such that $x + y = z$ or $x = y + z$

and indeed all the rest of the arithmetical truths that one thinks of as elementary. It can also express FERMAT'S LAST THEOREM.

What Gödel proved, then, is that no axiom system or other deductive apparatus can cover all the truths expressible even in that modest notation; any valid proof procedure will let some true statements, indeed infinitely many, slip through its net.

Further clarification is now called for. Since we have given up on self-evidence, why not just take all those truths as axioms? Is it because there are infinitely many? No, not exactly. Some infinite sets of axioms are admissible, and anyway there is no requirement that our deductive apparatus even consist of axioms and rules of inference. What is required is just that proofs admit of being checked. The rules of proof must be so formulated that a computer could be programmed to scan a purported proof, line by line, and determine whether it qualified as a proof of its bottom line.

Gödel's theorem is akin to the reflexive PARADOXES. Its proof hinges on coaxing the notation of elementary number theory into talking, in effect, about itself. Thus suppose the notation has been regimented in symbolic logic together with the arithmetical signs. We can *number* the total stock of single characters—digits, letters, logical signs, parentheses—in an arbitrary order, using say just two-digit numbers, of which there are enough and to spare. We can then assign numbers to expressions generally—strings of characters—by concatenating the pairs of digits for the component characters. Thus if the characters 'x', '$+$', 'y', '$=$', and '6' are numbered 13, 10, 27, 21, and 47, then the equation '$x + y = 6$' is numbered 1310272147.

Such is its *Gödel number*. Gödel's method was different, but no matter.

We begin to see that Gödel's proof will demand utter clarity over matters of USE VERSUS MENTION. The numeral '6' names the number 6 and is assigned the Gödel number 47. If we think of the Gödel numbers as going proxy for the expressions to which they are assigned, then the number 47 may be seen as naming the number 6.

Now that all expressions have been assigned their Gödel numbers, various syntactical operations on expressions can be mirrored by arithmetical operations on the numbers. *Appending* is a trivial example, on our approach: the appending of expression number 2147, namely '=6', to expression number 131027, namely '$x + y$', is mirrored by the arithmetical operation on those numbers that gives 1310272147.

Quotation is a subtler matter. Since it does not appear in the notation of symbolic logic and arithmetic, its parallel in terms of Gödel numbers cannot simply be read off by Gödel numbering; it must be worked out from scratch. Now the quotation of an expression is meant to name that expression, just as a numeral '6' names the number 6. Proxy-wise, then, 47 names 6. Similarly 47 is named in turn by 5361, if 53 and 61 happen to be the Gödel numbers of the characters '4' and '7'. Accordingly the quotation relation is represented by an arithmetical relation that 5361 bears to 47 and that 47 bears to 6. The general relation can be expressed in the notation of elementary number theory, though not easily. The arithmetical reconstruction of syntactical notions such as these was a substantial part of Gödel's achievement.

My two examples—appending and quotation—ominously echo my formulation of the Liar Paradox near the end of the entry on PARADOXES. That paradox is instrumental to one of two parts into which the proof of Gödel's theorem may, in retrospect, be resolved. His bombshell detonates when the parts are joined.

My cited rendering of the Liar Paradox, *q.v.*, can by Gödel numbering and a measure of ingenuity be translated into the notation of elementary number theory in its entirety, except for one word: 'truth'. If we could accommodate 'truth' too, we would have accommodated the Liar Paradox in full, discrediting elementary number theory itself. We must conclude rather that truth *for* elementary number theory is not definable, via Gödel numbering, *in* elementary number theory. Spelled out: *no formula in the notation of elementary number theory is true of all and only the Gödel numbers of truths of elementary number theory.* This, innocuous in itself, is one of two parts of the bombshell.

The other part treats of any proper proof procedure, that is, again, any whose proofs can be checked, as by a programmed computer. Gödel shows that, given any such proof procedure, *a certain formula in the notation of elementary number theory is true of all and only the Gödel numbers of provable formulas.*★

Combining the two parts, we conclude that the provable formulas do not coincide with the truths of elementary number theory. Either they include some falsehoods, God forbid, or they miss some truths.

Gödel's actual proof took a more direct line. He showed how, given any proper proof procedure, to construct a sentence in the notation of elementary number theory that says of itself, in effect, via Gödel numbering, that it cannot be proved. Either it is false and provable, God forbid, or true and not provable; presumably the latter. One could strengthen the proof procedure by adding this stray truth as a further axiom; but, by a repetition of the argument, there will always be others.

There is a final irony worth noting. It was implausible all along that a general mechanical routine could exist for checking for truth or falsity any and every statement in the notation of elementary number theory. Such a test would settle FERMAT'S

★ I slur over Church's Thesis; see RECURSION.

LAST THEOREM, along with a bundle of other stubborn conjectures. On the other hand Gödel's result, that there could not ever be a complete proof procedure, came as a bombshell. Now the irony is that the two lacks, the expected one and the astonishing one, could easily have been shown to be equivalent. For, if there were a complete proof procedure, then, as Stephen Kleene has observed, any statement could be tested for truth or falsity as follows. Program your computer to grind out expressions of the sort that qualify as proofs under the given proof procedure. Have it grind out the shortest ones first, in alphabetical order, and then continue into increasing lengths. Eventually, thanks to the completeness, it will print a proof of the statement in question if it is true, and of its negation otherwise. This is a finite test. It would be unfeasibly long for the fastest computer, but the point is theoretical.

I
—

Ideas

Ideas are supposed to be something in the mind. When we try to be more explicit about them, what we think of first are mental images. These are relatively clean-cut as mental things go. When we have a mental image of a red apple we are presumably activating or undergoing some neural processes in the brain that resemble, in a weak way, what goes into the actual seeing of a red apple.

But the word 'idea' as we ordinarily use it does not refer to mental images. Ordinarily its reference, if any, is much flimsier. When the White Knight

> . . . was thinking of a plan
> To dye one's whiskers green
> And then to wear so large a fan
> That they could not be seen,

he was indeed entertaining mental images, but they were not the idea; his idea was the plan itself, whatever a plan is. When someone says "I thought I might buy into Tronics" and we reply "I had the same idea," our mental imagery, if any, need bear little resemblance to that of our interlocutor; the "same idea" is rather, again, a plan. I suppose all plans, other than drawings, are ideas, though not vice versa. But to explain either by the other is to explain the obscure or flimsy by the no less flimsy or obscure.

Some clown says "I think allergies may be psychosomatic," and his equally misguided interlocutor replies "I have the same idea." Here the shared idea, so called, is not a plan; it is a BELIEF—which, we saw, is a pretty dim category too in its outer reaches.

The persistence of this phrase 'same idea' would seem to suggest that ideas are a familiar breed—familiar to the point of our being able to recognize sameness and difference among them. But actually our adeptness in talking of sameness of ideas is not traceable to any clarity in the idea idea. In many cases such talk comes to no more, in effect, than merely repeating someone's sentence. When the man in the last example said "I have the same idea," he just meant "I also think allergies may be psychosomatic." When the man in the preceding example said "I had the same idea," he just meant "I also thought I might buy into Tronics."

When a patent officer declares of two inventions that they hinge on the same idea, he is saying in effect that a single description or drawing, only negligibly less detailed than the descriptions or drawings that were submitted for the two inventions, would be equally true of both.

We are seeing, through these examples, that the way to clarify our talk of ideas is not to say what ideas are, but to show how to paraphrase talk of ideas into talk about language. It is ironical, then, to find the idea idea officiating in the purported clarification of linguistic matters, when the viable direction of clarification is the reverse; but we do find just that.

Thus we are told that sentences are equivalent, or synonymous, when they express the same idea. This is hardly to be gainsaid, but it would be more explanatory the other way around, as an explanation of sameness of idea. How then *may* we explain the equivalence of sentences? By saying that utterance of the one sentence would serve much the same purposes as utterance of the other in circles conversant with the language or languages. This is still rough, but its feet are on the ground. See MEANING.

We are told that the primary function of language is the COMMUNICATION, *q.v.*, of ideas. To communicate an idea, we are told, is to induce in the mind of the recipient of the message the same idea as was intended by the sender. And how do we tell that the idea is the same? Only by seeing that the message evoked an appropriate response, an appropriate answer or reaction. A serious analysis of language and communication will batten on perception, speech, and action, and make no use of the idea idea; for it is only a vaporous emanation from all that, and contributes only an illusion of explanation.

The idea idiom is an entrenched and consequently useful element of our vernacular. In daily discourse we cannot easily do without it, nor need we try. But it is a snare to the philosopher or scientist who admits it to his theory. Its fault, be it noted, is not its abstractness. There are abstract objects, or UNIVERSALS, *q.v.*, that figure indispensably in natural science. But there is no place in science for ideas.★

Identity

The term is used loosely. We speak of identical twins. We say that you and I drive identical station wagons. But for all the looseness of common usage, the term in its strict sense is as tight as a term can be. A thing is identical with itself and with nothing else, not even its identical twin.

David Hume was puzzled. Identity seems like a relation, but it does not relate things pairwise as a relation should; things are identical only to themselves. How then does identity differ from a mere property? Moreover, it applies to everything. How then does it differ from the mere property of existence, the property enjoyed by everything?

★I trust that my restraint in not italicizing this concluding sentence will not have gone unnoticed. People are going to have a field day, even so, quoting me out of context. Ah well, or *eh bien, vive le sport!*

It is hard to project oneself into the confusions of even so gifted a mind as Hume's, after those confusions have given way to the progress of science. A relation is now clearly conceived as consisting of pairs of objects; the uncle relation comprises all the uncle-nephew and uncle-niece pairs. The identity relation comprises all and only the repetitious pairs, $\langle x, x \rangle$; $\langle x, x \rangle$ is still not to be confused with x.

On confusions over identity see also USE VERSUS MENTION. And there are the makings of further confusion in the following reflection: evidently to say of anything that it is identical with itself is trivial, and to say that it is identical with anything else is absurd. What then is the use of identity? Wittgenstein put this question.

Genuine questions of identity can arise because we may refer to something in two ways and leave someone wondering whether we referred to the same thing. Thus I mention Simon, someone mentions Peter, and we explain that Simon *is* Peter; they are identical. It is neither trivial to say so nor absurd to doubt it.

There is little need to give a man two names, nor much interest in developing an identity concept solely for that contingency. What is more important is reference to something not by two names but by two descriptions, or by a name and a description. We need to be able to identify Ralph with the man who mows the lawn, and his house with the one nearest the station. Identities such as these permeate our daily discourse.

A philosophical riddle was propounded in antiquity about the identification, early and late, of a ship belonging to Theseus: was it the same ship despite successive replacement, over the years, of all its parts? The same riddle is familiar from Heracleitus in application to a river: you cannot step into the same one twice, he claimed, for its substance is continually renewed. For that matter, is Ralph as of now the same man that was mowing the grass eight years ago, if, as the saying goes, our bodily substance fully renews itself in the course of seven years? Are you indeed still you after all this time?

These three riddles—one, really—are wrongly reckoned as identity crises; they hinge not on the nature of identity, but on what we choose to count as a boat, a river, a person. Words are instruments, and their vagueness is tolerated where it does not impair their utility.

The continuing identity of a person over the years is predicated not on his retention of substance, but on the continuity of replacement of substance, and the continuity of change in his shape, mass, and habits. Continuity also of his memory is expected, but occasionally a lapse in this quarter is taken in stride. How far back to place a person's beginning—whether at birth or conception or somewhere between—is up for grabs, because the utility of the word 'person' has not hinged much on that detail until recent times.

A point that has seemed strangely in need of being driven home is that it is simply a question of the human use of the word 'person', whether the actual use or some use that is being proposed. It is not a question of discerning a hitherto undiscovered meaning of the word 'person'. Words, as Humpty Dumpty appreciated, are no more than what we make them.

I have dwelt here on persons, but the case is the same with the river of Heracleitus and the boat of Theseus. The truth of an identity statement hinges on the general term involved or implied—'person', 'boat', 'river'. Ralph is the same person now as eight years ago, but his stages are distinct. When on the other hand the ornithologist says 'This is the same as that', pointing in two directions, it would be absurd to accuse him of meaning what he says. He means that the species of this bird is identical with the species of that one.

A vital use of identity lurks unobserved in much of our use of 'only' and 'else' and 'nothing but'. When I say that the hiding place is known to Ralph and only him, nobody else, I mean to say two things: that Ralph knows the hiding place and that whoever knows the hiding place is identical with Ralph. To say that there is no God but Allah is to affirm, of whatever Gods there be, that Each, or He, is identical with Allah.

Idiotisms

Our word *idiom* is used to refer to a linguistic singularity: to a turn of phrase whose mode of use is not evident from broader regularities of the language nor from the use of its component words in other contexts. The word is also used, like *idiome* and *idioma* in Romance languages, to refer to a whole language or dialect. The first sense, linguistic singularity, gets a distinctive word in French: *idiotisme*. The beginner in French who copes with such idioms as *j'ai beau faire*, or learns that *le bel âge* is youth while *un bel âge* is old age, is apt to find the word *idiotisme* wryly appropriate.

Granted, the connotation of idiocy is fortuitous; idiosyncrasy is the soberer model. In Greek the word *idiot* itself bore no devastating connotation; an *idiotes* was just a layman, a man in the street, a population unit, whose distinctive trait was the want of distinctive traits. Through Latin and later languages the word gradually acquired its harshness by the grim process of EUPHEMISM, *q.v.*

What are commonly called idioms in the first sense, or idiotisms, exceed the bounds of my solemn definition at the beginning of this piece. A turn of phrase is sometimes so designated when it just reflects a point of view different from our own. In an opera we hear *"fin che non giunga il Re,"* and our first irresponsible guess is perhaps "in order that the King not come." We are startled by the simple translation: "until the King comes." Why the *non*? It all falls into place if we reflect that the period of time *until* the King comes extends precisely to the end (*fin*) of the period during which the King does *not* come. Anglophones think positively of what goes on up to the King's arrival. Donizetti and his compatriots think negatively of the King-free period and of when it ends. Both come to the same thing.

Another example in much the same spirit is likewise from song, this time Mexican: "*ya no puede caminar.*" Literally, "already he cannot get around"; freely, "he can't get around any more." To the Hispanophone he is *already* in the state of *not* getting around; to us he is *no longer* in the state of *getting* around. Both come to the same thing and are equally straightforward. But each might be put down by the other speaker as impenetrably idiotistic.

Impredicativity

It went without saying that you have specified a class beyond peradventure when you have clearly stated what is required for membership in it. So it went until Russell launched the twentieth century with his Paradox, which showed that there had to be exceptions to the rule (see PARADOXES).

In exchanges with Henri Poincaré in those early years, Russell attributed the paradox tentatively to what he called a vicious-circle fallacy. The "fallacy" consisted in specifying a class by a membership condition that makes reference directly or indirectly to a range of classes one of which is the very class that is being specified. For instance the membership condition behind Russell's Paradox is non-self-membership: x not a member of x. The paradox comes of letting the x of the membership condition be, among other things, the very class that is being defined by the membership condition. Russell and Poincaré came to call such a membership condition *impredicative,* and disqualified it as a means of specifying a class. The paradoxes of set theory, Russell's and others, were thus dismantled.

'Vicious-circle fallacy', however, is unduly harsh language. To specify a class, or whatever, is not to create it. In specifying something there is in general nothing wrong with appealing to a domain to which the thing has all along belonged. As I have remarked elsewhere, it is all right to determine the most typical Yale man by measurements and statistics of all Yale men including him. More generally, to move to the verbal level, what is required of a definition is just that the unfamiliar expression be equated to an expression couched wholly in familiar terms. When we specify Russell's paradoxical class—call it R—by its membership condition, we are simply defining the unfamiliar term 'R' as short for 'class of all objects x such that x is not a member of x', and thus far all is in order.

Prodded by the paradox, we must indeed take steps. One way is to defamiliarize the hitherto familiar defining expression, by desperately banishing 'x is a member of x' from the language (as Russell subsequently did). A better way is to preserve the language but repudiate the platitude, at the beginning of this article, that every membership condition determines a class. (Such was Zermelo's way.) The term 'R' then remains well defined but, like 'Pegasus', merely lacks an object; there is no such class as R.

For a genuine circularity see rather George Homans, *Coming to My Senses*, page 26: "A final club is a club election to which precludes election to other final clubs." If he is defining an unfamiliar phrase, the last two words of his definition are unfamiliar as well. Yet we do get his message, curiously enough. How to put it impeccably may be left as an exercise for the reader. I avail myself here of a favorite ploy by which mathematicians spare themselves sticky patches of exposition.

The banning by Russell and Poincaré of impredicative definition is to be seen, then, not as a mere clarification of previously muddy thinking, but as one of various ways of amending the erstwhile platitude that every membership condition determines a class. It is a new enactment in the face of a genuine antinomy (see again PARADOXES).

If adopted, the ban would need to be implemented by a hierarchical notation similar to the hierarchy of truth predicates that we were driven to by the Liar Paradox. We would attach indices to variables. The variables 'x^0', 'y^0', and so on would range over individuals. The variables 'x^1', 'y^1', and so on would range over certain classes, but in specifying a class in this range we would be allowed no such variables in our membership condition; only individual variables. The variables 'x^2', 'y^2', and so on would range over further classes, and in specifying these we would be allowed only variables of levels 0 and 1. And so on up.★ There is a certain naturalness to the plan, for it fits with a metaphor of progressive creation, as if the classes were not there until specified, and hence not present among the values of the variables used in specifying them.

But the trouble is that the restriction is far more severe than needed in barring the paradoxes, and so severe as to obstruct some eminently innocent and useful constructions. Thus imagine a multitude of classes that belong to some level of our hierarchy, say level 1, and suppose we want to specify their union—that is, the class formed by pooling the members of all of them. If we write 'Fx^1' to mean that x^1 is one of the multitude of classes in question, then the condition for membership in the pool, or union, is this: anything is a member thereof if and only if it is a member of some class x^1 such that Fx^1. But this membership condition uses a variable of level 1, forcing the class so specified to belong to level 2. The effect is that the union of a lot of classes of a given level cannot be counted on to belong to that level.

This particular failure spells failure for the proof of continuity noted near the end of the entry on REAL NUMBERS. Russell consequently abandoned his ban on impredicative membership conditions by the time he and Whitehead produced the first volume of *Principia Mathematica*. But the ban retains collateral interest, in the context of CONSTRUCTIVISM. There is interest in distinguishing between what can be achieved with our hands

---

★Readers aware of Russell's "theory of types" should note that classes of different levels can be of the same type and vice versa; see SENSES OF WORDS.

thus tied and what cannot. Predicative set theory, as it is called, keeps clear not only of the paradoxes, but of the whole extravagant multitude of unspecifiable classes and higher infinites that are the curse or glory of impredicative set theory. (See INFINITE NUMBERS. Regarding the vexatious terminological duplicity of 'sets' and 'classes', see CLASSES VERSUS SETS.)

Speaking of terminology, whence 'predicative' and 'impredicative'? Our tattered platitude about classes and membership conditions was, in Russell's phrase, that every predicate determines a class; and then he accommodated the tattering of the platitude by withdrawing the title of predicate from such membership conditions as were no longer to be seen as determining classes. 'Predicative' thus did not connote the hierarchical approach in particular, or the metaphor of progressive construction; that was just Russell and Poincaré's particular proposal of what membership conditions to accept as class-productive, or "predicative." But the tail soon came to wag the dog. Today predicative set theory is constructive set theory, and impredicative definition is strictly as explained in a foregoing paragraph, regardless of what membership conditions one may choose to regard as determining classes.

Infinite Numbers

Consider a lot of objects of some sort and the classes that can be formed from them. Think of the objects as correlated with various of those classes in some arbitrary fashion. An object may or may not belong to its correlated class; the only requirement is that no object be correlated with more than one class. Then there will not be enough objects to go around. One class that will get no correlate is the class of all the objects that do not belong to their correlated classes; for its correlate would have to belong to it if and only if it did not. Thus it was that Georg Cantor proved in 1890 that the classes of objects of any sort outnumber the objects.

The reasoning is reminiscent of the entry on PARADOXES,* but it shares neither the frivolity of the barber paradox nor, quite, the metaphysical portent of Russell's Paradox. But it is a runner-up in the latter regard, for it shows there are a multitude of infinities, indeed an infinity of them. Where the objects in the above reasoning are the integers, the argument shows there are more classes of integers than integers. But there are infinitely many integers; so the number of classes of integers is a higher infinite number. The same reasoning shows that there are more classes of classes of integers than classes of integers; so here we have a still higher infinity. The argument can be repeated without end, and successively higher infinite numbers emerge *pari passu*.

The argument hinged, we saw, on the class of nonmembers of own correlated classes; Russell's Paradox hinged on the class of nonmembers of selves. Take the correlation in particular as self-correlation, and Cantor's argument yields Russell's Paradox. This in fact was how Russell discovered his paradox. But Cantor's theorem is not an antinomy. Russell's Paradox is, and is barred by barring in one way or another the particular case of Cantor's Theorem that yields it; see PARADOXES.

A notable corollary of Cantor's Theorem is that there are unspecifiable classes: classes for which we cannot muster the membership condition, nor any other identifying trait. For, consider the infinite totality of grammatically constructible expression in our language, or any language. By Cantor's Theorem the classes merely of such expressions already outnumber the expressions.

Our criterion of larger and smaller in all this has been correlation: one class is larger than another if all its members cannot be paired off with members of the other. Nothing, surely, could be more reasonable. But then we are brought up

---

*Its conclusion even emerges as a case of the law (1) of the entry on PARADOXES, when the relation talked of in (1) is suitably specified. Its specification is left as an exercise for the reader.

short by observing that a class may be no larger, by this criterion, than one of its proper parts. For example the class of positive integers is no larger, by this standard, than the class of even ones; for we can pair off all the positive integers with even ones by pairing each with its double: 1 with 2, 2 with 4, and so on. Infinite classes behave in unexpected ways.

Should we reconsider our criterion? We have a choice: we can keep the criterion and conclude that an infinite class need be no larger than its proper part, or, changing our criterion, we can say that a class is always larger than any proper part but can sometimes be exhausted by correlation with members of a smaller class. The former option, with which we began, yields a simpler system of infinities, and it is standard procedure.

The resulting odd trait, then, of being no larger than one or another proper part, became Richard Dedekind's definition of infinitude. "An infinite class," a C student wrote, "is a class that is a proper part of itself." Not quite. An infinite class is a class that is no larger than some proper part of itself.

The positive integers, we saw, are no more numerous than the evens. Nor, by similar reasoning, than the multiples of three. Nor than the multiples of a million. So they all are equally numerous. But they are less numerous, surely, than the ratios, densely packed as these are between every integer and the next? Not so! The ratios can be exhaustively correlated with positive integers (and hence even with just the multiples of a million). We can see this by reflecting that each ratio can be expressed in the form x/y where x and y are positive integers, and that this pair of integers can be unambiguously represented by the single integer $2^x \cdot 3^y$. We can recover x and y uniquely from this single integer by seeing how many times the integer is divisible by 2 and how many times by 3.

Before learning from Cantor's Theorem that there are many infinities, we would not have been surprised that there are no more ratios than positive integers; their number is simply infinity, we would have said. Knowing Cantor's Theorem, however, we would have expected the ratios to outnumber the positive integers; and we were surprised that they did not. Now we would guess that the REAL NUMBERS altogether, rational and irrational, do not outnumber the positive integers either; but, surprisingly, they do. Cantor's proof hinges on the fact, noted under DECIMALS AND DIMIDIALS, that all the real numbers between 0 and 1 are represented by unending decimal expansions. Imagine any assignment of positive integers to those decimal expansions, numbering them first, second, third, and so on. Then we can describe an unending decimal expansion that was missed in the numbering. Its first decimal place is 5 or 7 according as the first place of the first of the numbered decimal expansions was or was not 7. Its second decimal place is 5 or 7 according as the second place of the second numbered decimal expansion was or was not 7. And so on. It differs from every one of the numbered decimal expansions.

So there are more real numbers than positive integers, and therefore more real numbers than ratios. It then follows easily also that there are more irrational numbers than ratios.

Since the real numbers outnumber the positive integers, it follows that they also, like classes, outrun all means of expression; there are unspecifiable real numbers. We see this by observing, as follows, that the available expressions do *not* outnumber the positive integers. Just order the expressions according to length and alphabetically within each length, and then tick them off one, two, three with the positive integers.

Cantor also showed that there are just as many real numbers as there are classes of positive integers. This is rather in line with something observed under DECIMALS AND DIMIDIALS, namely that the real numbers between 0 and 1 are in correlation with the infinite classes of positive integers.

Inflection

This is to say, declension and conjugation. When we are taught a foreign language, we are subjected to two quite unlike kinds of drill: SYNTAX and vocabulary. Distinctions not drawn by the one apparatus have to be drawn, if at all, by the other. Thus our verbs *come* and *learn* take both present and past in their stride, thanks to a simple syntactical inflection: *come* and *came*, *learn* and *learned*. Our verb *go*, on the other hand, is syntactically impoverished: it has no past. We have instead to seek elsewhere in our vocabulary. We come up with *wend*, past tense *went*. The verb *go* is defective in lacking the past tense, and the verb *wend* is defective nowadays in having only an obsolescent present but a vigorous past. Teachers tell us that *go* is an irregular verb, with *went* as its past tense; but this is mere bookkeeping. The two words are as unlike in origin as in form.

Our verb *be* shows the same phenomenon and more: *am*, *is*, *be*, *was* are a whole clutch of vocabulary, and not inflections of one and the same verb except for pedagogical convenience. Similarly for the *sum*, *esse*, *fui* of the Latin primer, and the memorable *ferre*, *tuli*, *latum*.

Our own verb *must* is so hopelessly defective that grammarians despair of patching it with parts of other verbs, and simply leave it in its tatters. It has no past tense, no participles, and, like the other modal auxiliaries, no infinitive. It is indeed the ultimate in defective verb; it has only the one form, unlike its German cognate, and does not inflect at all. It has its semantic troubles, too; see NECESSITY and NEGATION.

On the other hand even a "regular" or undefective verb like our old stand-by *amo*, *amas*, *amat*, for all its columns upon columns of conjugation in the textbooks, admits of still further columns of inflection or conjugation that are not usually tabulated as such. They are called ways of forming new verbs from old, but they could well be viewed on a par with the various tenses, moods, and aspects of the same old verbs. They are what have been called the negative, the iterative, the intensive, the diminutive, the desiderative, the inchoative.

Thus *scio* and *volo* have the negatives *nescio* and *nolo*, 'I don't know', 'I don't want'. The other *volo*, 'I fly', has the iterative *volito*, 'I flutter'. *Capio*, 'I take', admits the intensive *capesso*, 'I grab'. *Canto*, 'I sing', has the diminutive *cantillo*, 'I chirp'. *Pario*, 'I bear (progeny)', has the desiderative *parturio*, 'I am in labor'. *Caleo*, 'I am warm', has the inchoative *calesco*, 'I am warming up'.

There is also a causative inflection, but for it we must turn from Latin to English or German. We have *set* (to cause to sit), *lay* (to cause to lie), *raise* (to cause to rise), *fell* (to cause to fall), and *drench* (to cause to drink). But this inflection is on the wane; *set* and *lay* are conflated in the vernacular with *sit* and *lie*, and *drench* has lost its causative sense.

The six Latin inflections just noted were likewise weak, already in classical times. They turned up only sporadically, some on some verbs, others on others. This is one reason for not reckoning them as inflections in the textbooks, and it is why each of my examples was built on a different verb. But it is amusing to consider what could be done if they were freely applicable. *Volo*, 'I fly'; *volito*, 'I flutter'; *volitesso*, 'I flutter hard'; *volitessiturio*, 'I want to flutter hard'; *volitessituriesco*, 'I am beginning to want to flutter hard'; *nolitessituriesco*, 'I am not beginning to want to flutter hard'. It hardly seems worthwhile. And indeed it is not, which is why the forms are so sporadic.

Every beginner in Latin is gravely aware that it is much more highly inflected than English. Latin has inflections for future and imperfect, *amabo* and *amabam*; we Anglophones resort to auxiliary verbs, *will* and *am*. The Romance languages are at one with Latin in this score, though conspicuously less highly inflected in other quarters. If we look into the history of the Romance futures, however, we find a kink: they do not derive from the Latin inflections. They derive rather from an intervening stage similar to modern English, in which an auxiliary verb was used. The French future *aimerai* is obviously no derivative of *amabo*; it stands rather for the infinitive *aimer* plus the auxiliary verb *ai*, and thus harks back to the Latin *amare* plus *habeo*. Latin in its decay simply lost its future inflection and resorted, like English, to the use of an auxiliary together with the infinitive. Eventually the auxiliary and the infinitive got written together, to all appearances a simple inflection. In Portuguese there is still a trace of the separation: you can put an object pronoun between the two components. Thus *aprenderei*, 'I shall learn'; *aprendê-lo-ei*, 'I shall learn it'. What with one thing and another, the concept of inflection is less clean-cut than it would at first appear.

What is accomplished in one language by inflection is accomplished in another by circumlocution through auxiliary words; this remains true even if the boundary is not clean-cut. What is accomplished in neither way is not apt to be missed, it might be supposed: we simply lack the concept.

Actually this is not clearly the case. Our pronouns suffer grammatical lacks that can be acutely felt, and that can only be made up by prohibitively awkward paraphrases. We continually stumble over the ambiguity between plural and singular *you*, and between the *we* that includes the interlocutor and the *we* that excludes him. In these cases we are quite aware that we are limping. Our southern compatriots have conjured up *you all* in desperation, and the New York Irish *youse*. The French have accommodated the other problem with *nous autres*. The Spaniards also resorted to the latter expedient, with *nosotros*; but it lost its force and took on the indiscriminate sense again of *we*. It even induced an analogous second-person *vosotros*, though in the second person there was no similar distinction to be drawn.

We rightly wonder at the Darwinian finesse with which language has warped itself to our developing needs without our conscious intervention. We may wonder the more, then, at these cases to the contrary. The ambiguity of *you* (and *vous*) as between singular and plural is particularly remarkable, for it was only the effete use of plural for polite singular that brought it about; the distinction between singular and plural had been admirably under control with *thou* and *ye*, *thee* and *you*, *tu* and *vous*.

Information

How much information, true or false, novel or trite, have you gleaned since breakfast? or since opening this book? The question is meaningless; we have defined no measure. Relative to some firmly circumscribed situations, however, Claud Shannon and Warren Weaver did define a measure of something that they called information; such is their information theory. It has been prized by Bell Labs for its utility in communication projects.

A domain of ATOMS, *q.v.*, is supposed given. These may be finite or infinite in number, but they must be partitioned into a finite number of kinds. For the simplest case consider again halftones, already touched on under ATOMS. In halftones, the atoms are the positions on one or more halftone grids: the places where a black dot may but need not appear. The kinds of atoms are two: black positions and blank white ones. When we cite the color of a position—black or white—we thereby convey one bit of information as to the eventual picture on the grid. Each further position reported adds another bit. The number of such bits conveyed is the amount of information conveyed.

Each bit of information thus announces one binary choice. Less trivial systems of atoms comprise more than two kinds, and the method of measuring information varies accordingly. There is a general method, covering any finite number of kinds. Thus suppose there are eight kinds, and let us emulate Morse by labeling each kind with a dot-dash label. One kind is labeled '· · ·', another is '- · ·', another is '· - ·', and so on to '- - -'. Now the information conveyed in citing any one of the eight kinds amounts to announcing three binary choices: the label may begin with a dot or a dash, it may continue with a dot or a dash, and it may end with a dot or a dash. Since the announcing of a binary choice counts as one bit of information, the information conveyed in announcing any one of the eight kinds adds up to three bits.

There is an easy formula covering all cases where the information is relative to an atomism with a definite and finite number of kinds. Readers who think in logarithms will have surmised from the last example that in the case of n kinds the number of bits of information conveyed in announcing a kind is $\log_2 n$.

If the perceptual atomism of which we dream in the entry under ATOMS could be realized, it would provide an application of information theory that would enable us to speak objectively of the quantity of empirical information received by anyone on a given occasion or over a given period. As of now, however, the utility of information theory has lain mainly in work on communication and computers.

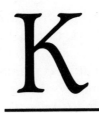

Kinship of Words

True etymology is, as the etymology of *etymology* attests, a pleonasm. (*Etymos*, 'true'.) A frequent obstacle to truth in ETYMOLOGY, *q.v.*, is, in very nearly Velikovsky's phrase, words in collision. The words in each of the following pairs turn out to be etymologically unrelated.

aperitive, appetite   discomfort, discomfiture
arch, architect   ghost, ghastly
argonaut, argosy   insolent, insult
author, authentic   jubilant, jubilee
bat, baton   rhyme, rhythm
bell, belfry   minimum, miniature
can, canister   trifle, trivial
contend, contest   victim, victor
council, counsel   whole, holism

These startling coincidences have in some cases been enhanced by contagion. The *h* in *author, ghastly,* and *rhyme* is unwarranted by origins, and came to be inserted in mistaken analogy to the other word of each pair. Similarly for the *l* in *belfry*. Kinship in meaning thus invites convergence in form. I have heard tell of a sprained *leg*ament, and of um*belly*cal cords. *Cold slaw* and *wrecking havoc* are further cases in point. The *neck of time* is not quite that; it is just a case of making half sense out of seeming nonsense. *Coupé*, 'cut back', was doubly destined to go monosyllabic in short order; the -*é* was exotic, and *coop* is descriptive. A similar case that made its way into standard English four centuries ago is *crayfish*. It is from *écrivisse*, and unrelated to *fish* except by contagion. And it may be noted in passing that *tuberose* and *primrose* are not from *rose*. The one is 'tuberous', and the other is related to the Spanish *primoroso*, 'top-drawer', 'elegant'. Less surprisingly, *titmouse* is unrelated to *mouse*; there was an Anglo-Saxon word *mase* for a kind of bird. However, expert opinion is divided on the last two examples. Some explain *primrose* as a 'prime rose' or a 'first rose' after all, and even derive *titmouse* from *mouse* despite the gulf between bird and rodent.

Conversely, some of the words that are paired in the above tabulation have no doubt converged in meaning because of outward resemblance. This is true of *trifle* and *trivial*. (For more on *trivial* see TRINITY.) It is also true of *insolent* and *insult*, of *jubilant* and *jubilee*, and of *minimum* and *miniature*. This last word originally connoted the use of red lead (*minium*) and had nothing to do with the size of the picture.

The pair *whole, holism* merits special notice. The one is from Anglo-Saxon and the other is from Greek, but we fully expect the Anglo-Saxon word and the Greek one to be cognate in their Indo-European origin. Even the *w* of *whole* is no deterrent, for it was not original; it was tacked on, Skeat estimates, around 1500. Yet the two are not cognate. They derive from different Indo-European roots.

Five further surprises of that kind are: the Latin *deus* and the Greek *theos*; our *day* and the Latin *dies*; our *main* and the Latin *magnus*; our *punch* and the Latin *pugnus*; and most remarkable, our *law* and the French *loi*. None of these are cognate.

I return to the purely domestic scene for a wild trio that was pointed out to me by Peter Geach: *pregnant, impregnate, impregnable*. In the medical sense *pregnant* is *pre-* plus the *gn-* of 'generation', but in the rhetorical sense it goes back rather to Latin *premere*, 'press'. The former sense reappears in *impregnate*, but *impregnable* goes back rather to *prehendere*, 'take'. I suspect a semantic contagion in the two senses of *pregnant*, comparable to *trifle* and *trivial*; but *impregnate* and *impregnable* present a curious picture rather of incompatibility.

Contagion or convergence can reach the point where two etymologies of a word can both be right. Thus the Spanish *querer*, 'to desire', 'to love', is perhaps accountable both to Latin *quaerere*, which spawned our *require* and *quest*, and to an unattested Late Latin *cariscere*, represented by our *cherish*. The Spanish *selvaje*, 'savage', is visibly a cross: it goes back to the Latin *salvare* like our *savage* and *salvage*, but shows infection from the Spanish *selva*, 'forest', Latin *silva*. Or take the other Spanish word for forest, *floresta*: Latin *forestis* well enough, but with a nod to Spanish *flor*, 'flower'.

The Spanish *flamenco* embodies a queer combination, imported from Provençal: 1. flamingo, for the bird's flaming hue, and 2. a Fleming. Add to this the songs and dances of Andalusia, which relate clearly to Gypsies and in no evident way to Flanders.

We have seen eighteen examples and more of seeming kinship on the part of unrelated words. There are also cases of the opposite kind, where a spelling has been changed apparently to hide a kinship—actually to distinguish a secondary use that a word has taken on. An example is *mettle*, which is the same word historically as *metal*; another is *flour*, which is the same word as *flower*; and another, indeed, is *too*, which is the same as *to*, as readers of German will have guessed.

There are more numerous cases of kinship where pronunciation as well as spelling have diverged. *Grammar* and *glamour* are an incongruous example; see SYNTAX. Again *attitude* is a mere corruption of *aptitude*. French goes along with English in this example, but in Spanish the corruption took a different line, yielding *actitud*, which again means 'attitude'.

Further examples are *deity*, *diary*, *Jove* and *Zeus*; they all go back to the same root. A more startling example is *black* and the French *blanc*, 'white': it is conjectured that they are identical in prehistoric origin. The semantic link would have to do with fire—its soot on the one hand and its blaze on the other. Another surprise is packed by the English verb *come*, its Latin translation *ven-*, and the Greek verb *bain-*: all three, so unlike in form, are identical in origin, stemming, Skeat tell us, from a prehistoric Indo-European root reconstructed as *gwem*, 'come', 'go'.

Knowledge

What counts as knowing something? First, one must believe it. Second, it must be true. Knowledge is true belief. However, as is often pointed out, not all true belief is knowledge. If something is believed for the wrong reason but just happens to be true, it does not qualify as knowledge. Knowledge has accordingly been described more specifically as *justified* true belief.

But this definition is still not narrow enough, as Edmund Gettier pointed out. The justification underlying a belief can be as reasonable and conclusive as you please and yet be contravened by some circumstance that nobody could reasonably have suspected. If this happens, and if by coincidence the belief is nevertheless true for other and independent reasons, then it is a justified true belief but still is undeserving of the name of knowledge. It is believed for the wrong reason.

An example is afforded by tabloids that appeared in the streets on November 7, 1918, mistakenly announcing an armistice. Two sportsmen set sail from Boston in their little sloop that day, with the newspaper on board and certainly no radio. They landed in Bermuda four days later in the well-founded belief that the war was over. They were right, too; it had just ended. But their belief was not knowledge, for its grounds, though reasonable, were wrong.

The notion of knowledge is beset also by a less subtle difficulty: a vagueness of boundary. Knowledge connotes certainty; what shall we count as certain? Even if one holds that some things are absolutely certain, and is prepared to specify a boundary between absolute certainty and the next best thing, still one would hesitate to limit knowledge to the absolutely certain. That would do violence to both the usage and the utility of the word.

We do better to accept the word 'know' on a par with 'big', as a matter of degree. It applies only to true beliefs, and only to pretty firm ones, but just how firm or certain they have to be is a question, like how big something has to be to qualify as big.

There is no place in science for bigness, because of this lack of boundary; but there is a place for the relation of biggerness. Here we see the familiar and widely applicable rectification of vagueness: disclaim the vague positive and cleave to the precise comparative. But it is inapplicable to the verb 'know', even grammatically. Verbs have no comparative and superlative inflections, *sequitissimur* to the contrary notwithstanding (see PREDICATE LOGIC). I think that for scientific or philosophical purposes the best we can do is give up the notion of knowledge as a bad job and make do rather with its separate ingredients. We can still speak of a belief as true, and of one belief as firmer or more certain, to the believer's mind, than another. There is also the element of justification, but we saw its limitations.

These reflections perhaps belong in their rudimentary way to the branch of philosophy known as epistemology, or the theory of knowledge. Rejection of the very concept of knowledge is thus oddly ironical.

It is not skepticism. Skeptics accept the concept of knowledge and deny its applications. What we are concluding rather is that the term does not meet scientific and philosophical standards of coherence and precision. The term retains its rough utility in the vernacular, like 'big', and, contrary to what the skeptic claims, there is plenty to which it then most emphatically applies.

The limitations of the concept have had insidious effects, however, even apart from philosophical contexts. Creationists challenge the evolutionists, who, being scientists, scruple to claim absolute certainty. The creationists then respond that the theory of evolution is therefore not *known* to be true, and hence that creationism should get equal time. Religious apologists and occultists on other fronts take heart in similar fashion. Sometimes also an unscrupulous criminal lawyer sees his way to exploiting the scientist's honest avowal of fallibility: it is not utterly and unequivocally *known* that the accused was in full possession of his faculties at the time of the atrocity. Beyond a reasonable doubt, perhaps? That, if justice is to prevail, is where the contest is resumed.

In closing I should acknowledge that there are two kinds of knowing: *knowing how*, as in swimming and bicycling, and *knowing that*. It is only the latter that has been exercising us here. *Knowing how* is a matter rather of what, thanks to one's training or insight, one can do. So in French; *on peut faire* is interchangeable, half the time, with *on sait faire*. Indeed our own *know* and *can* are ultimately the same word; compare the *kn* of *know* and the *cn* of *can*. In German, more obviously, we have *kennen* and *können*. The Greek and Latin *gno-* of *gnostic* and *ignorant* is the same thing again.

This last recalls a witty coinage by the biochemist Albert Szent-Györgyi, told to me by the biochemist John Edsall. The substance concerned was not yet wholly identified, but had to be in the sugar family along with sucrose, glucose, dextrose, levulose. He called it *ignose*, after considering and rejecting *godnose*. Our admiring chuckle is followed by wonder at the triple play: *ignorant*, *knows*, and the sugary *-ose*. But the first pair, we now see, is no accident.

L

Language Drift

Language is perpetually in flux. Each of us in learning his own language depends heavily on analogy, interpreting or fabricating further phrases by analogy with phrases we have learned before; and this same force of analogy reacts upon the language itself over the years, leveling exceptions and forcing odd forms into a more common mold. *Swelled* supplants *swole*, and *thrived throve*, because inflection by suffix is more usual in English than inflection by change of vowel. *Brethren* became *brothers* and *kine* became *cows* because pluralization by *-s* is so overwhelmingly the English fashion; and *oxen* would probably become *oxes* if the occasions to use the word at all had not become so rare. Language is always under pressure for regimentation, what the Nazis called *Gleichschaltung*. Granted, the trend is sporadic; we can continue to treasure *mice, lice, dice, geese, men, women,* and *children.*

Must the trend not reach an end where flat equilibrium is attained, with all anomalies set right? It would indeed, were it not for irruptions from the environment. Changes in natural environment and material culture affect the relative frequency of the occasions for using various words; and, as George Zipf has shown in *The Psychobiology of Language*, the form of a word is affected by its frequency. The more frequent a word, the more readily it is expected; the more readily expected, the more erosion it is apt to tolerate and still be recognized for what is intended. But the shortening is apt to increase its similarity to other words, which, being only runners-up in the popularity contest, then get decked out with redundant suffixes to distinguish them; for people like to make themselves understood without excessive enunciation or repetition. Such is one likely process, all unplanned, by which the linguistic equilibrium gets upset and restored. Thus it was perhaps that the Latin *cordem*, 'heart', got lengthened in Iberia to something like *cordationem*, giving rise to Spanish *corazón* and Portuguese *coração*; or that the Latin *diem*, 'day', gave way to the adjectival form *diurnum* and ended up in French and Italian as *jour* and *giorno*. (I cite Latin accusative forms because they are normally the source of the Romance forms.)

As Giuliano Bonfante has pointed out, the dialects in uplands separated by a valley are apt to resemble each other more than the dialect in the intervening valley. Moreover, they are apt to be more archaic. This, he explains, is because the changes in material culture that upset linguistic equilibrium come through the valley, by trade or invasion. More drastic disturbances of the equilibrium are in store if the traders or invaders speak a different dialect.

We have here a neat schema of linguistic change. The force of analogy progressively regularizes the grammatical forms, planing off the singularities, and bids fair to bring the language to a stable simplest state, but is prevented from doing so by disequilibrating irruptions.

Matters are not that simple. The forces behind linguistic change are not wholly understood, but one conspicuous one is the change undergone by a conqueror's language when imposed as a second language upon the conquered people. The differences between Portuguese and Spanish are attributable partly perhaps to differences in the Latin dialects of the conquering soldiers and settlers, but mainly to differences in the languages antecedently spoken by the Celts of western Iberia on the one hand and the proto-Basques, presumably, of most of Spain on the other. In the case of French there are both the original Gauls and the subsequent Franks to allow for.

Moreover, even the unconscious action of analogy is not always in the direction of simplicity or *Gleichschaltung*. It can also issue in mere confusions, in no particular direction. Our word *apron* came from *napron*, through a confusion of *a napron* with *an apron*, but our word *newt* came from *ewt*, or *eft*, by the same confusion in reverse.

Rich illustration is afforded by *orange*. The Persian for it was *naranj*, and is admirably preserved in the Spanish *naranja*. In Italian, French, and Portuguese, however, the initial *n* got lost through the same confusion as the *n* of our *napron*; for the indefinite article in Italian, French, and old Portuguese has *n* just as ours does. Thus we get Italian *arancia*. In French what would have been *arange* got further distorted to *orange* because of *or*, 'gold'; maybe those oranges were yellow, or there were thoughts of the golden apples of the Hesperides. The Conca d'Oro or Golden Shell that ensconces Palermo is said likewise to be named for oranges, though lemons are not wanting.

In Portuguese, much as in Italian, the fruit was presumably called *aranja*; but not for long. The confusion over the indefinite article was followed by a confusion involving the old definite article, *la*. So the Portuguese word is *laranja*. As a final irony, the definite article has lost its *l* in modern Portuguese; it is simply *a*. Portuguese is the one Romance language whose definite article lacks the *l*, and it is the one Romance language whose word for 'orange' has undeservedly acquired it.

Such was the career of one borrowed word. Another borrowing with an amusing career is *oboe*. It began with the French *haut bois*. The Italians called the instrument by its French name, which in seventeenth-century French was pronounced *oh bweh*. Eventually they took to rendering that pronunciation in Italian orthography, writing *oboe*. Finally, whereas the Italians had taken the spoken term from the French and respelled it Italian style, we borrowed the written word from the Italian and repronounced it English style: *oh bo*.

Italian was put to a test by the viol family. The basic word is *viola*. A somewhat smaller instrument was distinguished by the diminutive ending *-ino*, as *violino*, 'violin'. A much larger variant was distinguished by the augmentative ending *-one*, as *violone*, 'bass viol'. But then what to do about an interloper intermediate in size between viola and bass viol? Append a diminutive ending *-cello* to the augmentative *violone*, to get *violoncello*, 'little big viola'. See how wrong we would be to write 'violincello'; we want a little bass fiddle, not a little violin. No danger, since we generally rest noncommittally with 'cello'.

Language Reform

People have been casually reforming their language, I venture to say, almost as long as there has been language to reform. Where the process is unconscious, as it usually has been, I have relegated it to language drift. At an opposite extreme there is the deliberate fabrication of a new language out of whole cloth; see ARTIFICIAL LANGUAGES. I shall now note some intermediate efforts.

Within our own language there have been sporadic cases of enduring reform, derogated as schoolmarmism. One is *It is I*, predicated on the Latin contrast of nominative and accusative. If the reformers had thought in terms rather of the French contrast between conjunctive and disjunctive pronouns, they might have left us our more natural *It is me*.

And what then of *become*, not in the sense of going nicely with one's complexion, but in the sense of coming to be? It should be on a par with *be* so far as nominative complements are concerned. Must I then say of a long-forgotten fetus that *it became I*?

Again there is the banning of *ain't*. This form is the natural, even inevitable contraction of *am not*: the *a* is lengthened to *ai* in compensation for the deletion of *m* from the unpronounceable *amn't*. An intelligent schoolmarm might have banned *ain't* after *you, he, she, it, we,* and *they,* and she might have banned its use as a contraction involving the verb *have* (*ain't got, ain't seen*), but she would have honored it as a first-person singular negative copula. She might even have countenanced a niche for *hain't* in constructions built on *have*. But I do not mean to incite to action.

Another *bête noire* of the schoolmarm is the use of *like* as a conjunction: "like a cigarette should." The fringe cases are subtle, as Fowler's *Modern English Usage* attests, and consequently some bewildered souls have taken to avoiding the word altogether, as if it were as totally tainted as *ain't*. A faltering writer begins, commendably, thus: "Like the Dutch under Alva, they acquiesced . . .". But then, taking fright, he tries again: "As the Dutch under Alva, they acquiesced . . .". He senses that this could give the wrong idea, so he tinkers further: "As did the Dutch under Alva, they acquiesced . . .". Or even, plumbing the depths, "As with the Dutch under Alva, they acquiesced . . .". The counterculture, however, has been at pains to reinstate *like* with a vengeance, according it an obscure quasi-adverbial role, virtually an absolute construction or deconstruction. It sounds sort of groovy, like. You know what I mean?

Reformers of spelling have been at us intermittently from Theodore Roosevelt forward and backward. They point longingly to the scientifically reformed orthographies of Czech and Turkish, where letters are assigned to phonemes one to one. Spanish does almost as well; spelling settles pronunciation uniquely and almost vice versa. Italian spelling settles pronunciation except for stress and a bit about *e*, *o*, *s*, and *z*. A comparable orthography for English would indeed lighten the burden of teaching and learning, but we should also note, if only in the spirit of counting present blessings, that it would sweep away a wealth of little historical signs and relics that can reward contemplation. Examples are evident at every turn. Let me cite one of the less evident ones: the ending *-ar* in *beggar*, *burglar*, and *pedlar*. In our words of Old English origin the usual ending for agent is *-er*, and in words borrowed from Latin it is *-or*; what then of this deviant *-ar*? Looking up origins, we find that historically *beggar*, *burglar*, and *pedlar* are not even formed from verbs; there was no question of an agent ending. The three nouns came first, from other sources. Afterward we derived the verbs *beg*, *burgle*, and *peddle* from them by "back-formation," subtracting the *-ar* as if it had been an agent ending.

Some vagaries, certainly, are less readily accountable. We write *speak*, but *speech*. We write *accede*, *concede*, *intercede*, *precede*, *recede*, and *secede*, but *exceed*, *proceed*, and *succeed*.

Devious system is evident, on the other hand, in our rendering of long and short vowels. A vowel that is *checked* (that is, followed by two or more consecutive consonants, or by a final consonant) is regularly short. To mark a vowel long, then, when it is followed by a final consonant, we add a silent *e* so that the consonant will not be final; for another rule is that a stressed, unchecked penultimate vowel is long. These rules sound recondite, but most literate native speakers have wordlessly internalized them. Only to be put off, it must be said, by the treatment of various proper names by our English cousins: thus *Băsil*, *Cēdric*, *Cĕcil*, *Cŏlin*, *Bālliol*, *Wȳkeham*.

Likewise *Nĕvin*, might we add, and *Nīven*? Ah, but here we are caught up short by our own *seven*, *given*, *liver*, *ever*, and a host of others. We even outdo the British by rendering their *lēver* as *lĕver*. All these examples in *v* must simply be ruled out as irrelevant, because of an infirmity of English orthography: it cannot stomach *vv*, and hence has no way of marking the shortness of a vowel before *v*. The distinction between *līve* and *lĭve*, *even* and *ever*, *save* and *have*, has to be picked up independently of orthographic aids.

There is an opposite kind of bind where a long vowel is wanted before a consonant cluster: thus *bind*, *find*, *kind*, *wīnd*, *pint*, and even *ninth*—a far cry from *plinth*, *terebinth*, *labyrinth*, and *hyacinth*. We have been driven in desperation to write *ninety* rather than *ninty*, but we have stopped short of *nineth*. We could break the *-nd* cluster by writing *bined*, *fined*, and *wined*, but we resist this expedient because it smacks of conjugation of verbs. The distinction between *wīnd* and *wĭnd* thus just gets left to context.

The combination *ng* between vowels poses a trilemma, as witness *singer, finger, danger*. What with one thing and another, a phonetically univocal respelling of English would depart extravagantly from all we have known and much we have loved.

In the sixteenth century a reform was imposed on French that was the reverse of simplified spelling. The reformers prized the little etymological vestiges in spelling and proceeded to introduce still further silent consonants as reminders of Latin origins. Thus *poin*, 'fist', was respelled *poing* in memory of *pugnum*. Level heads prevailed in later years and rubbed out most of these Rococo intrusions, but some survived, including *poing*. An amusing further survival is *poids*, which memorializes a false etymology. The Latin origin of the word was not *pondus*, as supposed, but *pensum*.

Latin Pronunciation

Oxford's encaenia, or commencement, is conducted in Latin. I recall a counterpoint between the traditional English pronunciation of Latin and the reconstructed classical. The chancellor, Lord Halifax, used the one; the vice-chancellor, Sir Maurice Bowra, the other. Caesar's *Veni, vide, vici* would be *Vee nigh vie die vie sigh* for the one and *Way knee wee dee wee key* for the other.

It was early in this century that the former style gave way to the latter in English and American schools. We are apt to think of the traditional English or Halifax pronunciation as an outrageously provincial imposition on sturdily Continental and indeed old Italic syllables. Kenneth Jackson reminds us, however, that the Latin of the English monasteries has a mediaeval history concomitant with that of Middle English itself. Before 1400, vowels were pronounced in England much as on the Continent; and when the great sound shift took place it swayed the Latin of the monasteries no less than the English of the marketplace. This reflection induces renewed respect for the old *vee nigh* way. But the reconstructed classical way is clearly the one to teach, for it was the medium of the classical writings that are meant to be studied.

Some diehards scoffed at the reconstruction. Restoration of the Continental vowel qualities was plausible, but who can imagine the ancients calling Cicero Kick-a-row? In fact the evidence is copious and leaves no room for doubt. The phonetic transition in Vulgar Latin from classical to Romance has been meticulously traced by approximate centuries, in the light partly of pedantic complaints by ancient writers, partly of deviations in spelling, partly of early borrowings by other languages, and partly of divergences between Romance languages.

I shall present one example of the sort of consideration involved. I find this one of special interest because it was my own idea and, to my surprise, it turns out to be wrong. It hinges on the masculine and feminine plurals of Italian adjectives in *-ico*, such as *magnifico*. The masculine plural is *magnifici*, in which the *c* is soft, as always before *i* or *e*. The feminine plural, however, is not *magnifice*; it is *magnifiche*, where the silent *h* is merely a sign to keep the *c* hard. I proceeded, then, to reason as follows. The feminine plural in Latin was *magnificae*. The Latin diphthong *ae* reduces, in Italian and elsewhere, to *e*. But if this reduction occurred later than the transition from the uniformly hard *c* of classical Latin to the soft *c* before *e* and *i*, that would account for the survival of hard *c* in *magnifiche*: the ending *-ae* stayed long enough to preserve the hardness of the *c* through the softening century. Here, I conjectured, was evidence that the softening century preceded the reduction of *ae* to *e*.

I had one misgiving: Romance nouns and adjectives normally derive from Latin accusatives, so that *magnifiche* should come from *magnificas* rather than from *magnificae*. Anyway, scholarly sources give clear evidence that *ae* was well on the phonetic skids by the year one A.D., and that the decay of the hard *c* took a few further centuries.

The teaching of Latin has had a backlash of intrusive Latinity on some people's English. I have heard ignorant intellectuals say *spontanaiety*, *simultanaiety*, *Archimadian*, and *nuclaic*, as if the classicizing of Latin pronunciation were meant to drag with it the English words that were derived from Latin. And then I have seen the mistake compounded by misspelling some of them, as I have just done, to accommodate the mispronunciation.

Nuclaic, said of an acid, is quite another thing than *nucular*, said of a reactor. Illiteracy is many-faceted.

English derivatives from Latin, such as these, are one thing; straight Latin adoptions such as *fungi* are another. Even reasonable people can feel undecided whether to pronounce the adoptions according to the traditional English pronunciation of Latin or the reconstructed classical. I prefer the former for such cases, including *Cimex lectularius* and other biological binominals. But we hear intolerable hybrids of the two styles—thus *fun jee*, where the second syllable has the English soft consonant and the classical vowel, and *fun guy*, where the hybridization is reversed.

Similar hybrids are general practice in the naming of Greek letters by American fraternity men and mathematicians. My topic thus far has been Latin rather than Greek, but the same considerations apply. Consistent reference to Φ, Ψ, Ξ, B, and Θ in the traditional English fashion as *fy*, *sy*, *zy*, *beeta*, and *theeta* would be music to one's ears, and consistent reference to them as *fee*, *psee*, *ksee*, *bayta*, and *thayta* would be no less gratifying; but what we get is *fy*, *sy*, *zy*, *bayta*, and *thayta*.

Lines

One's heart leaps up when one beholds an unexplained correlation between familiar phenomena. Einstein's did so when he beheld the equality between gravitational mass, which shows itself in weight, and inertial mass, which shows itself in impact. In his general theory of relativity he promoted the

equality to outright identity and ascribed the apparent difference to the points of view of differently accelerated observers.

I move now from the sublime to a somewhat analogous
commonplace. My own heart leaps up a little when I behold
what radically dissimilar criteria all attest to one and the same
trite trait, the straightness of a line. I think of four.

One way of testing straightness is by use of a taut string.
This test recalls indeed the origin of our word *line*, Latin *linea*;
it is related to *linen* and *lint*. Sailors use the word in its primary
sense in calling their ropes lines. The same test is implicit in
our word *straight*, which is identical historically with *stretched*.
To the Greeks, more effete, a line was *grammē*, something
drawn. Still the taut string is what embodies Euclid's charac-
terization of the line as the shortest path between two points.

A strikingly different and independent way of checking the
straightness of a line is by sighting along it. If one speck blocks
your view of another, your eye and the two specks are all in
line. We have here a notable quirk of nature: the light ray,
which is our line of sight, matches the taut string. The tautness
was the mark of shortness of path, so we infer that light takes
the shortest path. Between yawns, try to recapture the fresh
sense of naive wonder that two such simple and disparate
phenomena, the taut string and the line of sight, should line
up so nicely.

General relativity theory tells us that light does not after all
go quite straight every time. But it tells us still that light takes
the shortest path available in a crumpled space-time. So any
aberration conceded to light by general relativity must be conceded equally to the taut string. They still agree.

A third embodiment of straightness is the crease of a folded
sheet of stiff cardboard. Here we have a manifestation of Euclid's proposition that planes intersect in a straight line. But
does this follow from the line's being the shortest path? Not
without outside help.

A fourth criterion of straightness is afforded by a sliding
edge. Thus suppose we are testing the straightness of a long

mark on the floor. We pass a card along the line. If the mark and the edge of the card are both in fact straight, then we can preserve full contact of the edge of the card with the mark throughout the length of the mark. This test is not yet conclusive; the mark and the edge might be curved, rather, with an equal and constant curvature. But if we repeat the test passing the card along the other side of the mark, then the test is conclusive. Constant curvature plus symmetry yield straightness of line. It would take quite a substantial chapter of geometry to show why the taut string, the crease, and the sliding edge all attest to the same simple quality. The remaining criterion, the line of sight, we leave in the lap of the physicist.

Longitude and Latitude

> "What's the good of Mercator's
> North Poles and equators,
>   Tropics, zones, and meridian lines?"
> So the Bellman would cry
> And the Crew would reply
>   "They are merely conventional signs.
> They are merely convent-
> They are merely convent-
>   They are merely conventional signs."

The last three lines are not to be blamed on Lewis Carroll. They are in anticipation rather of the eventual musical production of "Snark," if and/or when.

Almost everyone by now has been suitably surprised to hear that Reno, Nevada, is farther west than Los Angeles. Even those who haven't would guess right if asked, because they would spot the genre of the question. Similarly for anyone who is asked the less familiar question, whether all of Canada is farther north than California. Right: it is not. The forty-second parallel, legacy of the latter-day Portuguese explorer

John Dos Passos, is the latitude of the north boundary of California, but it grazes Canada's Lake Erie shore and clips Point Pelee, leaving its tip and Pelee Island south of the line—to say nothing (there being so little to say) of minuscule Middle Island, Canada's southernmost land.

Longitudes likewise have their ins and outs. Who, present company excepted, would ever think of eastern Florida as midwestern? Fernandina, on Florida's east coast, is due south of Akron, Ohio. Even Florida's easternmost outpost, Palm Beach, is a shade west of Pittsburgh's Golden Triangle. That meridian, the eightieth, is worth following on down. It grazes the western extremity of Jamaica and the entrance to the Panama Canal, and passes west of the entirety of South America except for a little fringe of Ecuador and a corner of Peru.

Time zones are the sport of meridians. They are what make Californians admire us easterners for our Yankee work ethic. Californians tune in the news at breakfast and find that we have been up and about the nation's business for two or three hours. The effect of meridians on time zones is pretty sketchy, however, as the wildly jagged time boundaries in this country bear out. And think of Spain: its longitudes are those of England, but its summer time is the standard time of Leningrad, Turkey, and Egypt. This helps to account for Spain's effete dining hours: ten o'clock in Spain is eight o'clock in solar fact.

The annual onset of daylight-saving time in our country is a perennial puzzle. If it is well to stay on daylight-saving time until the last Sunday in October, as indeed it is, then why would it not be equally well to start it on the third Sunday in February, instead of the last one in April? The daylight saved at beginning and end would be equal, and winter gloom might abate the sooner.

Longitude and latitude have their culmination, their true fulfillment, in antipodes. There are things about antipodes, as I hope to show, that give one pause. Inversion of the person, head to foot, is the least of it.

To have circled the globe is one thing. To have touched antipodes is another. Clearly any pair of mutually antipodal points must be separated by the equator, or joined by it. But the traditional world cruise has kept to the northern hemisphere, giving the equator its nearest miss at Singapore. For my own part, I have never quite circled the globe, but I have touched antipodal pairs of points in several parts of the world.

Would it be more correct to speak of touching pairs of *approximately* antipodal points? No, that would be overmodest. One can be quite certain of having been at exactly antipodal points.

To see why, note to begin with that any route from New York to Los Angeles, if not excessively devious, is bound to intersect any route from Winnipeg to New Orleans. Now let someone travel from New York to Los Angeles, and also travel from roughly the antipodes of Winnipeg to roughly the antipodes of New Orleans. These two routes do not intersect—far from it; but one of them intersects a route that is antipodal to the other. So our traveler is assured of having touched a pair of mutually antipodal points quite precisely, though he will know only approximately where.

Perth, Australia, is the remotest city on earth. I say this not primarily because Boston is the hub of the universe, but because 'remote' is a token-reflexive adjective, like 'here', and I am writing in Boston. Perth is roughly antipodal to Bermuda, but not exactly; for no land whatever, not a rock that I can detect, is quite antipodal to Australia. This is remarkable, for Australia is big, and the North Atlantic makes a pretty close fit. The antipodes of the bay at Perth accommodate Bermuda. The antipodes of the northwest coast run parallel to the West Indies, comfortably off shore. One of the Azores almost spoils the story, but not quite; its antipodes are in the Bass Straits, squeezed perilously between Tasmania and the rest of Australia.

Our familiar old United States, the pre-Alaskan forty-eight, very nearly return the compliment. Their antipodes, in the

Indian Ocean, are utterly aqueous except for uninhabited rocks and a northern slice of desolate Kerguelen Island, adding up to an area smaller than Rhode Island.

Imaginations have been fired by duller facts than these. One imagines a great cylindrical core of the earth, one end of it submerged under the North Atlantic and the other end protruding to form Australia—as if the core had got nudged downunderward. One imagines a similar core with one end under the Indian Ocean and the other protruding to form our fair land and environs, as if it had got nudged upoverward. And the South Pole, come to think of it, is on a high continent, while the North Pole is in a broad sea. Here we have a case for a third core, nudged southward. The three cores intersect at the center of the earth, and here one's imagination boggles and grinds to a halt. The monument at Chambéry, with its four life-size elephants impossibly intersecting in a four-square triumphal arch, presents a discouraging model. One savors the facts and lets the theory go.

Marks

There is a familiar use of the acute accent in mathematics to form new variables or other new signs for whatever purpose; thus x', read 'x prime'. Further signs are gained by doubling or trebling the accent; thus x'' and x''', which the latter-day mathematicians and philosophers I have known persist in reading 'x double prime' and 'x triple prime'. I even hear students and colleagues oblivious of origins speak of the accents themselves as 'primes'. My mathematics professors back in college read x'' and x''' rather as 'x second' and 'x third', in conformity with origins. The Latin for the three was 'x primum', 'x secundum', and 'x tertium'. Hence the otherwise puzzling 'prime'.

Most of us know about the absurd name *ampersand* for the sign '&' and its variants. The Oxford English Dictionary records no use of it earlier than 1837. The absurd but uncontested etymology is *and per se and*. The sign itself is a logogram of *et*.

The first and second marks '★' and '†' in the traditional footnote sequence, vulgarly known as star and dagger, rejoice in the prouder names *asterisk*, as we all know, and *obelisk*, as some of us may not. The one name is from the Greek diminutive for 'star', and fair enough. The other bespeaks a friendlier image than our own; it is from the Greek diminutive for 'spit'.

What is startling, rather, is our use of this same word for Egypt's gigantic monoliths. Little spits indeed! It is the same Gargantuan humor that recurs in our name for our imported specimen: Cleopatra's Needle. The humor dates clear back to Herodotus, who called the monuments *obeloi,* 'spits'. The further playfulness of the diminutive ending was borrowed into recorded English by 1549.

There is strikingly apt and imaginative imagery in the recent name for the sign '⊢'. The sign was Whitehead and Russell's adaptation in 1910 of a notation of Frege's from 1879, and was explained somewhat vaguely as indicating assertion. In current use it indicates demonstrability in some given deductive system, and the ingenious name for the sign is 'turnstile'. The credit goes, I think, to Barkley Rosser.

Use of the slant or slash '/' has waxed sensibly in recent years, to link or separate words in a noncommittal way. The typographers' term for the mark, from away back, is *solidus.* What, one may well wonder, is so solid about a slanting bit of line? The answer is that *solidus* is the Latin for 'shilling', and the slant is the traditional sign for that lamented monetary unit, being a degeneration of the old long *s.* Right down to the latter-day abandonment of the shilling, the regular notation for five shillings sixpence continued to be 5/6. The solidus here was no mere separator, as most modern users may have supposed; 5/6 was 5s6, *quinque solidi sex,* more fully 5s6d, *quinque solidi sex denarii,* five shillings sixpence.

And what was so solid about the shilling? Solid silver. *Eheu,* as I keep exclaiming, *fugaces.* Devaluation, moreover, has been bad all over; the humble *sou* likewise owes its name to *solidus.* Time was when the *solidus* could cut a figure in a soldier's pay; hence the French *soldat* and our *soldier.*

It seems suitable, if only coincidental, that a disquisition on marks should thus end on a monetary note. The etymological link proves to be genuine; the name of the German monetary unit is traced back by Kluge to the mark of authenticity stamped on a bar of silver. It is less clear that Marx was moved by his name to argue the economic determination of history.

Mathematosis

Some of my friends are mathematicians. In college I majored in mathematics myself, and for years afterward my efforts were largely mathematical in character. My admiration for some of the great mathematicians is unbounded, and my admiration for some of the lesser ones is genuine though bounded. If therefore I present the syndrome that I call mathematosis in an unfavorable light, let that not be put down to a general disaffection toward the profession.

Every mathematician knows a mathematician, himself or another, who manifests the syndrome. In a word it is overweening pride of profession. It stems in part from the fact, and more particularly from a widespread recognition of the fact, that mathematics is not only the most exact but the most exacting of the sciences. Awareness of this aura of the esoteric can implant in a susceptible mathematics major the germs of mathematosis even before he is out of college.

One likely manifestation of the syndrome is a pose of effortlessness. The impression is conveyed that the patient conceives the proofs of his theorems flat on his back or while strolling beside a brook. I do not question Poincaré's recollection of making a crucial discovery while boarding a bus, but he had already been working hard at his problem. Mathematosis induces a screening of the drudgery.

A related manifestation of mathematosis is a paucity of rigorous detail in the patient's presentation of his proofs. We may be expected to attribute this tendency to his generously assuming, in his modesty, that his readers and listeners are as perceptive as he. This tendency has the charm incidentally of sparing him some strenuous expository labor.

Mathematosis was thus bound to carry with it a disdain for FORMALISM, *q.v.* Formalism was seen as the pedantic grubbing of small minds. The attitude changed somewhat after formalism sparked the computer revolution, but diehards lingered on. A prominent mathematician was said to have said of the great Gödel that he did not belong in the Institute's school of mathematics, for he was no mathematician; he belonged in the school of historical studies. At Princeton's Institute for Advanced Study 'historical' means, primarily, nonmathematical.

Mathematosis fosters adherence to in-group fads of jargon and notation, at the expense often of mathematical elegance and simplicity. One of my friends in psychology was at a point in some investigation where he thought he needed to understand the mathematical term 'isomorphism', and he turned to me. Happy to oblige. No problem. But there had been a problem; my friend had first consulted a mathematician who, suffering from mathematosis, had offered this:

> An isomorphism is a bijective mapping; by bijective is meant a mapping which is both *surjective* (an epimorphism) and *injective* (a monomorphism). By surjective is meant a mapping which is onto and by injective is meant a mapping which is one-to-one.

There has been a tendency of late to sacrifice simplicity at the altar of model theory. For instance we find a *group* defined as an ordered pair $\langle A, f \rangle$ where A is a class and f is a FUNCTION, *q.v.*, whose arguments and values comprise A and fulfill certain axioms that I shall not pause over. This dragging in of a class A, and therewith of an ordered pair, is a gratuitous conformity to model-theoretic fashion; the function f is enough by itself, since A is definable in terms of f as the class of its arguments and values.

Another persistent case in point, given some class K, is

reference to "the functions from K to the truth values," that is, the functions whose arguments comprise K and whose values are the truth values. Those functions correspond one-to-one with the subclasses of K, and can serve no purpose not served more simply by the subclasses themselves. There is no call here for functions, for truth values, for anything beyond class inclusion. No call, that is, except in obeisance to fashionable jargon of model theory.

A particularly vexatious case of taking up fashion for fashion's sake has to do with the general notion of FUNCTION itself. We saw functions as the relations of values to arguments; $\lambda_x(x^2)$ as the relation of square to root. So it was with Peano in 1911, and so it has been down the subsequent decades with some writers, including Gödel and me. And so it most naturally should be: the function square-of is the relation of square to root, just as the relation uncle or uncle-of is the relation of uncle to nephew and niece. Others, however, have switched the function and taken it as the relation of argument to value, root to square. This is not just an arbitrary matter of right and left, starboard and port, fore and aft; it repercusses. Thus let f and g be two functions, say square-of and half-of. Their *resultant*, square-of-half-of, is written as the function $f \mid g$, so that $(f \mid g)$ of x should be f of (g of x). But on the fashionable perverse version of functions it comes out as g of (f of x). There are other awkward consequences as well.★ Nothing is gained, no gain is claimed, but the perverse switch is persisted in, if only as a hallmark of up-to-date professionalism. So the natural and the fashionable go on concurrently, and communication between communicants of the two styles is rendered laborious. One would happily ride with the tide were it not for the technical superiority of the old way.

★See my *Set Theory and Its Logic* (Harvard, 1969), p. 25.

Meaning

The meaning of an expression, we may be told, is the idea that it expresses. Evidently then meanings and IDEAS, *q.v.,* are the same things, if any. If we have thus reduced two nonconcepts to one, that is progress as far as it goes, but not progress enough. Anyway the two terms differ in respect of what the preposition 'of' relates them to: we speak of the meaning *of* an expression but the idea *of* any sort of thing—a condominium, a campaign, a vacation, a monument. We can speak of the idea of an expression, too, but it will not be the meaning of that expression; it will be the meaning rather, I suppose, of a name of that expression (see USE VS. MENTION). Likewise the idea of the Washington Monument is presumably the meaning of the expression 'Washington Monument'. It is still not the monument itself: that is rather the designatum of the expression (see REFERENCE). The Washington Monument, for all its marble, is a concrete object; meanings or ideas are not concrete at all.

Meanings, then, are meanings of linguistic expressions. The term also gets applied otherwise, but meanings of expressions will be more than enough to occupy us; and their advantage is that the expressions, anyway, if not the meanings themselves, are something we can get our teeth into.

People tend to think of the meanings of expression somewhat as if they were specimens in a museum of ideas, each labeled with the appropriate expression. Translation of one language into another consists in changing the labels. But John Dewey, and in later years Ludwig Wittgenstein, stressed rather that there is no more to the meaning of an expression than the overt use that we make of the expression. Language is a skill that each of us acquires from his fellows through mutual observation, emulation, and correction in jointly observable circumstances. When we learn the meaning of an expression we learn only what is observable in overt verbal behavior and its circumstances.

If the meaning of an expression is to be sought in its use,

what is it for two expressions to have the same meaning? They cannot have exactly the same use, for when we use one we are not using the other. One wants to say rather that they have the same meaning if use of the one in place of the other does not make any relevant difference. The question of sameness of meaning, then, comes down to the question what to count as relevant difference.

I see no prospect of a precise answer, nor any need of one. Everything real and objective having to do with our use of expressions, and hence with their meaning, can be said without positing any relation of full synonymy of expressions, or sameness of meaning. In describing ways in which an expression is used we may be said still to be explaining its meaning, but there is no lingering trace of a museum of labeled ideas nor of any clear and simple relation of paraphrase or translation.

Dictionaries, whether within English or between languages, are not to be lightly dismissed. But their business is not to be seen as synonymy, either for paraphrase or for translation. Their business is to help people achieve the various purposes for which they might use the language: giving or gathering information and instruction, persuading, making deals, devising plans and theories, and reveling in sound, image, and fantasy. Often a dictionary explains a word by citing another word or phrase that would serve much the same purposes in most situations or in situations of specified sorts, but no clean-cut relation of synonymy is called for.

I urged at the end of the entry on IDEAS that there is no place in science for ideas, and under KNOWLEDGE that there is no place in the theory of knowledge for knowledge. Now we find me urging that there is no place in the theory of meaning for meanings, commonly so called. Meaning, or use, yes; meanings, no. But I will not be thought to have belittled science or the theory of knowledge, and I would not be thought now to belittle semantics, or the theory of meaning. Cleared of encumbrances, it thrives the better.

See further COMMUNICATION.

Mind versus Body

It was widely held in Descartes's day that mind and body were two interacting substances, neither of them wholly dependent on the other. The view was sustained in part by a willful belief in the soul's survival of bodily death. But it had its embarrassing side. What conceivable mechanism could account for the interaction of the two substances? And interaction was scarcely to be denied. We may set aside Schiller's suggestion that mind creates body (see opening quotation under TYPE VERSUS TOKEN), but we are bound to see willful action as an effect of mind upon body. Sensation, conversely, is an effect of body on mind.

Besides the question of a mechanism, there was the law of conservation of energy to reckon with; for it served physicists well and was not to be lightly abandoned. It was destined to yield at last to relativity theory, but still not in such a way as to accommodate a dualism of mind and body.

Today's conventional wisdom is that no thought or feeling occurs without an impulse or twitch of some nerve or fiber as its bodily implementation. Many bodily events go forward without mental consequences, but every mental event reflects some bodily one, however subtle and however little understood. Granted this much, it becomes a flagrant breach of William of Ockham's maxim of parsimony to admit mind as a second substance at all; a *multiplicatio entium,* as Ockham would have it, *praeter necessitatem.* Better to drop the duplication and just recognize mental activity as part of the activity of the body. It is only thus, indeed, that the enigma of mind-body interaction is disposed of. Human bodies think, feel, decide, and act on their decisions, moving mountains.

I have been accused of denying consciousness, but I am not conscious of having done so. Consciousness is to me a mystery, and not one to be dismissed. We know what it is like to be conscious, but not how to put it into satisfactory scientific terms. Whatever it precisely may be, consciousness is a state of the body, a state of nerves.

The line that I am urging as today's conventional wisdom is not a denial of consciousness. It is often called, with more reason, a repudiation of mind. It is indeed a repudiation of mind as a second substance, over and above body. It can be described less harshly as an identification of mind with some of the faculties, states, and activities of the body. Mental states and events are a special subclass of the states and events of the human or animal body.

DEFINITION, we saw, is elimination; we define a term by showing how to dispense with it. The same may be said of explication more broadly. Are we dispensing with mental states and events *in favor of* bodily ones, or are we explaining mental states and events *as* bodily ones? The matter can be phrased either way: the hostile way or the friendly way.

This has been pretty easy. More has often been read into the proclaimed reduction of mind to body: something like a reduction of psychology to physiology, or more particularly to neurology. I see no hope of that, much less of a reduction of ordinary mentalistic talk to neurology. The age-old duality of mind and body has not dissolved; it has shifted from substance to concepts, or language. Let me sort this out.

Each individual episode of someone's thinking about Vienna, for instance, is a neural event, which we could describe in strict neurological terms if we knew enough about the specific case and its mechanism; such is the claim of today's conventional wisdom. But there is no thought of *ever* being able to translate the general mentalistic predicate 'thinking about Vienna' into neurological terms. Mental events are physical, but mentalistic language classifies them in ways incommensurable with the classifications expressible in physiological language.

Such is the doctrine of *anomalous monism,* in Donald Davidson's phrase. It is monistically materialistic, but only item by item and not systematically by general headings or rule (*nomos,* 'rule').

The age-old mind-body dualism goes on, then, transmuted and transplanted as a dualism of concepts or language. As such it remains irreducible; but it is out now where we can see where we stand and what we are dealing with.

Misling

At some point each of us has perhaps been misled, or has known some equally literate acquaintance to have been misled, by the preterite and participle *misled*. He encountered the word in reading, grasped its meaning by context, and even used it in his own writing. At length he even spoke it, as *mizzled*, never detecting that it was just the old familiar preterite and participle of *mislead* that he had been pronouncing correctly for half his life.

But the verb *misle* that is born of that misconception is too pat to pass up, descriptive as it is of the very circumstance that engendered it. Perhaps we can press it into service as a mild word for the restrained sort of deception, not quite actionable as fraud even in Ralph Nader's day, that has a respected place in enlightened modern merchandising.

A venerable case is that of the sardine, the *Sardinia pilchardus* of the French and Iberian coasts. The young of this species, oiled and tight-packed in tins, are so good that packers have found it expedient to extend the term *sardine* to other and humbler members of the herring family when similarly purveyed. Maine fisheries are permitted by law to apply the term to the local herring, and the Norwegians have followed suit, misling with the brisling. The sardine case has gone on so long and on such a scale that it perhaps no longer qualifies as misling; the word 'sardine' might simply be said to have come to mean the canned young of any species of the herring family. I have read that by international agreement every country's definition is now respected, and that twenty-one species are so countenanced. But then we need a distinctive word for those particularly succulent canned young herring, *Sardinia pilchardus*. Well, we have *pilchard*.

A no less venerable but less melancholy case, received certainly by present company as good-natured slapstick, is the soap that is represented as 99 44/100 percent pure. It floats. Is it so pure that it floats? They don't say that. Pure what? They don't say. It is just good clean fun.

The nostalgic curvaceous Coca Cola bottle was an eloquent case of wordless misling. Its fluid capacity of six and a half ounces was modestly marked in conformity with the law, but what uninquiring mind would dream that a whole Coke could be got into a little paper cup? A likely reaction, on downing a bottle, was "I was thirstier than I thought, I guess I'll have another." I picture the second nickel (*eheu fugaces!*), and not the piddling saving in water and syrup, as the payoff of the imaginative packaging.

A startlingly barefaced try at misling has lately appeared on some soup cans. The cans are generous in size, because the soup is not concentrated; it has its full aqueous bulk. So far so good. But how is this explained on the can? "Full strength; no need to add water." Bewildering, yes; but misling? None will be misled who does not richly deserve it.

I saw a companion piece on a billboard for vodka. "Now in 80 proof," it screamed, making this sound like an extra special added feature attraction.

I turn to a more sinister case. I am told of a canner of salmon whose product was persistently white instead of the canonical pink. He made a spurious virtue of this chromatic deficiency by proclaiming "Guaranteed not to turn red in the can." How many neophytes may he have turned against good pink salmon?

To that sad tale there is again a companion piece. This time the can contains the little black lumpfish eggs that look like caviar. The label says "It's real caviar. Lumpfish, not sturgeon." The last half is true. The first half, therefore, is false, putting the case beyond the pale of mere misling, except as the Food and Drug Administration may see fit to generalize the word *caviar* after the manner of *sardine*. The label may initiate two grave misconceptions—first that sturgeon caviar is not the real thing, and second that the lumpfish product is entitled to the title in a way that the larger and more flavorful salmon-pink alternative, salmon eggs, is not. The real thing is indeed out of reach, but I give you salmon eggs.

N

Natural Numbers

Traditionally the term was a synonym for 'positive integer'. But there is more occasion to speak collectively of the positive integers and zero than of the positive integers alone. The conjunctive phrase 'positive integers and zero' is awkward, and 'non-negative integer' is ugly. The phrase 'natural number', superfluous as a synonym of 'positive integer', has consequently been warped over increasingly to the inclusive sense; and it is thus that I shall use it. So the natural numbers are 0, 1, 2, and so on.

Pleistocene man presumably had a working knowledge of a few of the natural numbers. Gottlob Frege, however, seems to have been the first to offer a coherent account of what they are, and that only as recently as 1884. They may be seen as sizes of classes, and so properties of classes. The number 12 is the property of twelvefoldness. Or, exercising our well-founded preference of classes over properties (see CLASSES VERSUS PROPERTIES), we end up construing the numbers as classes of classes. Thus 12 is the class of all dozens.

The numerals so construed are translatable into the notation purely of elementary logic and class theory, or set theory; they add nothing. Clearly 0, to begin with, comes out as the class of all empty classes, hence the class $\{\Lambda\}$ whose sole member is the empty class Λ. Next, given any natural number n, a class will belong to the next number if removal of a member leaves a class that belongs to n. We can thus define, for each n, the successor of n; and each natural number is thus defined, step by step. As noted under RECURSION, then, natural number in general becomes definable as well: the natural numbers are the members shared by all classes that contain 0 and the successors of all their own members. All this translates into symbolic logic (see PREDICATE LOGIC) plus the two-place predicate '∈', 'is a member of'.

In 1923 John von Neumann came up with a trickier version of the natural numbers. They are for counting, and each is simply the class of the counters needed in counting that far—these being natural numbers in turn. Each number n is simply the class of the first n numbers. This works thanks to 0; thus n is the class of the numbers from 0 through $n - 1$. Each number is the class of all earlier numbers. 0 is now Λ itself rather than $\{\Lambda\}$ as with Frege, and the successor of each number n is now formed from n by throwing into it, as a further member, n itself.

All this, again, translates into symbolic logic and '∈'. On either version, Frege's or von Neumann's, we can then go on to define sum, product, and power, along lines sketched under RECURSION. Both versions lend themselves likewise to application outside mathematics, which is to say, primarily, the measuring of finite classes. Frege's version applies immediately: to say that a class x has n members is to say that $x \in n$. On von Neumann's version, to say that x has n members is to say rather that x and n are alike in size, which means that there is a one-to-one correlation between the members of x and the members of n. This again can be done ultimately in symbolic logic and '∈', exploiting the developments noted under FUNCTIONS.

The reasoning behind Frege's version seems more natural than the other, but von Neumann's version is far more efficient and elegant when we proceed to develop arithmetic within set theory. All that we can demand of natural numbers is provided by either version, and by infinitely many alternative versions as well, all formulable in terms of logic and the '∈' of set theory. All that is required is that the numbers form a *progression*—that is, an infinite series each member of which has only finitely many precursors. Well, Paul Benacerraf points out one further requirement: the relation of earlier and later in the sequence should be *effective,* that is, testable by observation or computation (see again RECURSION). Given any such series, we can immediately apply it to class sizes by saying that a class has *n* members if its members can be correlated with the precursors of *n*.

The multiplicity of ways of construing number, then, is best looked upon as follows. In the beginning the word 'number' and the numerals were defective, in that there was no saying what the objects were that they denoted. We now simply dispense with the defective idiom and talk, instead, of some clearly identified objects to the same purpose: Frege's classes, perhaps, or von Neumann's. For convenience we carry over the familiar word 'number' and the numerals, but none of the old quandary. In our daily use of numbers apart from philosophical or set-theoretic concerns, our choice between Frege's version, von Neumann's, and others can simply be left unspecified.

Necessity

'Must', we are told, implies 'is'. Whatever is necessarily the case is the case. Yet I say "He must be halfway home" precisely to allow for my missing my guess and his not being halfway home. Otherwise I would say "He's halfway home" flat out. Clearly something must give, and what must give is 'must'. The word may express necessity half the time, but half the time it connotes precisely the lack of necessity, or the lack anyway of certainty. 'Must' is a law unto itself, if 'law' is the word I want. See INFLECTION and NEGATION.

Leaving 'must' then to its fun and games, let us come to grips with necessity as such. It is not easy. A leaf that latter-day philosophers have taken from Leibniz's book explains necessity as truth in all possible worlds. Whatever clarity can be gained from explaining necessity in terms of possibility, however, can be gained more directly: a sentence is necessarily true if it is not possibly false. 'Necessarily' means 'not possibly not'. And we can equally well explain possibility in terms of necessity: 'possibly' means 'not necessarily not'. We understand both adverbs or neither. Each is perhaps the more useful in that it affords an explanation of the other, but we must cast about still for outside help.

David Hume despaired, two centuries ago, of distinguishing between what is necessarily so and what just so happens. It is commonly said that the truths of mathematics and the laws of nature hold necessarily, along with all their logical consequences. However, this only pushes the problem back. Which of the truths about nature are to count as laws of nature, rather than as just so happening? Well, we are told, they should be general. No, this does not help; even the most typical singular sentences are equivalent, trivially, to general ones. 'Garfield was born in Orange' is equivalent to the generality 'Everyone was either born in Orange or is other than Garfield'. The further requirement is then proposed that a law of nature single out no specific object, such as Orange or Garfield. But the trouble with this requirement is that it would disqualify the laws of geology, which cite our planet, and the laws that hinge on specifying the sun and the solar system. It would leave us with the broadest laws of physics, and few occasions to apply the adverb 'necessarily'.

Hume was right, I hold, in discrediting metaphysical necessity. Laws of nature differ from other truths of nature only in how we arrive at them. A generality that is true of nature qualifies as a law, I suggest, if we arrive at it inductively or hypothetico-deductively (see PREDICTION) rather than by the sort of trickery seen in the Garfield example. *Sub specie aeternitatis* there is no necessity and no contingency; all truth is on a par.

The adverb 'necessarily' is much more frequent in daily discourse than called for by laws of nature, let alone metaphysical necessity. In this vernacular use the human element that I have ascribed to law is more marked; necessity commonly so called comes and goes from occasion to occasion. In the course of a discussion we are apt to attach this adverb to a sentence that can be seen to follow from something on which we and our interlocutor are agreed, in contrast to the points that are still moot. In expository writing we are apt to attach it to a sentence that clearly follows from something farther up the page, in contrast to what is conjecture or still in the course of being proved.

There remains a loose end that wants picking up. Two paragraphs back I noted the purported necessity of the truths of mathematics and the laws of nature, and proceeded to dispose of the laws of nature. But mathematical necessity calls for quite another account, hinging on something in the theory of evidence called *holism,* over which let us now pause for a while. The point of holism, stressed by Pierre Duhem eighty years ago, is that the observable consequence by which we test a scientific hypothesis is ordinarily not a consequence of the hypothesis taken by itself; it is a consequence only of a whole cluster of sentences, among which the hypothesis in question merely happens to be the one in *question.* To put it in the terms of the piece on PREDICTION, the hypothesis does not by itself imply an observation categorical.

The bearing of this on mathematical necessity is as follows. Within the cluster of sentences needed to clinch the implication there are apt to be not only sentences from the particular science in question, physics perhaps, but also something from mathematics, and various commonsense truths that go without saying. If the predicted observation fails, the failure could in principle be accommodated by recanting any one of the cluster. We would try to choose in such a way as to optimize future predictions, and this will have been why the particular hypothesis was fingered in the first place. The considerations that guide these guesses are not well understood, but one conspicuous maxim is the maxim of minimum mutilation: disturb overall science as little as possible, other things being equal. Truths of mathematics, in particular, are pretty sure to be safeguarded under this maxim, for any revision in that quarter would reverberate throughout science.

This accounts pretty well for the air of necessity that we attach to the truths of mathematics. Mathematics shares the empirical content of the rest of science, insofar as it contributes indispensably to the joint implying of observation categoricals; but it owes its air of necessity to our prudence in not excessively rocking the boat.

Negation

An imaginary dialogue, no less brief than coherent, runs thus: "Mommy, must I finish my Breakfast of Champions?" "No, dear, you mustn't."

Our nearly all-purpose negative, *not,* overshoots its mark when applied to *must.* To get a proper negation we have to supplant that verb by a more tractable synonym, *have to* or *need,* and negate it instead. The mother knew this, however inarticulately, and was being mischievous; the child alone was bewildered.

The German cognate *muss* of *must* shows no such recalcitrance; *muss nicht* means 'need not', quite as one might wish.

The case of *think* is somewhat similar. *I don't think so* overshoots negation of *I think so* and means *I think not.* But in addition to sharing this awkward trait with *must, think* differs from *must* in a yet more awkward way: *must* enjoys a true and compact negation in *need not,* but *think* has no such. In an effort to deny *think so* without committing ourselves to thinking not, we stammer something like "Well, I have no opinion one way or another"; and this undershoots the mark, since a proper negation of *think so* should be compatible with both thinking not and open-mindedness.

Another difference from *must* is that the speaker is less likely to be aware of the pitfall of *think* than of the pitfall of *must*. I can imagine some simple soul being thus trapped in a negative commitment that he never intended, and ending up scrambling to rationalize an unconsidered opinion.

"Our nearly all-purpose negative," said of *not,* was perhaps an overstatement. Another place where the word fails of that purpose is in application to *some; not some* is not English. Instead we have to say *no* as an adjective and *none* as a substantive. If we want to negate a compound sentence of the form '*p* and *q*' or '*p* or *q*' or 'if *p* then *q*', simple application of *not* is again not English. We can expand *not* artificially to *it is not the case that* or we can dig into the structure and apply *not* judiciously to the components. Readers initiated in logic, and some uninitiated, will know that '*p* and *q*' under negation becomes 'not *p* or not *q*', and they will know about '*p* or *q*' and 'if *p* then *q*' as well.

Negation itself, unlike the *not* that we think of as expressing it, is admirably simple. Either a statement or its negation is true, and not both. Yet *not* is not alone in its strange vagaries; the negative prefixes *un-* and *in-* have their share of complexity as well. See PREFIXES.

Even the negative two-letter sentence *No* and its lengthier opposite number *Yes,* said in answer to questions, can fail to communicate when the question itself is negative. "Didn't he like it?" "Yes." I think we would all take this as denying, not affirming, the queried sentence "He didn't like it"; and conversely we would take "No" as expressing agreement: that he didn't like it. Still, we are shaky on the point; we are apt to bolster our answer, saying "Yes, he did" or "No, he didn't."

The Japanese line is opposite. In answer to "Didn't he like it?" the Japanese say "Yes" (*Hai*) in agreeing that he didn't like it, and "No" (*Iye*) to say that, on the contrary, he did.

But how then can I say that *hai* is Japanese for 'yes' and *iye* for 'no'? Objection sustained. Let me then say that the Japanese use *hai* where we use *yes* except in answer to negative questions, where they use *iye*; and that they use *iye* where we—but need I go on? It was an easy question to answer, but I applaud the semantic sophistication that prompted it.

The French and Germans are like us in responding to "Didn't he like it?" with "No" (*Non, Nein*) to mean that he didn't, but they are unlike both us and the Japanese in their way of responding that on the contrary he did. For this the French say neither *Oui* nor *Non*, but *Si*, and the Germans say neither *Ja* nor *Nein*, but *Doch*. (For more on French negation, see SEMANTIC SWITCH.)

P

Paradoxes

Nothing can bear a relation to all and only the things that do not bear it to themselves. It is not a point that would have occurred to most of us, but the proof is easy. Pick any relation ("helps," "attracts," "activates," . . .) and suppose there were something x that bore it to all and only the things that do not bear it to themselves. So x would bear it to anything if and only if that thing did not bear it to itself. So, in particular, x would bear it to x if and only if x did not bear it to x. A contradiction.

Imagine, contrary to a familiar saying, that God helps all and only those who do *not* help themselves. Then God would help himself if and only if he did not help himself. A contradiction. We still have not proved that God helps those who help themselves, but we have certainly disproved something else.

We can extend our logical law a bit by relativizing it:

(1)   Nothing *of a given kind* can bear a relation to all and only the things *of that kind* that do not bear it to themselves.★

The proof proceeds essentially as before.

★ *Technology Review*, 1941, pp. 16f. I cite this little-known piece of mine only to forestall a misapprehension.

One can hold without fear of logical contradiction that God helps all and only those *mortals* that do not help themselves; it would then follow from (1) that God is not mortal, but that we may accept.

In (1) we have a firm and elementary law of logic. Some of its instances, however, have packed surprises. Thus take the relation as that of shaving, and take the kind as men in the village, and we have the well-known paradox of the barber: a man in the village who shaves all and only those men in the village that do not shave themselves. It is propounded as a puzzle: does he shave himself? (1) answers the question by undercutting it: there is no such barber. We are not surprised that there is in fact no such barber; certainly we had none in mind. But we are perhaps surprised that such a barber is logically impossible; hence the sense of paradox.

A more serious instance of (1) is got by taking the kind as classes and the relation as that of a class to its members. What (1) then tells us is that no class has as members all and only the classes that are not members of themselves. Such was the burden of Russell's Paradox (1901), the thundering heptameter that shattered naive set theory:

the class of all those classes not belonging to themselves.

From time immemorial it had been plain common sense, and had gone without saying, that you have determined a class when you state its membership condition; but here is a clear membership condition, namely non–self–membership, that does not determine a class. Russell's Paradox, unlike the barber paradox, is an *antinomy*: it discredits a previously accepted principle of reasoning.

An easy revision comes to mind: just say that classes are determined by all membership conditions except one, namely, non–self–membership. This will not do. Russell's Paradox is just the first and simplest of a series. With a little more effort we can derive a contradiction also from assuming a class of all those classes that are not members *of members* of themselves.

This series can be continued without end. Further membership conditions that engender antinomies can be constructed outside that series. Worse, there are membership conditions that are harmless separately but lead to antinomies together. There is no formula for minimum restraint of the naive principle of omnipermissiveness. Different systems of set theory differ in the exclusions adopted to preserve consistency.

Back now to (1), for we have not done with its strange fruit. Take the kind now as adjectives, and take the relation as denotation, or truth-of. The adjective 'short' denotes each short thing. It even denotes itself. On the other hand 'long' does not denote itself, not being a long adjective; it is a non–self–denoting adjective. The adjectives 'right' and 'rong' denote themselves; the adjectives 'rite' and 'wrong' do not. And what about the adjective 'non–self–denoting'? This is where (1) comes in. Take the kind in (1) now as adjectives, and the relation as denotation; (1) tell us that

(2)   No adjective can denote all and only the adjectives that do not denote themselves.

Yet we have the very adjective: 'non–self–denoting'.

This paradox is due to Kurt Grelling and is known as the Heterological Paradox, *heterologisch* being Grelling's word for non–self–denoting. It is an antinomy, and perhaps a more startling one even than Russell's. There is no arguing with (1), nor therefore with (2); how then are we to come to terms with 'non–self–denoting'? The line taken is polysemy of 'denote': there is denoting, we may say, at this level and that. Attaching numerical subscripts to mark the levels, we may say indeed, with (2), that no adjective can denote$_0$ all and only the adjectives that do not denote$_0$ themselves; but then we can go on to say after all, without fear of contradiction, that 'non–self–denoting$_0$' denotes$_1$ all the adjectives that do not denote$_0$ themselves. In principle the levels mount without end. Adjectives that do not mention denotation or kindred notions do their denoting at level 0, and all is well; but those which do mention some level of denotation do their own denoting only on the next. Clearly these are desperate accommodations.

The paradoxes that we have been scanning are all of a type, which we may call *reflexive*. Most of them are covered by (1), in which the reflexive or self-directed twist is evident. The variant of Russell's Paradox that treated of members of members did not fall directly under (1), nor do the further paradoxes of the series thus initiated; but still the reflexive quality is there.

I turn finally to one more reflexive paradox, again not covered directly by (1), but notable as the patriarch of the whole family: the ancient Paradox of the Liar. In its simplest and crudest form it is 'I am lying', or 'This statement is false'. The quality of antinomy is right on the surface here; the statement is true if and only if it is false.

Unlike Russell's Paradox and the Heterological, however, the Liar calls for some tinkering to secure it against scoffers. Thus it is objected that the demonstrative 'this' in 'This statement is false' is a coupon that wants cashing; the statement that it refers to needs to be named, say by quotation. When we try to do so, we get nowhere:

'This statement is false' is false.

The version 'I am lying' turns equally on demonstratives, implicitly: the present tense in 'am' means 'at this moment'. At *what* moment? *Name* it. A glance at our quartz-crystal calendar wristwatch takes care of that in a way, but it appeals to mundane matters of casual fact that sully the logical purity of the paradox. Similarly for the expedient of printing 'Line ___ of page ___ of ___ is false' with the blanks so filled as to make the sentence specify itself.

The problem is to devise a sentence that says of itself that it is false without venturing outside the timeless domain of pure grammar and logic. Here is a solution:

(3) 'Does not yield a truth when appended to its own quotation' does not yield a truth when appended to its own quotation.

The eleven-word quotation, with its quotation marks, is a noun and the subject of (3). The quotation names that eleven-word expression. (3) tells us that if we append those eleven words to the quotation itself, the result will not be true. Carrying out the instruction, we end up with (3) itself. (3) achieves self-denial.

The Liar, thus purified, does to TRUTH what the Heterological did to denotation. The accommodation is similarly desperate: levels again. Truth and denotation go along together in this hierarchy, closely interlocked. Denotation, after all, is just truth-of.

Phonemes

The twenty-odd alphabetical representations of consonants and vowels are a drastic abstraction for the phonetics of actual speech, where sounds grade off pretty continuously. There are gradations in accent among speakers of the same language, and detectable differences even between purported repetitions by the same speaker. Abstraction has necessarily underlain not only the ALPHABET, *q.v.,* but all written representations of speech from the rebus onward. We reduce sounds to a manageable number by selectively disregarding innumerable small differences.

This abstraction, however, antedates writing and is prehistoric with a vengeance. It is as old as language, and is mastered by three-year-olds without explicit instruction. Spoken sounds within an appropriate acoustical neighborhood of one another, or anatomical neighborhood in respect of execution, are accepted as interchangeable; one of them may even be offered as a repetition of another. The continuum of spoken sounds curdles, perceptually, into discrete globules, called *phonemes.*

The mastery of one's phonemes may be compared to the violinist's mastery of fingering. The violin string lends itself to a continuous gradation of tones, but the musician learns the discrete intervals at which to stop the string in order to play the conventional notes. We sound our phonemes like poor violinists, approximating each time to a fancied norm, and we receive our neighbor's renderings indulgently, mentally rectifying the more glaring inaccuracies.

This phonematic clustering of phonetic variations is vital to the unlimited relaying of messages, for it provides standards to which we can rectify shaky enunciation at each further relay. It is vital even to the learning of language, which hinges on repetition and feedback; for repetition cannot be counted on to be exact, hi-fi aside, and the phoneme determines what counts as near enough.

The ALPHABET, then, is roughly a register of phonemes, though old Cadmus was no more aware of that than was M. Jourdain that he had talked prose. But 'roughly' wants heavy underscoring; alphabets do full justice to the phonemes only for languages such as Czech and Turkish, for which orthographies were devised in the enlightened recent decades.

The partitioning of speech sounds into phonemes differs somewhat from language to language. Aspiration of an explosive consonant (see PRONUNCIATION) turns it into a different phoneme in Hindi; not so in English. A first step in the scientific analysis of a language is the determining of its phonemes—typically twenty to forty in number; for these are the units of which all expressions of the language are composed. They are its spoken alphabet.

Two distinguishable sounds belong to the same phoneme, for a given language, if switching them does not change the MEANING of any expression of that language: such is the ordinary uncritical definition of the phoneme. But meaning is a frail reed; surely the phonemes, the very building blocks of the language, are firmer than that. They are indeed, despite occasional misgivings over the point. There is an easy behavioral criterion of sameness of phoneme that presupposes no general notion of sameness of meaning. Two sounds belong to the same phoneme if substitution of one for the other does not affect a speaker's disposition to assent to any sentence.

Deeply rooted though the phoneme principle is in the very nature of language, oscilloscopes reveal that speech is not a simple succession of self-sufficient phonemes. Each sound reverberates, rather, affecting the neighboring sounds to a degree inversely proportional, one is tempted to say, to the square of the distance. It reverberates not only forward but also backward, by anticipation. Martin Joos found that if he replayed the recording of a phrase after delicately excising a consonant, the consonant was not missed; its presence was simulated by its effects in modulating the auditory context.

Our subjective interpolation of absent consonants owes much to the modulation of adjacent vowels, but much also to our creative imagination. A burglar alarm was idly skirling in a car outside my window, and I heard it for a while as 'sorry, sorry, sorry, . . .'. I marveled that the subtle modulations could make the missing consonants so convincing. Presently, however, I was hearing it rather as 'grade three, grade three, grade three . . .'. Each 'sorry' had given way to 'three, grade'. I found that by taking thought I could switch back and forth. The utter dissimilarity of the two versions shows how undependable the interpolated consonants can be.

Technology has shown further that the naive conception of speech as a string of phonemes has experimental reality too. Strings of self-sufficient phonemes, unmodulated by one another, have been synthesized on tape, and the result is clearly intelligible, though lacking in human timbre as well as in the phonetic redundancy that is so welcome to weak ears.

The concatenation of phonemes, with or without modulation, is not the whole of what makes up intelligible speech. The lilt of the voice and the hint of a pause can make the difference in meaning between "What's cooking? sugar?" and "What's cooking, Sugar?" Stress and timing can make the difference in meaning between "The elephant is a great *lum*bering beast" and "The elephant is a *great, lum*bering *beast.*" A subtle modulation is all that marks the difference between plucky little Jack the Giant Killer and hulking Jack, the *giant killer.* So-called suprasegmental phonemes are invoked for the analysis of such refinements.

Plurals

In Hungarian, Japanese, and other exotic languages, the distinction between singular and plural is optional. A plural ending is applied only when plurality matters and cannot be inferred from the context. In our Indo-European family the distinction is obligatory, except for a few such words as *sheep,* and even there we have to fiddle with the verb. Sometimes our noun is stubbornly plural in form but singular in feeling, whereupon we may find ourselves hemming and/or hawing over the verb. We say "Mathematics *is* (not *are*) child's play." "Physics *is* (not *are*) a tissue of God knows what." "Biometrics *is* (not *are*) the answer to a maiden's prayer."

The United States has (have?) had its (her? their?) vicissitudes in this regard. Our inconvenient name had previously been applied to the Netherlands, whose diminutive United Provinces were sometimes referred to in the seventeenth century as the United States. I see by the Oxford English Dictionary that the name governed a plural verb in those days, as *United Nations* does today. The name continued to behave as plural when applied to our own sprawling federation, even long after our thirteen sovereign states had been congealed under a constitution in 1787. Politicians still differed over how much unity to reckon to the Union, until the Civil War clinched matters. Since then the singular verb has prevailed. Our states, still so-called, are now provinces that enjoy a measure of autonomy over internal affairs. Pursuant on the minor Dutch precedent and this major American one, the word *state* has been demoted to denote similar subdivisions elsewhere, notably the ten *Länder* into which West Germany is now divided, as well as the divisions of Austria, Australia, India, Nigeria, Mexico, and Brazil.

So much for nouns that are plural in form but somehow singular in feeling and consequently singular in syntax. In the opposite case, where the noun is singular in form but plural in feeling, the British and Americans part company. The British say "The Queen Insurance Company are pleased to announce"; we say "is."

On the other hand Americans agree with Englishmen in giving *people* a plural verb when the sense invites it. *People* has simply come to function as two homonymous nouns, grammatically singular in the sense of 'nation' and plural in the sense of 'persons'. Its translations into the Romance languages have fared similarly. French is lucky with its *gens,* which already looks plural thanks to having been spelled to match the Latin singular; see LANGUAGE REFORM. The other Romance languages are less comfortable with *gente*; it works out as a singular mass word like *water,* as if we were to say "much people."

The substandard tendency to say that everyone should behave *themselves,* or that somebody dropped *their* ticket, has an independent and obvious cause: a flight from gender. There was hesitation over the masculine singular when the indefinite protagonist might so well be female. This was true even before feminism became militant, and despite teachers' assurance of a neutral use of *he, his,* and *him.*

It is hard to say whether *riches* is singular or plural in feeling, but it is unequivocally plural in its form and its grammar. Even so, it owes its plurality to a confusion; the word is a deterioration of *richesse.* Its sister word *largesse* has held up better.

Data, media, and *agenda* are notorious current instances of the opposite shift: plural to singular. Someone begins a sentence, and its subject is "The data." So far so good; he didn't say "datta." But our definite article *the* is indistinguishably singular and plural, unlike the definite article in German and the Romance languages. So we sit there in suspense, hoping against hope for a plural verb. If it comes through, we settle down to his lecture with redoubled interest.

If someone were moved to condone the subliterate treatment

of *data, media,* and *agenda* as singular nouns, he could cite a lofty precedent; for neuter plurals in Greek were regularly governed by singular verbs. A score of nouns in Italian show a related and trickier phenomenon; see GENDER.

Data, media, and *agenda* are corrupted as singulars each in its own way. *Data* is treated as a mass noun, like *water*: 'There was some data', never 'There was a data'. *Media* is treated like *sun* or *firmament,* as a name of something unique and overarching. *Agenda* is treated as an ordinary count noun: 'There is a short agenda'. Thus *agenda* is the only one of the three that gets pluralized over again: *agendas.* I am now on the lookout for the crowning irony, a learned re-Latinization of *agendas* as *agendae.*

The double plural, be it *agendas* or *agendae,* is not without precedent. *Children* is another. *Child* originally enjoyed the plural *childer,* Scandinavian style, and this, not being typical enough to Anglo-Saxon ears, got further pluralized with the Anglo-Saxon *-en.* A factor may have been false analogy with *brethren,* which is not itself a double plural; its *r* is part of the stem.

Though *agendae* is still in merciful abeyance at last reports, other pseudo-Latin plurals assail us. I have encountered *definientes.* We have all heard *octopi,* and I am braced for duck-billed *platypi.* Read *definientia, octopodes,* and *platypodes,* or, excusably, *octopoda* and *platypoda.* We hear *rhinoceri* and perhaps *rhinoceroi,* but both are wrong; the Greek lexicon rewards us with *rhinocerotes* and impels us to go out of our way to refer to the grim beast in the plural whenever occasion can be contrived.

Quora and *ignorami* I have yet to encounter. *Quorum* and *ignoramus* are already Latin plurals in irrelevant ways, the one being a plural genitive pronoun ('whereof', 'desquelles') and the other a first-person plural verb. *Cauci, doldra,* and *hoodla* I have likewise been spared.

Census, consensus, and their kin give a sensitive speaker pause, for the choice between plural *-i* and plural *-us* (with imagined long *u*) requires us to know whether the Latin declension was second or fourth. Sometimes we can shortcut the Latin lore by thinking of a related adjective that betrays a *u* stem, symptomatic of a fourth-declension noun. Thus *sensual* assures us that the Latin dictionary would yield *consensus, -ūs,* 4. In an extremity we retreat to an unaesthetic *-usses.*

Such are the pitfalls besetting the pluralizing of Latin and Greek words in English contexts. Singulars, conversely, are a danger zone when the familiar form is plural. I have seen *sensibilia* singularized as *sensibilium*; read *sensibile*. Epistemological writing is a trap for the Latin dropout.

Confusion between singular and plural can subsist unsuspected and then abruptly emerge. Someone has been uneasy about her appendix, so she says, and we can share her misgivings on that score while having none about her command of the language. Then she goes on to wonder if she "should have them out," and with a flash her ignorance transpires: *appendics.*

The mandatory agreement in number between noun and pronoun was what exposed the woman's misconception. The agreement between noun and verb was what we counted on to resolve our suspense about *data.* The latter requirement does not figure in Norwegian, nor, usually, in the past and future tenses of English. On the other hand German and the Romance languages, like Latin and Greek, go further than we in requiring agreement in number also between noun and adjective. This is useful, like agreement in GENDER, *q.v.,* in helping to show which adjective goes with which noun. I encountered a phrase in Spanish that illustrates this advantage with a curious twist: *plomo y hierro fundidos.* The plural here shows that the adjective modifies neither of the singular nouns, but their whole conjunctive combination. We in English would be driven to the ugly 'molten lead and molten iron' or to casting about for some way to circumvent it.

An ignorant refinement that has unaccountably infested academic circles in recent decades is *prŏcessēs,* or *prōcessēs.* I have no quarrel with the British *prōcess,* nor with its adoption by Americans; for it is clearly more in conformity with the basic patterns of our joint language than the American *prŏcess*. To put it technically, a stressed unchecked vowel (see LANGUAGE REFORM) may be expected to be long. (*Prŏgress* is irrelevant; its vowel is checked.) But my quarrel is with the *-ēs* of *prōcessēs* or *prŏcessēs*. Why in God's name? It is not something these people grew up with. Do they think they are being scholarly about a Greco-Latin plural, as in *basēs, crisēs,* and *proboscēs*? Will they venture a singular *processis*? Or will they move on to *horsēs* and *assēs*?

The prize irregular plural, to close on a more cheerful note, is the Norwegian for 'little': singular *lille*, plural *små*. Little child, small children.

Predicate Logic

"*Non sequitur,*" protested Tweedledum. "*De contrario,*" countered Tweedledee, "*sequitissimur!*" His Latin, for all its faultiness, was not unimaginative. At any rate their logical bone of contention, whatever it may have been, would no doubt have crumbled in short order if they had had modern predicate logic at their disposal. Predicate logic markedly expedites the business of settling what follows from what and what does not.

What follows from what is largely a question of the patterns formed within a text by various grammatical connectives and operators, and of the patterns in which the verbs, nouns, adjectives, and pronouns recur and interweave. Predicate logic abstracts those patterns from the embedding texts by substituting neutral letters '*F*', '*G*', and so on for the *predicates*—that is, for the verbs, nouns, and adjectives that bear all the burden of subject matter. Just one of the predicates is retained intact, namely, the two-place predicate '=' of IDENTITY, *q.v.*, as a distinctively logical predicate.

Pronouns are likewise retained as part of the abstracted pattern, for pronouns carry no subject matter beyond what would have been thrust upon them by the predicates that have gone by the board. The pronoun contributes rather to structure. It serves to mark different positions where some one and the same object is referred to, unspecified though the object now is.

In symbolic logic these pronouns are rendered as VARIABLES, *q.v.*, and serve for referring back to a *quantifier*: perhaps to '∃x', 'there is something x such that', or to '∀x', 'everything x is such that'.

Other structural members that are left standing after the dismantling of subject matter are the sentence connectives 'and' and 'or' and a sign for negation, as most of my readers know from a first course in logic. The grammar of the resulting predicate logic is familiar to them and readily stated. Its atomic formulas consist each of a predicate letter with one or more variables appended as subject or complement—thus 'Fx', 'Gxy'. These atomic formulas are compounded without limit by 'and', 'or', 'not', and the quantifiers.

Paraphrasing and trimming, we can coax vast reaches of language into this skimpy structure. A celebrated example of paraphrase is that of 'if p then q' into 'not (p and not q)', which is faithful enough for most purposes. Our identity predicate '=' comes to the fore in paraphrasing 'else', 'except', and the singular 'the'. A complex segment of discourse may, on the other hand, be swept into the framework of predicate logic as a seamless whole and be treated as atomic when its internal structure offers nothing to the logical argument in hand.

Nouns, verbs, and adjectives are represented indiscriminately: 'Fx' might stand for 'x is a dog', 'x is fierce', or 'x bites'. Verbs are treated as tenseless; see SPACE-TIME. Proper names and other SINGULAR TERMS can be taken in stride, as explained under the latter heading. Adverbs can be insinuated into the scheme, Donald Davidson has shown, by converting them to nouns or adjectives that denote events. Prepositions, on the other hand, are logically unproductive and can be left out of sight as fragments of unanalyzed predicates. Thus '*Fxyzw*' might stand for '*x* sold *y* to *z* for *w*'.

Much remains, however, that cannot be regimented to fit the structure of predicate logic. 'Because' cannot, nor 'necessarily', nor 'possibly', nor the strong 'if-then' of the contrary-to-fact conditional. There is no place for the idioms of propositional attitude: '*x* believes that *p*', '*x* regrets that *p*', and so on. There is no place for 'shalt' and 'shalt not', nor for questions.

Despite such exclusions, all of austere science submits pliantly to the Procrustean bed of predicate logic. Regimentation to fit it thus serves not only to facilitate logical inference, but to attest to conceptual clarity. What does not fit retains a more tentative and provisional status.

Discourse fitted to predicate logic carries all its subject matter in its predicates. The rest is logical structure. The effect of the regimentation is to reduce grammatical structure to logical structure. One sentence logically implies another, in the regimented language, when their grammatical structures are such that no two sentences having those same structures are respectively true and false. Complete procedures have been in hand since 1879 (Frege) for proving logical implication in this sense, and their completeness has been known since 1930 (Gödel).

These considerations make for a neat demarcation of logic from the rest of science, but the demarcation need not be insisted on. It is customary to reckon the business of logic as exceeding grammatical structure to the extent of claiming also one of the predicates, as we saw, namely '='. Less defensibly, some imperialistic logicians claim set theory as well, thus reckoning the predicate '$\in$' as logical where '$x \in y$' means that *x* is a member of *y*. In either case the grammar stays the same; it is just a terminological question of whether to classify certain of the predicates, perhaps '=' or perhaps '=' and '$\in$', as logical along with the grammatical structure.

But the name of logic is commonly extended also beyond

what can be fitted within the grammatical structure of predicate logic at all. We encounter a logic of necessity and possibility, a logic of questions, of 'shalt' and 'shalt not', of propositional attitudes, and of strong conditionals. Insofar as the grammar of predicate logic is in principle adequate as a vehicle of austere scientific theory, these ulterior endeavors have no part to play in our theoretical system of the world. They can serve still as clarification of various other aspects of ordinary language.

Prediction

A prediction may turn out true or false, but either way it is diction: it has to be spoken or, to stretch a point, written. Etymology and the dictionary agree on the point. The near-synonyms 'foresight', 'foreknowledge', and 'precognition' are free of that limitation, but subject to others. Foreknowledge has to be true, indeed infallible. Foresight is limited to the visual when taken etymologically, and is vague otherwise. 'Precognition' connotes clairvoyance.

'Prediction' remains the usual word for my present topic, and we had best limp along with it. When treating of babies or other dumb animals we can retreat to 'expectation', ignoring its less obtrusive etymology, or to 'anticipation'.

Prediction is rooted in a general tendency among higher vertebrates to expect that similar experiences will have sequels similar to each other. Similarity, however, for all its seeming familiarity, is a hard notion to pin down. Can we say that things are more or less similar according as they share more or fewer properties? Well, how many properties are shared by two peas, or by Boston and Philadelphia, or by my brother and me? When it comes to enumerating properties, we don't know where to begin. The notion of a property, for all *its* seeming familiarity, is as dim a notion as that of similarity.

CLASSES, we saw, stand in for properties when there is work to be done. They likewise are of no help, however, in defining similarity. Things cannot be said to be more or less similar according as they are fellow members of more or fewer classes. One pair of things may be expected to be fellow members of just as many classes—countless, namely—as another pair.

We see a neat way around the obstacle when we take note of the particular context of similarity that concerns us: the creature's expectation that similar experiences will have similar sequels. What matters is only what counts as subjective similarity of experiences for the creature in question. This, providentially, admits of definition, or testing anyway, even if objective similarity does not.

Our own handles on the creature's experiences are the stimulations that engender them. By experimenting in stimulation, reward, and punishment we can compare the stimulations in respect of how similar they are for him. We reward his response to one stimulation and we penalize the same response on the occasion of another stimulation; then we conclude that a third stimulation is more similar to the first for him than to the second if it again evokes the response. There would seldom be profit in doing this, but the point of describing it is to give experimental meaning to the notion of subjective similarity. It was more than we could do for objective or absolute similarity.

In our expectation that subjectively similar events will have similar sequels, we and other animals are often deceived. "Life," in the words of A. E. Housman, "is uncertain. Life, I repeat, is not a stranger to uncertainty." What is uncanny, however, is how overwhelmingly much more often our expectations are fulfilled than disappointed. We take their fulfillment hour in and hour out as a humdrum matter of course; the occasional unexpectedness is what we notice. Our standard of similarity, for all its subjectivity, is remarkably attuned to the course of nature. For all its subjectivity, in short, it is remarkably objective.

In the light of Darwin's theory of natural selection we can see why this might be. Veridical expectation has survival value in the wild. Innate standards of subjective similarity that promote successful expectation will tend to be handed down through the survival of the fittest. The tendency will have favored us and other species as well. These considerations offer no promise of future success if nature takes what we would regard as a sudden turn, but they do account plausibly for how well we have been doing up to now.

Such was prediction, or better, expectation, when the jungle law of tooth and claw held sway in man's primordial day. A man sees the dawn's early light and, in the light of past experience, he expects birds to sing. Or, blessed with language, he sees the dawn and *says* "The birds will sing." This *is* prediction. In the fullness of time he verbalizes his habitual expectation and says "When the sun comes up the birds sing." This, which I call an *observation categorical,* is the first step in scientific theory. It is a hypothesis that generates predictions and can be refuted by failure of prediction.

Such generalization, called simple induction, distinguishes us none from other high mammals except that we verbalize it. It only puts words to their habitual expectations. Sophisticated science far transcends simple induction. It interpolates unseen interim careers of seen things (see THINGS) and fabricates terms for fancied things unseen. It posits abstract objects, notably numbers, and with help of these devises measurement. Thus arises a powerful and virtually conclusive refinement of induction, the method of which John Stuart Mill called concomitant variation. An intricate web of hypotheses is devised which together imply a host of observation categoricals. Such is the "hypothetico-deductive method."

Science, for all its refinement, does not lose the common touch. The observation categorical is still the touchstone. It says that if the experimental condition is set up, observable by the scientists concerned, then the predicted observation will ensue. If the prediction fails, then the theory, which implied the observation categorical, is refuted. The empirical meaning or content of the theory, we might say, is the set of all implied observation categoricals. In practice of course the links of implication are not explicitly set forth, and many of the contributing hypotheses themselves are commonsense platitudes that one does not stop to state.

Hypotheses about history, even of the remote past, are part and parcel of science in the inclusive sense, and the arbiter is still prediction. Occasionally this is evident, as when a hypothesis about ancient history implies the findings of some future excavation. More often the historical proposition will link up only very indirectly with prediction, through participating in a large, cohesive section of scholarly and scientific lore and common sense which has its ultimate links with observation categoricals and prediction somewhere outside the historical quarter. But prediction is always the bottom line. It is what gives science its empirical content, its link with nature. It is what makes the difference between science, however high-flown and imaginative, on the one hand, and sheer fancy on the other.

This is not to say that prediction is the *purpose* of science. It was once, we might say, when science was young and little; for success in prediction was, we saw, the survival value of our innate standards of subjective similarity. But prediction is only one purpose among others now. A more conspicuous purpose is technology, and an overwhelming one is satisfaction of pure intellectual curiosity—which may once have had its survival value too.

Prefixes

The warning "inflammable" on the backs of tank trucks was changed in recent decades to "flammable" for the protection of semiliterate tailgaters who might confuse the two senses of the prefix *in-*. Few will protest meddling with a word when human life is at stake. Semiliteracy, however offensive, is not a capital offense. Besides, a perfectly literate fellow passenger or passerby might get burned as well.

The prefix *in-* inherits its awkward ambiguity intact from its native Latin. Its one sense is the negative and its other is that of the preposition *in,* commonly with some metaphorical stretching. Before *l* and *r* the *in-* changes to *il-* and *ir-*, and before *b, m,* and *p* it changes to *im-*; but the same ambiguity carries over. The prefix has the one sense in *irreverent* and the other in *irrigate*; the one in *illiterate* and the other in *illocutionary act*; the one in *impregnable* and the other in *impregnate.* (On this last case see, further, KINSHIP OF WORDS.)

Besides the variants *il-*, *ir-*, and *im-* there is the curious variant *i-*. It is used only before *gn* and it has the power to restore a lost *g*. We negate *noble* as *ignoble* because *nobilis* was archaically *gnobilis*, 'knowable'. So also *ignorant, ignominious*— ugly words.

NEGATION, *q.v.*, has an awkward tendency to veer into contrariety. This happened to *immoral*. The word has taken on rather the sense of 'anti-moral', thus prompting the coinage *amoral* to take up the slack. Robert Louis Stevenson, to whom the coinage may be due, evidently trusted the Greek negative *a-* to retain the simple logical negativity that *im-* in this context had lost. Further, he evidently experienced no revulsion on juxtaposing a Greek prefix and a Latin stem.

The negative *in-* and its variants apply almost exclusively to adjectives. The *in-* of such words as *incompetence, invalidate,* and *incapacitate* is to be seen as part of an adjective from which the noun or verb was subsequently formed: thus the adjectives *incompetent, invalid,* and the Latin *incapax.* The verb *ignore* is a rare exception.

Corresponding to our Latinate negative *in-* there is also our negative *un-* of Anglo-Saxon origin. It likewise is restricted to adjectives, with a few exceptions: *unemployment, unreason, unrest.* Nouns like *unkindness* are not exceptions; *unkindness* is an adjective *unkind* plus *-ness*.

Verbs here are yet another matter. *Un-*, like *in-*, has two meanings. In its second meaning *un-* is different in origin from the simple negative *un-* and *in-*, and cognate rather with its

German equivalent *ent-*. This *un-* does attach to a verb, and it expresses an undoing of what the verb expresses. Usually it carries an air of liberation, as in *unbend, unbuckle, unburden, unbutton, undress, unfasten, unfold, unhinge, unlace, unload, unlock, untie, unzip.* Thus it is that *unloosen* in the vernacular has the sense not of 'tighten' but of 'loosen'. Similarly for *unravel.*

There are occasional contexts, such as *unseat* and *unsettle,* that are neutral in respect of liberation, but in such cases refuge is often taken in another prefix, *dis-*; thus *disappear, disarrange, discount, discover.* This prefix is Latin in origin. On the other hand *dys-* is Greek, and has the sense rather of 'bad', as in *dysentery, dyspeptic.* An equivalent from the Anglo-Saxon side is *mis-,* as in *mishap, misshape, misfortune.* On the other hand *miso-* harks back to the Greek and connotes hatred, as in *misogyny.*

Our prefix *re-*, like *in-*, is Latin in origin and double in meaning. It can mean 'again', as in *recreate* and *reiterate,* and it can mean 'back', as in *rebound.* The full form is *red-*, and the *d* is kept before vowels; thus *redeem* (*red* plus *emere,* 'buy back') and *redintegrate.* In French the two senses tend to be distinguished by the vowel: *re-* for 'again' and *ré-* for 'back'. This could help us remember which words have *re-* and which *ré-*, but regrettably it is not dependable.

It is a remarkable coincidence, if any, that the duplicity of *re-* is matched in German by utterly different words: *wieder* is 'again' and *wider* is 'back' or 'against'. But this brings us to an equally remarkable coincidence, if any, in English itself, if 'back' is thus akin to 'against'; for we have *again* on the one hand and *against* on the other.

Our most richly ambiguous prefix is *for-*. Its most obvious sense is the sense it bears in the anomalously spelled *forward*; usually the prefix is spelled *fore-* when used in this sense. It has a second sense, if any, and certainly not readily defined, in *forbid, forfend, forget, forgo.* It has the first sense in the noun *forbear,* or, better, *forebear,* and the second in the verb *forbear.* German distinguishes: *vor-* for the one, *ver-* for the other. A third sense of the prefix is not found in *fornicate,* for *for-* here is not a prefix, but part of the stem. Again in *foreign* it is stem rather than prefix, but in this case it is a stem that recurs elsewhere as a prefix, namely in *foreclose* (where I should have liked *forclose*) and *forfeit.* The prefix in this third sense is from *foris,* 'outside'.

Prizes

There are prizes for lucky numbers and there are prizes for promise or achievement. Public lotteries have projected prizes of the first kind into a stratosphere of megabucks. Prizes of the second kind have not attained quite that in the hands of the Nobel Commission, the MacArthur Foundation, and later comers, but they have soared to dizzy heights nonetheless—heights very nearly commensurate with inflation.

Public lotteries are beneficial to society in one way (see GAM-BLING), but detrimental in another. A solid citizen who earnestly devotes his energies and careful judgment to laying up a modest competence is dismayed by the widely publicized cases, however sparse statistically, of striking it rich in the lottery. There are easier, quicker, and more rewarding ways, he sees, than his patient plodding. Even if he has better sense than to be impelled into the lottery at that point by dreams of glory, he is somewhat demoralized. Horatio Alger's legacy has lost its lustre.

Similar considerations apply on the other side, to the great prizes for scholarly and scientific achievement, for they are bound to provoke envy, which is demoralizing to a degree. The consequent loss to science and scholarship is more than made up, surely, by the motivation afforded by the prospect of reward, so long as the prizes are judiciously awarded. Envy and self-conceit will engender criticism of the awards even in the best case, but we can be confident that it is only in really unjust awards that the harm will outweigh the good.

In view of the inevitable fallibility of even the best of judges, a reasonable precaution might be to curb the size of the prizes and spread them more widely. The risk of unjust discrimination can thereby be lessened, and the engendering of envy as well. This policy seems especially advisable when we move from awards for achievement to awards for promise. Hindsight serves judges relatively well on the whole; foresight less so. An overweening confidence in one's foresight is called for in betting a hundred and fifty thousand dollars on the future of any budding student short of a proven young Mozart. Better to hedge one's bets by electing two promising graduate students, for that sum, to a three-year term in Harvard's Society of Fellows.

Pronunciation

Hans Kurath, pioneer in the study of American regional English, was telling me about the phonetic gradations of the diphthong *ou,* as in *sour.* In Virginia it sounds *thus,* he said, and rendered it convincingly. Cross the Potomac into Maryland and it sounds *thus,* he went on, and gave a distinct and delicate modulation. He pursued the diphthong up across the Mason-Dixon line into Pennsylvania, and across the forty-second parallel into western New York, and across the lake into Ontario, producing the subtly different local allophone at each stage. His ear and mouth were indeed finely tuned. But the English in which he discussed these fine points—his *metalanguage,* in the regrettably hybrid jargon of latter-day logicians—retained the strong Austrian accent of his native Villach. Speaking with an eye to speech is one thing, and speaking with an eye to content is another.

Similarly, and more obviously, for listening. When one listens to a lecturer with an odd accent or unusual diction, one's grasp and retention of the content suffers from the division of attention even though each word is clearly understood. I carry less away from a lecture in a foreign language, for this reason, than my conversance with the language would seem to warrant. Reading presents no such problem, for one can savor both the words and the meaning on one's own time.

But there is also a feedback from semantics to phonetics that is sometimes uncanny. I once listened to a lecture in Spanish by Mario Bunge while I had an English version in my hand. I am comfortable with the Spanish of Mexico, but Argentine speech such as his is harder for me to catch. To my surprise, my eye on the English text caused his Spanish words to come through to my ear clear as a bell. The phonetic clarification was immediate and without conscious thought, though the words used in the two languages were on the whole phonetically unrelated. Comprehension instantaneously adjusts perception, warping the heard sounds into better conformity with our prior standards.

Accents can bewilder, and they can cause misapprehension without bewilderment. Mrs. Alfred North Whitehead had not been long in America when she was struck by the forthrightness of American women: a new acquaintance had spoken of some third woman as a horror. It was indeed a forthright description, to the point of unkindness; but less so than Mrs. Whitehead thought. What she heard was "a whore."

Once in Mexico my writing came to an abrupt stop for lack of paper, and I rushed over to the *papelaría* to buy more. I asked the girl carelessly for *papel,* still caught up in my half-written thoughts, and she did not understand. Coming to grips, I cleaned up my three consonants and my syllabication, and all was well. That little word had presented no fewer than four hurdles. Our English *p,* when not next to another consonant, explodes with an aspiration; you can test this by pronouncing it into a lighted match. (Similarly for *t* and *k*.) Spanish omits the aspiration. A hurdle, then, at each *p*. Our *l* is struck by the tongue against the roof of the mouth; the Spanish *l* is struck nearer the teeth. Syllables tend in English to break after a consonant, audibly if not orthographically; in Spanish they break before the consonant. Incomprehension on the part of a girl with little experience of foreigners is no cause for wonder.

American travelers often complain that the French are haughty about their language and feign not to understand our imperfect renderings of it. Observation of an occasional confrontation of this kind has persuaded me that the charge is unjust. Though French has long been the main foreign language to which Americans are exposed in school, phonetically it is far more alien than Spanish, Italian, or German. There is the delicate matter of *liaison*—to link or not to link. The prize in this quarter is the so-called aspirate *h*, which is as silent as its silent partner, but recognizable by further silences in respect of *liaison*. Further there is the wandering stress, sensitive rather to the phrase than to the word. Hardest of all are the vagaries of pitch and pace. A French interlocutor more worldly wise than the Mexican shopgirl could still be stymied in all sincerity by our violation of these elusive norms across the board.

The American traveler's defensiveness can be exacerbated by a curious French custom regarding stress. Utter an iambus, and the Frenchman in his response will utter the same word as a trochee; also vice versa. "À Par*is*?" "Oui, à *Pa*ris." The embattled traveler thinks he is being corrected and later indeed discorrected, not appreciating that the switching of stress in the response is standard procedure.

But let me dwell further on that amusingly miscalled aspirate *h,* distinguished by an asterisk in French dictionaries. Actual aspiration in French steers clear of any written *h*; I hear it rather in their uvular *r* and an occasional emphatic *oui*.

We can do at this point with what M. Michelin is wont to call *un peu d'histoire*. The Franks moved in on the Latinized Gauls and took on their culture with Germanic nuances. *Haut,* the most familiar locus of the enigmatic *h*, derives from the Latin *altum* of like meaning, but Meillet tells us that it owes its *h* to the echo of some Frankish equivalent on the order of *hoch*. The Franks really sounded it, and it blocked liaison as would any other consonant. But acculturation wore on, and in the fullness of time the vigorous Germanic *h* succumbed to the Romance conspiracy of silence. For the most part we may look to Germanic origins for these phantom French aspirates. The letter is silent and yet, in its resistance to liaison, phonetically operative—a mute salute to Frankish forebears.

I have been concerned here with accent in one of several senses of the word. A second sense is syllabic *stress*; happily we have this unambiguous word for it. In a third sense, evidently derivative from the second, the word 'accent' denotes the diacritical marks by which stress is indicated. In Spanish and Portuguese, stress is punctiliously marked whenever it departs from certain easily remembered regularities. Similar aids are sorely missed in Italian, where the mark is limited to words that end in a stressed vowel. One soon gets some feeling for Italian stress anyway, thanks to internal parallels and to cognates in other languages; but the feeling does little for proper names. Who could guess that Taranto and Otranto are Táranto and Ótranto? I was startled lately to hear a Harvard art professor, no less, refer to the early Italian painter Cimabue twice as Cimábue. Prepared to unlearn my Cimabúe of perhaps six decades' standing, I consulted a pronouncing dictionary and an encyclopedia. They sustained Cimabúe.

The marks are still called accents when used in French to indicate not stress but quality, and in classical Greek to indicate pitch. They are still called accents even when used in mathematics, to no phonetic purpose; see MARKS.

Real Numbers

The name 'Pythagoras' conjures up first of all the Pythagorean Theorem, which has been the mainstay of surveyors and the point of departure for FERMAT'S LAST THEOREM. It also conjures up the irrationality of the square root of 2; for Pythagoras is credited with discovering that shortcoming, and is said to have sworn his followers to secrecy regarding it. But the truth would out.

The square root of 2 is irrational, however, only in a rather innocuous sense in which we may all be said to be irrational; namely, in the sense of not being a ratio. There are no whole numbers *m* and *n* whose ratio, *m/n*, is the square root of 2. Nor is 2 peculiar in this respect. Pick any integer at random and it is likelier than not that its square root is irrational, and its cube root too, and so on down. Nor is irrationality peculiar to roots of integers, as witness π and a nameless host of others.

A ratio, clearly, is just a relation between numbers. The ration 2/3 is the relation in which 2 stands to 3, and 4 to 6, and so on. But what then, precisely, is an irrational number? We can best grasp these matters by putting ourselves in the position not of exploring what was there, but of deciding what to use for a preconceived purpose.

What Pythagoras discovered was that the ratios 7/5, 141/100, 707/500, and so on come closer and closer to squaring to 2 but no ratio quite makes it. No ratio is the exact limit of the infinite class of ratios m/n such that $(m/n)^2 < 2$. If we want to enjoy the luxury of being able to extract square roots, and other roots, indiscriminately of 2 and other positive integers, we are going to have to enlist other objects than ratios to serve as those roots. It is a question of fixing upon some extraneous object for the office of limit of the class of ratios m/n such that $(m/n)^2 < 2$ and, more generally, a question of assigning something systematically as limit to every class of ratios. The objects thus assigned (as we shall proceed to do) are what we thereupon *call* "real numbers," with one conventional exception: the one assigned as limit to the class of *all* ratios is not called a real number. It would be a highest real number, ∞. The honorific 'real' is only by way of contrast with "imaginary numbers," which are a further extension of the number system for the purpose of affording square roots of negative numbers (see COMPLEX NUMBERS).

An object that is ready to hand, for us to press into service as limit of any class of ratios, is simply the class itself. This will not quite do, but only because distinct classes of ratios sometimes call for the same limit rather than distinct ones. For instance the infinite class of ratios m/n such that $(m/n)^2 < 2$ can be thinned out in countless ways without disturbing the convergence upon 2 of the squares of its members. In a word, there are *co-final* classes of ratios. We need a rule for picking out one from each family of co-final classes, to play the role of the "limit" of each of those classes, including itself.

There is an easy rule: take the thickest class in the family. It will be the one that skips no ratios along the way. It contains all the ratios that belong to any classes in its co-final family. In particular our old standby, the class of all ratios m/n such that $(m/n)^2 < 2$, is such a class. So on the present construction it is reckoned as its own "limit", the real number $\sqrt{2}$.

A further refinement is needed, for examples other than this one. The class of all ratios less than 2/3, and the class of all ratios less than or equal to 2/3, are co-final; they have the same commonsense limit 2/3, and should therefore not count as two real numbers. So we add the requirement that to qualify as a real number a class must not have a highest member.

To sum up, then, a real number is any class of ratios that meets these three conditions: (1) it contains every ratio less than any of its members, (2) it contains no highest member, and (3) it does not contain all ratios. This third requirement is just the conventional disqualification of ∞.

The real numbers thus defined are not just the irrationals. They include also a counterpart of each ratio. Corresponding to 2/3 there is, we saw, the real number that is the class of all ratios less than 2/3. Such real numbers are the rational real numbers, or, briefly, again the ratios; we now have ratios in two senses of the word. It is only this second sense that permits us to say, as one does, that the real numbers comprise the ratios and the irrationals.

For that matter, we are now getting positive integers in three senses. There is the positive integer 5 in the primary sense of NATURAL NUMBERS, there is 5 in the sense of the ratio 5/1 which is the relation of 5 to 1, of 10 to 2, and so on, and there is 5 in the sense of the real number that is the class of all ratios less than 5/1. This multiplicity of senses is pertinent only to studies in the philosophy of mathematics. The sense appropriate to applied mathematics is usually that which reckons the integers and ratios among the real numbers, or even among the COM-PLEX NUMBERS, *q.v.* In the practice of mathematics there is no thought of those distinctions, nor of the underlying construction of the real numbers such as we have been reviewing. This is but one, moreover, of various related versions to the same effect. The basic idea goes back no further than Richard Dedekind (1888).

The real numbers are *dense:* between any two there are more. But that was true already of the ratios, without benefit of the irrationals. What the irrationals add is *continuity,* in the full technical sense; namely, every class C of real numbers has a limit which is in turn a real number or, at worst, ∞. For a real number, it will be remembered, is any class of ratios that fulfills conditions (1), (2), and (3); so C is a class of such classes. Its limit can be got simply by pooling those classes. The result, the class of all ratios belonging to members of C, can be seen to fulfill (1) and (2), and thus to qualify as a real number in turn, unless it is ∞.

Another notable contrast between ratios in particular and real numbers in general is that whereas any ratio is specifiable by two Arabic numerals and a fraction line, the real numbers outrun all means of expression. See INFINITE NUMBERS.

Recursion

If you know that something is true of zero, and you know further that if it is true of any integer then it is true of the next, you can conclude without further ado that it is true of all the integers from zero up. This recursive form of argument was used as far back as Euclid's day, and it was expressly recognized as a rule of reason three centuries and more ago by Fermat. It is a persistent refrain in elementary number theory.

It is called *mathematical induction,* but numbers are a special case. The same principle tells us that if Dustin Judson had sickle-cell anemia, and if the sons and daughters of persons susceptible to sickle-cell anemia are likewise susceptible, then all descendants of Dustin Judson are susceptible. Note that this example even differs in structure from the numerical one; a number has only one successor, but a person's sons and daughters can be many.

A companion piece to mathematical induction is *inductive* or *recursive definition.* Example: we define

(1) $x + 0 = x,$ (2) $x + Sy = S(x + y)$

where Sy is the successor of y. We thus explain $x + 0$ and then x plus each succeeding number, step by step. We start with (1) and then we explain $x + n$ for any n by n steps of (2). Recursive definitions of product and power follow the same pattern:

$$x \cdot 0 = 0, \quad x \cdot Sy = x + xy; \qquad x^0 = 1, \quad x^{Sy} = x \cdot x^y.$$

From these recursive definitions the familiar laws of calculation are derivable by mathematical induction. Such are the recursive definitions of the familiar operations on natural numbers. Predicates also may be defined recursively—notably 'natural number' itself:

(3)   0 is a natural number, and successors of natural numbers are natural numbers.

Strictly speaking we should also impose a lid:

(4)   There are no natural numbers but what (3) requires.

For a further example we may look outside arithmetic. Here is a recursive definition of 'ancestor'.

(5)   The parents of x are ancestors of x, and the parents of ancestors of x are ancestors of x.

(6)   There are no ancestors of x but what (5) requires.

Recursion is vital also to one's command of language. There are countless sentences, never yet uttered, that we stand ready to utter if occasion arises, and countless sentences as yet unheard that we would understand if we heard them; and the key to this infinite store is recursion. We internalize our grammatical constructions early in life and accrete our vocabulary over the years, thus building up a tacit recursion that is boundless in its potential output. The grammar book and dictionary are an explicit rendering of such a recursion for the ideal speaker. Together, in all their bulk, they constitute a recursive definition of 'sentence' for the language concerned, together with a recursive explanation of what all the sentences mean.

Recursive definitions are definitions only in the weaker of two senses of the word. Addition is defined by (1) and (2) in the sense that they fix $x + y$ uniquely for each choice of x and

y. Definition in the full sense, however—*direct* definition—does more: it shows how to eliminate the defined notation at all points in favor of the previous notation on the basis of which it was defined. Recursive definition fails this test; (1) and (2) show us how to eliminate the plus sign when it is followed by '17' or any other numeral, but not when it is followed by a mere variable 'y'. This distinction can make all the difference between consistency and contradiction; see TRUTH.

Recursive definition formalizes the idea of 'and so on'. Thus (1) and (2) tell us that $x + 0$ is $x,$ and $x + S0$ is $Sx,$ and so on. (3) and (4) tell us that the natural numbers are 0, its successor, *its* successor, and so on. (5) and (6) tell us that x's ancestors are his parents, their parents, *their* parents, and so on.

Now it turns out that these two recursive definitions (3)–(6) can be neatly embodied in direct definitions, thereby putting the finishing touches on the analysis of 'and so on'. We can define the ancestors of x as the members shared by all classes that contain the parents of x and the parents of all their own members. We can define the natural numbers as the members shared by all classes that contain 0 and the successors of all their own members.

This was indeed a praiseworthy maneuver, and a hundred years ago there was some acrimony between Charles Sanders Peirce and Richard Dedekind as to which of the two deserved the credit. Ironically, Gottlob Frege had scooped the two of them in 1879.

The same idea can be used, more laboriously, to directify other recursive definitions. Thus look again to (1)–(2) and think of the relation that x plus any number bears to that number. (1) and (2) tell us two traits of that relation, namely, that x bears it to 0, and that whenever one number bears it to another, the successor of the one number will bear it to the successor of the other. Now we can define $x + y$ directly as the number that bears to y every relation that has those two traits.

But if recursive definitions can always be thus directified, how can I have said that the difference between recursive and direct can make all the difference between consistency and contradiction? For answer we must look to the auxiliary apparatus involved. Frege's directification of (3)–(6) appealed to all *classes* meeting certain conditions. The directification of (1)–(2) appealed to all *relations* meeting certain conditions. If we are working within elementary number theory, whose variables range only over numbers, our formalism affords no such recourse to classes or relations.

Classes and relations are the business of set theory, and set theory comes in various strengths (see PARADOXES); so even when we are working in a domain that draws on set theory, we may not have at our disposal the particular classes or relations that would enable us to directify some recursive definition. So it is with the recursive definition of satisfaction, *s.v.* TRUTH.

Sum, product, and power have come to be called recursive functions, along with all others that are recursively definable in similar fashion. Derivatively, a *class* of numbers is called recursive if it is determined by a recursive function—say as the class of those numbers to which the function assigns 0. I could be more rigorous, but a better use of the reader's patience is in noting what it all came to. In the mid-thirties of this century it came to an explication of *effectiveness*.

A trait is effective if there is a hard and fast routine by which we can check for it, without guesswork or imagination. In affirmative contexts this notion of effectiveness stands up well, without need of sharper definition. We show that a trait is effective simply by explaining how to check for the trait; everyone can agree that the routine is cut, dried, and free of guesswork and imagination. Need is felt for a definition of effectiveness only for negative contexts, where it is claimed that some trait is not effective. The impossibility of a hard and fast routine, free of guesswork and so on, can be argued only from precise standards of what these things mean. One such negative context was Alonzo Church's proof in 1936 that logical validity is not effective. Another was GÖDEL's THEOREM, according to which no proof procedure for elementary number theory can be complete so long as we require, as we must, that the assessment of proofs be effective.

It came to be appreciated, in the mid-thirties, that recursiveness affords a sharp explication of effectiveness. This has come to be called Church's Thesis. To say that logical validity is not effective is to say that the class of Gödel numbers (see GÖDEL'S THEOREM) of the valid logical formulas is not recursive. To say that the assessment of proofs is effective is to say that the class of Gödel numbers of proofs is recursive.

By its nature, Church's Thesis was not open to formal proof; for the thesis equated a precise property, recursiveness, with a property—effectiveness—that was to be rendered precise only by the thesis itself. But the thesis was supported by such instances as could be mustered, and soon it was pretty well clinched by Alan Turing's pioneer work in the abstract theory of computing machines. His formulation of mechanical computability, in terms of ideal mechanization, turned out to be equivalent to recursiveness. Mechanical computability, surely, is very much what our intuitive talk of effectiveness was aiming at all along; so Church's Thesis is well sustained.

Redundancy

Teachers of English composition have given redundancy a bad name, as this poignant exchange reminds us. "Help, Ma, I'm drownding to death." "Don't be redundant, dear."

A redundancy of redundancy is dismal, admittedly. I have sensed this in an ill-documented song in praise of my alma mater, despite the soundness of the sentiment.

> Oberlin forever, we will always be
> Faithful, true, and loyal in our love for thee.

Forever, always; faithful, true, loyal. One of each would convey the idea. The redundancies served to fill out the measures of the melody, but surely there were better ways. However, see also TRINITY.

A lecturer lately came out with the frustratingly redundant phrase "freedom, liberty, and so forth." In what direction do you continue forth when you haven't moved an inch?

A judicious redundancy, even so, is the breath of life. It is the judicious excess over minimum requisite support. It is why a good bridge does not crumble when subjected to stress beyond what reasonably could have been foreseen. It is fallback and failsafe. It is why we address our mail to city and state in so many words, despite the zip code. One indistinct digit in the zip code could spoil everything.

A single letter, at the hands of a careless or malicious compositor, can play havoc. "The book is of cosmic significance," "The book is of comic significance." "His point is worth noting," "His point is worth nothing." "She was neatly dressed," "She was nearly dressed." "Five milestones of empiricism," "Five millstones of empiricism." A kingdom, legend tells us, was lost for want of a horseshoe nail. Redundancy is our safeguard against such instability.

Redundancy at its crudest, in speech, is direct repetition. Sometimes it is the effect of a tic or a bad memory, and sometimes it is elicited by a listener's apparent failure to catch the message. In the first case it is tiresome for the listener and bad; in the second case it is good, but tiresome for the speaker. Speakers spare themselves this tiresome recourse in some measure, deliberately or unconsciously, by resorting to some other sort of redundancy that promises to obviate the need for repetition. One such alternative is a redundant effort in the enunciation of some easily mistaken word; but this is tiresome too. Another alternative, which has evidently been a factor in the changing of language down the centuries, is the lengthening of an inconveniently short word by adding a redundant suffix; see LANGUAGE DRIFT.

There is a valuable phonetic redundancy that pervades language and was nobody's invention. As we saw under PHO-

NEMES, a consonant can be excised from a tape recording and not be missed. The consonant is redundant in view of the accommodating distortions of the sounds before and after it. Conversely, the distortions are redundant given the consonant; a tape constructed without distortions is still intelligible. The redundancy is valuable, however, for it enhances intelligibility when acoustics are bad. Our comprehension of foreign speech declines more abruptly under poor acoustics than our comprehension of English, because we are less adept at rounding out foreign sounds from sparse residual clues.

This redundancy, however, is far from complete. If we were to depend for our consonants wholly upon the quality of the neighboring vowels, our creative imagination would promptly lead us astray. See further under PHONEMES.

Redundancy, paradoxically, is commonly an economic measure. This is evident in the case of the bridge: the redundant struts can be cheaper than the actuarially estimated fraction of the cost of replacing a crumbled bridge. In subtle and far-reaching ways redundancy is a source of economy also in scientific theory. Thus consider REAL NUMBERS, rational and irrational. The irrationals differ only infinitesimally from rational ones, and so contribute nothing to the accuracy of physical measurements. Moreover, while the rationals are infinitely numerous, the irrationals are infinitely more numerous; see INFINITE NUMBERS. Evidently then the recourse to irrational numbers in natural science is an exorbitant redundancy. Yet it engenders vast economy in the smoothness and simplicity of theory. Practically it is indispensable; the alternative is unthinkable. See DISCRETENESS.

Redundancy engenders economy likewise in the theory of grammar. When we formulate the SYNTAX of a language, *q.v.*, we count as grammatical countless strings of words that would strike the native ear as unnatural, as witness Bertrand Russell's "Quadruplicity drinks procrastination." It is a matter again, as in the case of irrational numbers, of simplifying a theory by redundantly rounding out its content.

Redundancy to this purpose permeates science. Our ultimate evidence for scientific theory is limited to the stimulations that are undergone by our sensory surfaces; yet we stuff our theoretical universe with everything from imperceptible quarks and electrons to black holes and galaxies. We have embedded our "blooming, buzzing confusion" into a manageable order by rounding it out (see THINGS).

Reference, Reification

It is convenient that these words come in alphabetical succession, for the two topics are not easily separated.

Terms, some of them, *refer* to objects of one sort or another—stones, people, or abstract ones such as numbers. To declare there to be objects of a given sort, for purposes of one's theory, is to *reify* them. Zoologists reify wombats and not unicorns, thereby reckoning the term 'wombat' as referring and 'unicorn' as not.

Reference by general terms—common nouns, adjectives, intransitive verbs— is *denotation*. 'Wombat' denotes each wombat. Reference by a singular term or a proper name is *designation,* singling out one object. The real numbers are all denoted by 'real number', but we saw under REAL NUMBERS that they cannot all be designated. A third species of reference is the taking of values by VARIABLES, *q.v.;* a variable refers to its values. The variable has its literary prototype in the relative pronoun and its subsidiary pronouns.

We say, or I anyway, that there are wombats, numbers, and classes, but no unicorns and no properties (see CLASSES VERSUS PROPERTIES). I reify those and not these. What does this distinction come to? I conclude under UNIVERSALS that the key is the variable. What we reify are what we reckon as admissible values of 'x' in 'object x such that'; in other words, what can be referred to by the 'which' and 'it' of relative clauses.

What I want now to look into is the role of reification in science: what is contributed to scientific theory by sweeping one or another multitude of putative objects into the range of variables, or, for that matter, what is contributed by the variables and their pronominal prototypes at all.

In the piece on VARIABLES we see that they and the pronouns are for marking and linking up various positions in a sentence, so as to extract from the sentence a complex predicate for use elsewhere. The node or pivot of the extracted predicate, the x of the 'such that' clause, is contributed by reification. What may usefully be reified for this purpose depends on what complex predicates may usefully be extracted.

Another contribution that reification confers is an indispensable tightening of links between scientific theory and the observations that support it. To appreciate this we must begin by reflecting on the nature of that support.

Under PREDICTION I depict the rudimentary repository of scientific lore as the observation categorical. It is formed of two observation sentences, as I call them, such as 'The sun is rising' and 'Birds are singing', each of which has come to be associated directly with some range of stimulation of the speaker's sensory receptors. He has learned, whether through direct conditioning or in more devious ways, to assent to 'The sun is rising' whenever queried while observing the sunrise, and to assent to 'Birds are singing' when hearing them sing. It is just these sentences as seamless wholes, without regard thus far to reification of birds, sun, or songs, that are associated with the stimulatory situations. Reification of objects for the component terms to denote or designate may or may not have originally helped him to associate these sentences with the situations; but it is just these associations themselves, however acquired, that are the first link in the chain from sensory stimulation to scientific theory.

Scientific theory, finally, connects with the observation sentences by implying observation categoricals; such, as noted under PREDICTION, is the observational support of science. What is now to be noted is that it is a matter of sentences first and last: observation sentences here, theoretical sentences there. Terms, variables, and reference enter only in an auxiliary role, contributing somehow to the elaborate network of implications that connect the sentences at the one extreme with the sentences at the other.

They do so by tightening the links by which sentences are joined to form compound sentences. Thus consider two sentences joined in conjunction by 'and'. It is a loose connection; the compound is true provided merely that both components are true, however irrelevant one to the other. A quantified conjunction, of the form 'Something x is such that Fx and Gx', affords a tighter connection. Again alternation, 'or', is a loose connection. Quantification tightens it: 'Everything x is such that Fx or Gx.'

Thus it is that quantification helps to knit up the logical fabric of sentences that connects theory with evidence; and it is quantification, with its variables, that embodies reification.

It is startling to reflect that this contribution is purely structural. Other objects would have served the purpose as well as ours, as long as they were in one-to-one correlation with them. No evidence, therefore, could be adduced for reification of the one lot rather than the other.

It is not to be wondered, still, that we start reifying where we do: reifying middle-sized bodies in the middle distance. They contrast with their background in color and movement. Here we get our start in the primitive equivalent of quantification and variables. Developing further theory little by little, we impute endurance and recurrence to these bodies; see THINGS. Need of further links in the evolving theory prompts reification of invisible analogues of bodies, and eventually even abstract objects such as numbers. We talk of discovering objects, and discovery indeed there is; but ultimately it is discovery of a need of further nodes in the developing structure. What the theory is ultimately answerable to, early and late, are sensory stimulations and the observation sentences that are keyed to them without benefit of reference and reification.

Rhetoric

Rhetoric is the literary technology of persuasion, for good or ill. It is the rallying point for advertisers, trial lawyers, politicians, and debating teams.

Debating teams are promoted in schools as a spur to effective language and incisive thought. They serve that purpose, but only by setting the goal of persuasion above the goal of truth. The debater's strength lies not in intellectual curiosity nor in amenability to rational persuasion by others, but in his skill in defending a preconception come what may. His is a nefarious knack of disregarding all the discrepancies while regarding every crepancy. The same skill, along with legal lore, is the strength of the trial lawyer or barrister, and the strength also of the successful politician, one or the other of which careers the captain of the debating team is clearly destined for. Happily there are lawyers who will take on only such cases as they deem to be just, and politicians who will espouse only a cause that is righteous; but these scruples are not adjuncts of the rhetorical pole, nor are they keys to success in the legal or political profession.

When an electorate or a jury is in the sway of a demagogue's rhetoric, cold reason and the marshaling of facts bear little promise in rebuttal. Marshaling more rhetoric, then, in a contrary vein, we fight fire with fire. Rhetoric is invaluable homeopathically in withstanding its own assaults.

In scientific circles there is little demagogy to combat, but rhetoric is sometimes of service even there; for in an extremity it may happen that a scientist needs more than a cold statement of his theory and his evidence if he is ever to shake the stubborn and mistaken preconceptions of some of his students, let alone his dissident colleagues. But rhetoric in the wrong scientist's hands can do disservice to science. It can help him put his theory across for his reputation's sake despite some shakiness in the evidence.

Rhetoric, then, is sometimes nefarious and sometimes not. In its nefarious use it is the art or practice of defending a proposition on grounds other than one's own reasons for defending it. An auxiliary device is innuendo. A *referentially translucent* expression, as Randal Marlin calls it,★ is subtly ambiguous: it can be taken as objectively stating a result of an action, and it can be taken as accusing the agent of intending that result. One of Marlin's examples is the headline "Pope Fouls Up Bar Mitzvah." The Pope's arrival in town caused a traffic jam that rendered the synagogue inaccessible for the bar mitzvah; but the headline can be taken as hinting unjustly of hostility on the Pope's part toward Jews. It is an insidious device, effective in warping unsuspecting minds while still adhering, in a sense, to the verifiable.

Nefarious rhetoric is rife not only in tendentious journalism, television commercials, courts of law, Congress, political rallies, and the United Nations, but also in homelier settings. In a New England town meeting a citizen will describe in glowing terms the public advantages that would accrue from some proposed measure, when what is at stake deep down has to do with his own interest as proprietor, abutter, investor, or contractor. In such a case we do not cope with the abuse by meeting rhetoric with rhetoric, fire with fire; we just expose the man's motives. What is important is to be alert to what is going on, and not accept insincere argument at face value. This much applies to the august cases and the humble ones alike.

What I have been calling nefarious rhetoric recurs in a rudimentary form also in impromptu discussions. Someone harbors a prejudice or an article of faith or a vested interest, and mar-

★"The Rhetoric of Action Description," *Informal Logic* 6 (1984), pp. 26–28.

shals ever more desperate and threadbare arguments in defense of his position rather than be swayed by reason or face the facts. Even more often, perhaps, the deterrent is just stubborn pride: reluctance to acknowledge error. Unscientific man is beset by a deplorable desire to have been right. The scientist is distinguished by a desire to *be* right.

S

Semantic Switch

We have no pat suffix for ability. Predictability is not the ability to predict. Our suffix *-ble* or *-ile* expresses a passive trait: susceptibility. One is lovable or despicable who can *be* loved or despised. Similarly for their Latin originals *-bilis* and *-ilis*. The Latin *terribilis,* then, is a curious exception; for the verb *terrere* means 'terrify', but *terribilis* does not mean 'terrifiable', it means 'can terrify'. This oddity comes over into English with *terrible,* except that we did not inherit the corresponding verb *terr*. In *horrible* we have a different anomaly: the underlying Latin verb is intransitive, meaning 'be afraid'. We would not expect an intransitive verb to make sense with *-bilis* or *-ble*.

Usually an adjective in *-ble* carries with it a noun in *-bility;* but we do not find *terribility* or *horribility*. This anomaly is perhaps linked with the other.

It is odd that we have this pat suffix *-ile* or *-ble* for susceptibility, applicable to any and every transitive verb at the drop of a hat, and no corresponding one for ability. Similarly for Latin and the Romance languages. Why cater thus to the passive, to the neglect of the active? It is to be wondered that the strays—*terrible, horrible*—are so few.

German does have a symmetric pair of suffixes, -*bar* for susceptibility and -*fähig* for ability, though the latter is less often used. Something capable of absorbing is *saugfähig;* we lamely say *absorbent,* conflating the ability with the activity. Custom makes us unaware that we limp.

The semantic inversion noted in *terrible* and *horrible* has sometimes invested also the suffix -*ful.* To be fearful is indeed to be full of fear, and fear is fright; yet to be frightful is not to be full of fright, but to inspire it. *Frightful* is *fearsome.* To call a dog or a follower *faithful,* again, is quite parallel; it is not to say that he is full of faith, but that he inspires it. *Faithworthy* would be more to the point.

Wonderful, again, is parallel: the wonderful is what inspires the wonder, and it is rather the onlooker that is full of wonder. The straightforward word for *wonderful* would be *admirable,* in its primary sense; for to admire was to wonder at, as in *nil admirari.*

Awful, in its original and formal sense, is parallel again to *fearful, faithful,* and *wonderful.* To be awful is to inspire awe. To be awful in the vernacular sense is to inspire revulsion. Can the word have been influenced by *offal?* It is curiously sensitive also to word order; thus we happily put up with an awful lot of people, but less happily with a lot of awful people. For other reflections on *wonderful* and *awful,* see ANOMALY.

Shameful, again, is of a piece with *awful, fearful, faithful,* and *wonderful.* These inversions are running into such numbers that they may begin to seem right side up. But *shameful* adds a reflexive twist: the shame that a shameful act inspires, or should inspire, is in the perpetrator. Another twist is that the *shameful* and the *shameless,* for all the opposition of their suffixes, are not unlike.

A transitive verb is sometimes used in both its active and its passive senses without recourse to the grammatical contrast of active and passive forms. Tribulations are experienced *by us,* as is their wont, and *we* are said to *be* very experienced. A sinner *confesses* to a priest, and is said to be *confessed* by him. I mistake a thing, so the thing is mistaken by me; yet I say that *I* am mistaken. I am registered in a hotel or am graduated from college, but then I say that I registered or graduated. English is quite tolerant of such a switch. We can subject a verb to it for the first time without provoking offense or perplexity.

There is one case, however, that bears especial interest: *please.* We have 'It pleases *him*' and we have 'He does as *he* pleases'; insofar the switch is true to form. But what is interesting is that in the polite cliché 'If you please' itself the *you* is direct object, historically, and not subject. In the second person singular of yore the cliché was 'If thee please', not 'If thou please'. (I write the subjunctive *please* in both cases, rather than *pleaseth* and *pleasest.*) Thus the original sense of 'If you please' is 'If (it) please you'. The smart aleck responds to 'If you please' with 'Oh, but I don't'; historically 'Oh, but me doesn't' would be better. The indiscriminate takeover of *thee, thou,* and *ye* by *you* is the source of the confusion.

French vernacular has engendered semantic switch *en masse* by the simple expedient of omitting the negative particle *ne,* than which little could be more effective. By this expedient *pas,* 'step', comes to mean 'not a step' even in the absence of *ne,* and finally just 'not'. Similarly *point,* 'speck', comes to suffice for quite the contrary, 'not a speck'; *personne* for 'nobody'; *rien,* originally Latin *rem,* 'thing', for 'nothing'. The mechanism is evident: these words came to occur much more frequently with *ne* than in other contexts, so in many cases the *ne* could be taken for granted. It is a paradox of our garrulous species that a man will save a syllable where he can.

Our *any,* similarly, occurs mainly in negative contexts. If the tendency so marked in French were operative also with us, *any* might have been expected to come to mean 'none'. Or perhaps it is saved by its use with *if;* a semantic switch to 'none' would wreak havoc with *if any.*

In the present century the word *labor* seems to have undergone an odd switch. Labor unions are not prolabor and never were; they are for the limitation of labor and the promotion of pay and leisure. Similarly for so-called prolabor legislation. The labor movement stimulates "automation" and labor-saving devices.

These last quotation marks are shame quotes. *Automation* disowns its Greek origin in *automaton* and feigns Latin origin in a spurious verb *automare*. It is as perverse in its way as *operatic* in its. *Operatic* disowns its Latin origin in *opus, operis*, and feigns Greek origin in a spurious *opera, operatos*.

Semantic switch was once overestimated, in the strategem of *lucus a non lucendo*; see ETYMOLOGY.

Senses of Words

We are accustomed to being told of some word that it is used in several senses, three perhaps. How do they know what to count as one broad sense and what to count as two or three narrower ones? We speak of a cool drink, a cool breeze, and a cool reception; and we are told that 'cool' has the same sense in the first two contexts, but a different sense in the third. Again we speak of hard benches, hard liquor, and hard problems, and are told that 'hard' has a different sense in each. Is it just a question of how unlike the things are that the adjective is applied to? Receptions are indeed very unlike drinks and breezes, and problems are very unlike benches and liquor; it is the abstract versus the concrete. But benches and liquor are surely no more unlike than drinks and breezes; why in these cases is 'hard' said to occur in two senses and 'cool' in but one?

Technology answers the question, in these happy cases, by actually offering the three pertinent senses in operational terms. The breeze and the drink are cool in the sense measured by the thermometer. Benches are hard in the sense in which a thing is harder than the things it can scratch. Liquor is hard as measured by alcoholic content.

But these measures are modern. The distinct senses that they measure could already be distinguished without them, simply in terms of comparability. A drink may be cooler or less cool than a breeze, but liquor can be neither harder nor less hard than a bench. Likewise drinks and breezes are neither cooler nor less cool than receptions, and liquor and benches are neither harder nor less hard than problems. Comparability thus serves as a convenient touchstone of sameness of sense, however arbitrary. But it is limited to such adjectives as 'cool' and 'hard', that admit comparatives.

A still more compelling consideration for ascribing difference in sense is difference in origin. Thus 'sound' would be ascribed three senses on this score alone; see ETYMOLOGY. The three are reckoned even as distinct words, in the commonest though not the simplest sense of the word 'word'. They are homonyms. An equally compelling and more frequently available basis for distinction of sense is grammatical role; thus 'smell' as a transitive verb, an intransitive verb, and a noun.

But these criteria, for all their diversity, are not seen as covering the ground. A further and vaguer criterion, noted by L. J. Cohen, is resistance to parallel construction, as in the *syllepsis* 'He took a deep breath and an aspirin', or 'He took his briefcase and a taxi'. It is a subjective criterion, and it grades off; but in so doing it promises to accord some words, such as 'take', a great many senses.

A naive respect for dictionaries induces a false air of objectivity in the numbered subdivisions of a dictionary entry. The so-called senses thus enumerated are for the lexicographer the merest expository convenience in his effort to coach his reader in the use of the word on all and sundry occasions. Thus a Latin–English dictionary would list two senses for *altus*, (1) high, and (2) deep, though from a Latin point of view a single inclusive sense covers the matter; see ETYMOLOGY. The lexicographer's purpose is simply to help the Anglophone with his Latin in the most efficient way.

Deeper philosophical significance came to attach to certain differences of sense, however, as an effect partly of Russell's "theory of types," which was his eventual way around the PARADOXES of set theory. Individuals made up the lowest type, classes of individuals the next type, classes of such classes the third type, and so on up. Sentences of the form '$x \in y$', affirming membership, were ruled out as ungrammatical and meaningless except where the terms in the position 'x' and 'y' referred to things of consecutive types.

Russell's expedient gave way to neater ones involving no such grammatical gerrymandering (see IMPREDICATIVITY), but meanwhile it encouraged, by its example, an excessive respect for purported categories and a readiness to declare a sentence meaningless if it crossed them up. "Category mistakes" were scouted by Gilbert Ryle and other no-nonsense philosophers as a major source of metaphysical inconsequence.

For instance Ryle and others held the verb 'exists' to have one sense or another according to the category of the purported object: concrete or abstract. To apply the verb jointly to something abstract and something concrete was to use it simultaneously in two senses, and hence was meaningless. I remarked elsewhere that I was impressed less by what such philosophers so stoutly maintained than by the stoutness of their maintenance. A nominalistic animus was doubtless a factor; see UNIVERSALS. But we do see under CONSTRUCTIVISM, oddly enough, that a respectable role for a distinction between abstract and concrete existence may eventually be established after all.

If drastic difference of objects makes for differences of sense, then I must concede that the differences between abstract and concrete should indeed do so. If senses are to be rigidly conceived, than I must concede further that the use of a word simultaneously in two senses may be fairly rejected as its use in none. What I reject is the rigid objectification of sense. Leave it, I say, as a lexicographic convenience, and let grammar run over it roughshod. Nothing but vagueness and complexity is lost by declaring it simply and trivially false, rather than meaningless, to say that the breeze was cooler than the reception or vice versa.

Singular Terms

Asked whether Pegasus flew, whether he had horns, and whether he had pin feathers, we are apt to say that the first is true, the second false, and the third neither. This is an elliptical way of saying that the ancient myths affirm the first, that they rule out the second, and that they take no stand on the third.

But what then are our own verdicts on the three statements, speaking for ourselves and not for our fanciful forebears? Presumably that none of the three is either true or false, there being no such creature as Pegasus. Still we hesitate to reject them as meaningless. We understand the word 'Pegasus', after all, and we even recognize some statements as true that contain it, notably the statement 'There is no such creature as Pegasus'.

There is a clear reason not to opt for meaninglessness, and it becomes evident when we move from Pegasus to such examples as Camelot and Prester John. We know there never was Pegasus, but are less sure whether there was or was not such a place as Camelot or such a man as Prester John; and it is undesirable to let the question of meaningfulness of sentences of our language hinge on such unsettled questions of nonlinguistic fact.

A better line, evidently, is to reckon all the above sentences about Pegasus as meaningful, but still to reckon the first three as neither true or false. The question what sentences about Camelot or Prester John are true or false, then, and what ones are neither, will hinge on the factual question of existence of such a place or person. This is better, since truth and falsity, unlike meaningfulness, normally do hinge on matters of fact and commonly do remain open questions.

We had to give 'There is no such creature as Pegasus' special status. Similarly for its contradictory, 'Pegasus exists', and other sentences equivalent to these; they do qualify unequivocally as true or false. I pause here for a theological interlude. An old argument for the existence of God, known as the ontological argument, was that God is by definition perfect. Failure to exist would be an imperfection, so God exists. Kant was no more impressed than we by the argument, and his rebuttal was that existence is not a predicate. We have now noticed again the special status of singular existence statements, however their status be phrased.

As for other statements about Pegasus—ones that might in a Kantian spirit be called "predicative" if that word were not preempted (see IMPREDICATIVITY)—we concluded that the most natural way of representing everyday language is to regard them as neither true nor false. This means taking a negative stand in the matter of the EXCLUDED MIDDLE, *q.v.* But when for purposes of logical analysis we are concerned to regiment scientific language along logically economical lines, as in PREDICATE LOGIC, there is a better way of dealing with names and other singular terms. It conforms to the law of the excluded middle, and it is more explicit on matters of existence and uniqueness.

It is a matter of absorbing singular terms into predicates. 'Pegasus', 'Napoleon', and the rest are treated as inseparable fragments of the predicates 'is Pegasus', 'is Napoleon', and so on. 'Pegasus flies' becomes:

(1) $\exists x(x$ is Pegasus and x flies),

that is, 'Something is Pegasus and flies'. See PREDICATE LOGIC. This sentence is simply false, along with '$\exists x(x$ is Pegasus)' itself. The three sentences about Pegasus that we accounted neither true nor false now turn out false.

Might we not have simply ruled them false at the outset,

without paraphrasing? Might we not have agreed to account all sentences about Pegasus as false outright, except for ones like 'There is no such thing as Pegasus'? No, this line would have led to trouble. It would account 'Pegasus flies' and 'Pegasus does not fly' both as false, contrary to logic. The point of the paraphrasing is to sort out such conflicting cases. 'Pegasus does not fly' admits of two opposite paraphrases; for it is true that

$$\text{not } \exists x (x \text{ is Pegasus and } x \text{ flies})$$

but false that

$$\exists x (x \text{ is Pegasus and } x \text{ does not fly}).$$

Sentences formerly deemed neither true nor false thus do not all get paraphrased as false. Distinctions emerge.

A singular term connotes uniqueness. It purports to designate just one thing. On the present approach uniqueness, like existence, gets separate attention. When wanted it is expressly stated:

(2) $\forall x \forall y (\text{if } x \text{ is Napoleon and } y \text{ is Napoleon then } x = y),$

that is, only one thing is Napoleon. First and last, thus, the effect of absorbing names into predicates is an explicit sorting out of logically pertinent features. It is reminiscent of what happens to tense under logical regimentation; see SPACE-TIME.

Complex singular terms can be similarly absorbed. The dominant form of complex singular term is singular description, for example, 'the author of *Waverley*'. This is the ever-recurring example, stemming from Bertrand Russell's pioneer work in paraphrasing singular terms. Here again the term gives way to a predicate—in this case 'wrote *Waverley*'. Then, just as 'Pegasus flies' became (1), so 'The author of *Waverley* is Scottish' becomes:

$$\exists x (x \text{ wrote } Waverley \text{ and } x \text{ is Scottish}).$$

Again, as in (2), we can add a stipulation of uniqueness when we need it.

Similarly for the idiom of singular description generally. Its general form is 'the object x such that Fx'; and to ascribe any further predicate 'G' to the object thus described we have merely to write '$\exists x(Fx$ and $Gx)$'. Again we can stipulate uniqueness of the described object when we need to:

$$\forall x \forall y (\text{if } Fx \text{ and } Fy \text{ then } x = y).$$

Singular terms in forms other than singular description are ubiquitous in mathematics—thus '$z + w$', 'zw', 'z^2'. But they can all be disposed of in essentially the way we have been seeing. Thus '$z + w$' gets absorbed into a three-place predicate 'Σ', meaning 'is-the-sum-of-. . . -and. . .'. A sentence about $z + w$, say '$G(z + w)$', becomes '$\exists x(\Sigma xzw$ and $Gx)$'. A theorem or postulate of uniqueness, again, can be cited as needed:

$$\forall x \forall y \forall z \forall w (\text{if } \Sigma xzw \text{ and } \Sigma yzw \text{ then } x = y).$$

Such is the elimination of singular terms. It is part of the process of paraphrasing ordinary language into the straitjacket of PREDICATE LOGIC, in the narrow form in which I have sketched it under that heading. It makes for a streamlining of logic and for a reconciliation, as we have seen, of EXCLUDED MIDDLE with questions of nonexistence.

Its practical drawbacks, however, must be noted and heavily stressed. Substitution of polynomials and other complex singular terms directly for variables and for one another is the very life of computation and algebraic manipulation. Mathematics would be immobilized by the straitjacket of predicate logic without singular terms. In principle the work can all be done in the paraphrased idiom, but the clumsiness and the resulting barrier to intuition would be prohibitive. The dilemma has a happy solution, however, in the reversibility of the rules of paraphrase. We can switch back and forth, enjoying the best of both worlds. Logical elegance and clarity of analysis this side, efficient practice that.

Space–Time

Bind two straight sticks together, one across the other, so as to form a big plus sign. Then bind a third stick to the two of them at their intersection, perpendicular to both. The three sticks are perpendicular each to each. Clearly this can be done. But now can a fourth stick be bound to the three, at their intersection, and perpendicular to all three? Clearly not. Here we observe a remarkably simple and basic law of nature: the tridimensionality of space. It is not a law of pure geometry; geometry works nicely for any number of dimensions. It is a physical law. There are physical tests of straightness of sticks (see LINES) and of perpendicularity, and it is an experimental fact that, try as we will, we cannot bind a fourth stick perpendicularly to the three.

The man in the street, baffled by talk of a fourth dimension, blames his want of visual imagination. He might better credit his insight into nature. He can see, in his mind's eye, that three is all there are.

Barring, of course, double-talk. The mathematician generalizes, as is his wont. He begins by noting that we can specify any point in space by assigning values to three independent variables: (1) how far up, (2) how far out, and (3) how far over. Such is the tridimensionality of space. Generalizing, then, he speaks of a class of entities of any sort as n-dimensional if there are n independent variables such that each member of the class is specifiable by assigning values to all n variables, and each assignment of values to all n variables specifies a distinct member of the class. Predictably the mathematician also generalizes the word 'space' correspondingly, calling the class an n-dimensional space.

One instance of this extended usage lies nearer home than others, namely, the four-dimensional manifold whose dimensions are the three dimensions of space ordinarily so called and the single dimension of time; in a word or two, space-time. This modest supplementation of vulgar space is imperative for

Einstein's special theory of relativity, but it conduces greatly to clarity and simplicity also apart from that. It was propounded by Boscovich already two centuries ago.

When time is thus viewed, an enduring solid is seen as spreading out in four dimensions: (1) up and down, (2) right and left, (3) forward and backward, (4) hence and ago. Change is not thereby repudiated in favor of an eternal static reality, as some have supposed. Change is still there, with all its fresh surprises. It is merely incorporated. To speak of a body as changing is to say that its later stages differ from its earlier stages, just as its upper parts differ from its lower parts. Its later shape need be no more readily inferred from its earlier shape than its upper shape from its lower.

Our ordinary language insists on tenses for verbs, even when, as in pure mathematics, time is irrelevant. Our mathematical notation is mercifully free of tense, and its tenselessness carries over into symbolic logic. When symbolic logic is used in contexts where time does matter, then, any needed temporal information is provided rather by explicit predicates such as 'later than', just as any needed spatial information is provided by predicates such as 'north of'. Our regimented logical notation thus takes on just the style that the four-dimensional view would prescribe. The cumbersome alternative of importing tense into the logical notation serves no purpose, unless that of modeling ordinary language because of an interest in it.

The spatializing of time serves logic in more than simplicity and convenience. Mustn't the truly tense-bound mentality feel uneasy about relations between noncontemporaries? A relation between Mark Antony and Cleopatra, despite their nonexistence, is perhaps condoned by the past tense; for they coexisted back then. But what about the great-great-great-grandfather relation? Two people have seldom if ever existed, simultaneously, to sustain it. What, again, of a class of noncontemporaries, such as the class of all the great generals of history? There are doubtless various ways of coping, but the one before us is the simplest and best: that of recognizing all denizens of space-time, however remote in any dimension, as tenselessly coexistent. We transcend tense by escaping into the fourth dimension.

We have gained all this by treating time as a dimension on a par with the spatial ones but still, in an important sense, independent of them. In space we recognize not only the directions up and down, right and left, forward and back, but also all the intermediate oblique directions: thus up and left, forward and down. The spatial directions can be blended in all proportions. If the time dimension were to be thoroughly amalgamated with that congenial old threesome, so as to enable us to treat freely of oblique directions up and ago, forward and hence, and the rest, we would have to set up equations between units of distance and units of duration: so many miles equal an hour. For the benefits thus far noted, this full integration of time with space has not been needed. It is needed, however, for the theory of relativity.

To see why, consider to begin with two stakes five yards apart. One observer, from where he stands, correctly describes one stake as four yards to the left of the other and three yards beyond it. Another observer correctly describes the one stake as only three yards to the left of the other but four yards beyond it. One man's left is another man's straight ahead. It is a question of orientation.

Turning now to relativity theory, consider not two stakes but two flashes of widely separated lamps. One observer correctly states the distance and the time lapse between the flashes; another observer, traveling by at a different velocity, equally correctly ascribes a greater distance and a greater time lapse. So says the theory. The difference between space and time also ceases to be absolute and becomes relative to the circumstances of the observer, like the difference between left and straight ahead in the case of the stakes. The temporal dimension must thenceforward be fully integrated with the three spatial ones. We must accommodate all sorts of spatiotemporal diagonals.

Relativity theory turns out not to admit measurement, not

even across four dimensions, that is analogous to distance and independent of the observer's velocity. An "interval" between events is indeed defined that is independent of the observer's velocity, but it is very unlike distance; it can be zero even when the events are far apart.

Looking out on the momentary scene with a painter's eye, one might even describe it in just two dimensions: up-down and left-right. This is all very well for the one scene; a camera can do no better. But if we want to accommodate different viewpoints while preserving the identity of the trees and houses, we have to invoke all three spatial dimensions. The three will serve us well as we explore and measure the world, as long as we maintain a sedate pace. If we change our pace drastically, then relativity theory tells us that any distance measurements made thus far will require correction. Distances are reconcilable with varied velocities only by invoking time as a fourth dimension, and not just as an independent fourth. The fully integrated four are needed, complete with measurable diagonals.

Not that we in our daily rounds ever change pace sufficiently to detect this need. Maintaining the even tenor of our ways, we can leave the time dimension independent of the spatial ones as we always have. But we do well still to keep it firmly alongside, treating the world and its denizens tenselessly as four-dimensional, simply for logical clarity and quite apart from relativity.

Syntax

Who and/or what could be less glamorous than a pedantic old rule-happy grammarian? An English grammarian at that? The truth of the matter is, however, that *glamour* and *grammar* are in origin one and the same word.

Elementary schools have been called grammar schools, particularly in their upper grades, and it seems that there were secluded stretches of eighteenth-century Scotland in which the grammar school, or its master, came in the shepherd's mind to epitomize learning. Through hyperbole and liveliness of imagination the word then came to connote magic, and it was with this connotation that the word, distorted by then to *glamour,* was insinuated into standard English by Sir Walter Scott. In reporting this I rely implicitly on the *Oxford English Dictionary,* as is my wont; but sources disagree.

Even the word *grammar,* quite apart from *glamour,* is used variously. In its narrow use it designates the system of uniformities or rules that say what strings of words, or strings of PHONEMES, *q.v.,* are coherent specimens of a given language, as opposed to those strings which are gibberish. In its broader use, no less venerable, the word denotes rather the entire "art of speaking or writing language . . . according to established usage." I for one have habitually understood the word in the narrow sense, but providentially there is no need to insist or depend on it; for the word *syntax* is at our disposal in just that sense and no other. I shall try to abide by it instead.

The syntactician's task, then, is to say what strings belong in the language. But this way of describing such a task is utterly indefinite in two ways. Consider an analogy: the task of saying what people you know. Might you accomplish it tautologously by simply saying "Those whom I know"? No, there is a tacit requirement that you enumerate them by name. But the task remains indefinite even so, until we get clear on what counts as knowing someone. Visual recognition? Mutual visual recognition? Use of first names? So we have to settle two things: how the individuals are to be specified and what qualifies them for specification.

Similarly for the task of syntax. Here the answer to the first of the two questions is that the strings belonging to the language are to be specified *formally;* that is to say, by reference purely to their component words or phonemes and how these are arranged. I shall come back to this.

The second question is as to the conditions for belonging to the language. Intelligibility is too liberal a standard. "You are very; I am mere" is a clear and touching tribute, but not English. And people just down the street, with whom we grew up, are said to speak ungrammatically at times. If the language under consideration is to exclude even them, it must be demarcated very narrowly; it will be the dialect of a literary elite on their best verbal behavior.

We settle, then, on some seemingly typical members of the narrowly chosen speech community, whether ours or some exotic one in the bush. But the strings that our syntax is to cover are not just the few that we hear from these informants; they embrace also the multitude of further strings that might be elicited from such informants by describable circumstances. Those circumstances must not themselves be of a linguistic nature in turn, such as might deflect the informant from his own dialect; but they can extend to the fantasies of fairy tales. William Haas has suggested such a demarcation: if there is no way of fabricating a story in which the string might plausibly occur, it may fairly be accounted ungrammatical.

In particular we would have to stretch our creative imagination to the breaking point to accommodate Bertrand Russell's seemingly grammatical example "Quadruplicity drinks procrastination." But we round out and round off. A dubious string may be counted as grammatical or ungrammatical with a view to the smoothness and simplicity of the overall syntactical system that we are formulating. Accustomed as one is to the austerity of the language teacher and her rule book, one fails to appreciate that the rules themselves, insofar as defensible, are generalizations drawn by empirical scientists from the observation of verbal behavior. Drawn, rounded out, and rounded off.

These rules are the fulfillment of the syntactician's task of specifying what strings qualify as grammatical under the tentative standards we have been reviewing. The task, as we saw earlier in answer to the first of the two questions, is to specify them formally.

He does it mainly by RECURSION, *q.v.:* a method resembling that of genealogical trees. He begins with single words, which are his simplest strings, and proceeds to describe various *constructions* that generate longer strings from shorter ones. He partitions the growing store of strings into categories, called parts of speech, as an indispensable aid to describing the constructions that generate the store. Thus he wants to be able to say that attachment of an adjective to a noun, simple or complex, yields a noun; that attachment of a noun to an intransitive verb yields a sentence; that the joining of sentences by a conjunction yields a sentence.

Such is the sketchiness of grammar-school syntax, with its eight parts of speech: noun, pronoun, verb, adjective, adverb, preposition, conjunction, and sentence. We already see that one of these, the verb, needed subdividing into transitive and intransitive. Further subdivision is needed for languages requiring agreement in GENDER; for the goal, always, is to say what strings belong to the perhaps idealized language that we are describing. Such divisions and subdivisions, indeed, are barely a beginning. Even the abstract nouns *cognizance* and *exception* are syntactically unlike; for we can coherently take cognizance *of* but not *to,* and take exception *to* but not *of.*

If the syntax of our language were to be formulated in full by explicit recursion, the parts of speech would have to be construed very narrowly indeed. They would have to be so narrow that two strings would never be reckoned to the same part of speech unless they were interchangeable everywhere *salva congruitate.*

This nice ablative absolute, one of my many debts to Peter Geach, means that the interchange would always preserve grammaticality: never yield gibberish. If parts of speech were defined that narrowly, *cognizance* and *exception* would be different parts of speech; also *of* and *to.* Surely there would be hundreds of parts of speech, many of them singletons. A reasonable and usual alternative is to abandon recursion after the first broad sketch of the language, and then add the refinements

simply as supplementary observations as in the present example.

The grammarian Noam Chomsky has developed a method
other than recursion, or trees, for systematizing such refinements. He formulates rules for transforming strings into other
strings, with a view to equating the multifarious sentences of
our actual language to sentences of a fabricated core language
that does submit to recursive formulation.

Something like this happens, along other lines and for other
purposes, when we paraphrase into PREDICATE LOGIC, *q.v.* In
this logical case the procedure of paraphrase is not sharply
codified, however, for our eye is then on the cognitive content
or momentarily intended use of the sentence rather than its
linguistically interesting features. Moreover, our sentences do
not all submit to that Procrustean bed. Such as do submit,
however, thereupon lend themselves to a recursive syntax of
childish simplicity, as seen under PREDICATE LOGIC.

T

Things

William James pictured the baby's senses as first assailed by a "blooming, buzzing confusion." In the fullness of time a sorting out sets in. "Hello," he has the infant wordlessly noting, "Thingumbob again!"

Thingumbob: a rattle, perhaps, or a bottle, a ball, a towel, a mother? Or it may only have been sunshine, a cool breeze, a snatch of maternal babytalk; they are all on an equal footing on first acquaintance. Later we come to recognize corporeal things as the substantial foundation of nature. The very word 'thing' connotes bodies first and foremost, and it takes some effort to appreciate that the corporeal sense of 'thing' is peculiarly sophisticated.

People and other animals do indeed react instinctively and distinctively to animals and other bodies from early infancy, but my point is that the question of its being the *same* bottle or ball or wolf or lamb the second time around does not arise, any more than does the question of its being the same sunbeam or the same irruption of cool air. Seeing a body again means to us that it or we or our glance has returned from a round trip in the course of which the body was out of sight. This is what is sophisticated about the corporeal sense of 'thing'. The baby's wordless 'again' is innocent of that.

Innocent of similarity it is not. Similarity of events, or identity of phenomena, does come in at the ground floor (see PREDIC-

TION). The baby's unspoken 'Thingumbob again' is well on target when the thingumbob is the general and repeatable phenomenon of sunshine or fresh air or, for that matter, the general attribute of being a red ball or a bottle.

We in our sophistication make good sense of the question whether the penny now in our pocket is one of the utterly similar ones that were there a week ago, little though we may care about the answer. It is bound up with a theory of the continuity of bodily form and motion between observations. Answering such a question can require ransacking one's systematic knowledge and beliefs. In the present case we would probably try to remember what interim transactions may have involved odd pennies.

We reduce the bewildering flux of observable events to system and simplicity, comparatively speaking, by interpolating an unseen intermediate career or trajectory between our observations of what we choose to regard as the same body or substance. We adjust and readjust our reifications and our reidentifications with a view to contriving the simplest and laziest of all possible worlds: the simplest and laziest of all worlds, that is to say, compatible with our observations. Our tacit maxim is the law of least action—a law which, therefore, is one not so much of our discovery as of our own unconscious enacting. There is no denying, even so, that the maxim suits the whims of nature well. Our overwhelming success in predicting and controlling our environment, for good or ill, bears ample witness.

Rudolf Carnap gave us a masterful schema or caricature, in *Der logische Aufbau der Welt,* of how this law or maxim governs our conceptual construction of the world. His construction begins with basics; for present purposes, with the color patterns in one's visual field. These constitute a two-dimensional array, as in a painting. He proposes to project these spots of color into three-dimensional space, assigning each spot of color to a position in space that is to be deemed to be sending that ray to the eye. The direction from the eye to the position in space is fixed by the position of the spot in the visual field, but the distance remains an open question. The question is to be settled, Carnap explains, by adjusting all the distances in such a way as to keep the color changes as few and gradual as possible from place to place and from time to time. Retrospective revisions of the distances will be called for as new visual displays emerge, in order to maintain the smoothest overall history. Carnap's construction is a model in miniature of our projection of the world of enduring things, observed and unobserved, from the data of observation.

This is no game for babies, nor for other dumb animals young or old. The animal responds distinctively, by instinct or training, to qualitatively different stimulations: distinctively to sunshine, to rain, to cats, to people. The dog will recognize the recurrence of one person as distinct from another, but only because of a qualitative criterion, the smell, and not by virtue of any conceptual interpolation of unobserved excursions. The question will never arise whether some object is the old familiar one or another just like it. Dogs do ponder simple problems and solve them, I believe, but the scope of their thought can scarcely exceed that of the human infant, for want of the conceptual matrix of unseen but enduring things.

Tolerance

The state of the world, present or imminent, is in Albert Wohlstetter's chilling phrase a delicate balance of terror. Wary of tipping that balance, we face another: a delicate balance of tolerance. Democratic regard for civil rights and due process affords a shelter for subversive efforts of enemy agents and for seditious activities of native sympathizers. An enemy despot can send his fifth column through democracy's open gates while keeping his own gates secured.

Some restraints on democratic tolerance are thus vital to the survival of democracy. Excessive restraints, on the other hand, would be an abdication of democracy. Such, then, is the delicate balance of tolerance. All of us, governors and governed, appreciate the weighty considerations on both sides of the balance. I am not one of those, if such there be, who know how best to strike the balance. I can only appreciate its delicacy.

The balance of tolerance is no less delicate, though less desperately urgent, in spheres other than national security. A conspicuous sphere is that of sexual mores. Pressed by the rebellious youth of the sixties, the courts summoned literary experts for professional testimony on pornography. Being professors and hence liberals *ex officio,* the experts did not hesitate to set their faces steadfastly against censorship in every shape, form, and manner. Not for them the mawkish prudery of psalm-singing shopkeepers and unschooled rustics. Their forthright stand was readily bolstered by *ex cathedra* pronouncements on human nature: strip away the taboos and sex will dwindle to its just proportions; licentiousness will lose its charms. The solons, touchingly deferential to academic authority, accordingly proceeded to devise a supportive reinterpretation of the federal constitution.

Moral censorship down the years had monitored an ill-defined limit of legitimacy that was regularly pressed, tested, and moderately violated by the literary, artistic, and popular forces for prurience. Burlesque skits had made merry with sexual themes by *double entendre* and thinly veiled allusion that brought down the house. Press the bounds, however narrowly drawn, and titillation was assured.

Withdrawing the bounds did away with the titillation. So far, perhaps, so good; but this was the least of the effects. Pornography burgeoned, ready with ever more extravagant lures lest custom stale. Also apart from such excesses the public prints, films, and broadcasts relaxed their restraints to a marked degree. General standards of taste in speech and behavior could then be counted on to evolve or dissolve apace, dictated as they are by the public prints, films, and broadcasts.

It was a bewilderingly abrupt relaxation of the restraints of centuries, and no small achievement on the part of vocal students, liberal English teachers, and a few docile jurists. There were deeper social forces, also, that have yet to be understood. One conspicuous factor, superficial still, was the widespread spirit of rebellion induced by the Vietnam war, when sympathy with the enemy was open and defiant. Insofar, tolerance of the sort that we first considered played a role: tolerance of subversion.

The sudden sexual revolution was not just the lifting of censorship. Landlords and hostelers, long forbidden by law to accommodate unwed couples, could now be told not to ask personal questions. It was a refreshing change. But the courts were left facing stubborn new problems regarding marital or quasi-marital responsibilities and titles to property. Deeper dislocations of a social kind are being wrought by the weakening of the family.

Restoration of a new and optimum equilibrium calls for a thoughtful and painstaking balancing of gains and losses. Tolerance there must be, and some manner of restraint. Good social scientists have a golden opportunity here to distinguish themselves in the interests of society.

A third domain for tolerance or for talk of it, and a proverbial one, is religion. Here the question of a proper balance of tolerance is peculiarly delicate, because the answer varies abruptly with the point of view. Militant atheism aside, religious tolerance tends to be inversely proportional to religious faith. If someone firmly believes that eternal salvation and damnation hinge on embracing his particular religion, he would be callous indeed to sit tolerantly back and watch others go to hell.

If on the other hand someone subscribes to no religion, and is appalled by the inhumanity of religious intolerance, then his moral course of action would evidently be to try to stamp out religion and, therewith, religious intolerance. This puts him in the paradoxical position of religious intolerance in turn—intolerance of all religion. Such, then, is the militant atheist. Let us just hope that he exercises his intolerance humanely.

Yet I am not prepared unequivocally to cast my lot with the militant atheist either, however humane his militance. There remains a burning question of the social value of the restraints and ideals imposed by some religions, however false to facts those religions be. If this value is as great as I suspect it may be, it poses a melancholy dilemma between promoting scientific enlightenment and promoting wholesome delusion. The remote desideratum remains clear enough: imbue some future generation with moral values independent of religious myth or mysticism. Meanwhile perhaps a delicate balance of religious tolerance is called for after all: a delicate balance between militant atheism on the one hand and all manner of reasonably humane religions on the other. For the placing of the point of balance we must look again to the wisest of the sociologists, whichever they may be.

A question of tolerance closely parallel to the religious one recurs at a less consequential level in the teaching of controversial subjects such as philosophy. There should be a balanced representation of rival philosophies, it is urged. True enough, if one is concerned only with the history or sociology of philosophy; correspondingly for the history and sociology of religion. But if one pursues philosophy in a scientific spirit as a quest for truth, then tolerance of wrong-headed philosophy is as unreasonable as tolerance of astrology would be on the part of the astrophysicist, and as unethical as tolerance of unitarianism on the part of the hell-fire fundamentalist.

Still, in staffing a philosophy department and setting up a curriculum, other considerations intrude. Philosophy enjoys less firmness and conclusiveness than astrophysics, so that there is some lack of professional consensus as to what even qualifies as responsible philosophy. The astrologer's counterpart in philosophy can enjoy a professional standing such as the astrologer cannot.

Thus pressed, the philosophy department convenes to elect a representative of a prominent philosophical movement or tradition that none of those present finds intellectually respectable. Short of refusal, how might one make the conscientious best of the predicament? I once put it to Sir Stuart Hampshire, and he suggested appraising the candidate on his scholarly command of his benighted philosophical persuasion. Scholarship is a matter on which an objective and essentially scientific consensus can prevail, however disreputable its subject matter.

Might one better just resist the appointment? Perhaps so in most cases, but the cases are not to be lightly chosen. Grave danger lurks of pernicious dogmatism. What if the philosophy that we are bent on snubbing were better than we think? I can only conclude this last phase of my topic inconclusively, again, as to where to strike the delicate balance of tolerance.

Trinity

A predilection for threes has invested song and story. We have the Three Fates, the Three Graces, the Three Magi, the Three Musketeers, the Three Bears, the Three Little Maids from School.

Immanuel Kant's metaphysical categories came in threes. Those of Quantity were Unity, Plurality, and Totality. Those of Quality were Reality, Negation, and Limitation. I could go on. He even boggled at a dichotomy of judgments into affirmative and negative, if only for its want of trinity, or threeness. He settled for affirmative, negative, and infinite. And where would Hegel have been without thesis, antithesis, and synthesis?

Semiotic or the theory of signs, according to Charles Sanders Peirce (1839–1914), was concerned with a three-way relation. What were related were the *sign,* the *object,* and the *interpretant.* He trichotomized the *signs* into *qualisigns, sinsigns,* and *legisigns* according to what sorts of things they were in their own right (no questions, please), and into *rhemes, dicent signs,* and *suadisigns* according to how they were represented by their interpretant,

and into *icons, indices,* and *symbols* according to how they sig-
nified their objects. *Symbols,* in particular, he classified further
into *terms, propositions,* and *arguments*; and *arguments* in turn he
classified into *deductions, inductions,* and *abductions.*

Charles Morris, an admirer of Peirce and a fellow admirer
of the number three, produced *Signs, Language, and Behavior*
(1946), in which he divided the domain of semiotic into *syntax,
semantics,* and *pragmatics.* This trichotomy, taken up by Carnap,
has been faithfully cited and adhered to for forty years, despite
the fact, as I see it, that the separation between semantics and
pragmatics is a pernicious error. I suspect that the durability of
this trichotomy is due to its trinity.

Another durable trichotomy, somewhat outside of semiotics,
was drawn in 1933 by Max Black in the philosophy of mathematics: there are *logicism, formalism,* and *intuitionism.* To this
day any general account of the philosophy of mathematics from
south of our border, and most from north or northeast of it,
can be counted on to begin with this trichotomy. I venture to
say that, among other strengths, 3 is a prime factor.

An air of strength and stability is conferred by trinity. Thus
Liberty, Equality, Fraternity; also Life, Liberty, and the Pursuit
of Happiness; Faith, Hope, and Charity; and again Spirit,
Mind, and Body. Would spirit have had to be invoked here as
a supplement to mind, or vice versa, if a need had not been
felt for a triad? Or take the example on page 177, where we
style ourselves "faithful, true, and loyal." One of the three
would seem to have covered the ground if trinity had not been
reckoned as independently valuable. Well, that and the melody.

Trivial, then, injects an odd irony. Little strength or stability
there. It is from *trivium,* the fork in the road, where three ways
(*tres viae*) converge and passers-by pause in their passing by to
bandy trivialities. Still, *trivium* resumes its supportive role in
the medieval schools, the *tres viae* being grammar, logic, and
rhetoric.

Last but scarcely least, we have the Holy Trinity. Father and

Son make good substantive sense, at least by analogy (cf. Thomas Aquinas), but there is something tenuous about the Holy Ghost, suggestive again of trinity for trinity's sake.

The stability of three legs is symbolized in the *triskelion,* a heraldic device consisting of three legs radiating swastika-wise from a hub. It was an emblem in ancient Sicily, where it was encouraged by the triangular shape of the island, the ancient Trinacria. But it appeared also in the Isle of Man, where its connotation of stability became explicit in the motto *Quocunque jeceris stabit.*

The stability of three comes down to brute and homely fact when we look upon the three-legged stool and contrast its firmness with the wobbly four legs or the toppling two. The underlying geometry is elementary. Three points always lie in a plane; four need not. Three points lie in *only* one plane; two lie in many.

Again there is the rigidity of the triangle. The geometry of this is that two triangles with matching sides are bound to be congruent, while other polygons with matching sides are not.

Truth

Philosophy primers tell of two opposing doctrines as to the nature of truth: the coherence theory and the correspondence theory. Neither theory, when naively stated, can be taken seriously. The coherence theory would have it that the truths qualify as such simply by all hanging together as a logically consistent system. The correspondence theory would have it that they qualify as true by corresponding to reality.

The coherence theory, thus baldly stated, seems to rest on an irrational rationalism—on the absurd idea that the infinite totality of possible statements admits of only one overall distribution of yesses and noes that is logically consistent. Moreover, the theory makes no visible demands on observation and experiment. On this showing we can receive it only as a dummy doctrine, a straw man or whipping boy.

On the other hand the correspondence theory, as thus far stated, is vague or vacuous. What on the part of true sentences is meant to correspond to what on the part of reality? If we seek a correspondence word by word, we find ourselves eking reality out with a complement of abstract objects fabricated for the sake of the correspondence. Or perhaps we settle for a correspondence of whole sentences with *facts*: a sentence is true if it reports a fact. But here again we have fabricated substance for an empty doctrine. The world is full of things, variously related, but what, in addition to all that, are facts? They are projected from true sentences for the sake of correspondence.

But let us ponder this last maneuver for a moment. The truth of 'Snow is white' is due, we are told, to the fact that snow is white. The true sentence 'Snow is white' corresponds to the fact that snow is white. The sentence 'Snow is white' is true if and only if it is a fact that snow is white. Now we have worked the fact, factitious fiction that it is, into a corner where we can deal it the coup de grace. The combination 'it is a fact that' is vacuous and can be dropped; 'It is a fact that snow is white' reduces to 'Snow is white'. Our account of the truth of 'Snow is white' in terms of facts has now come down to this: 'Snow is white' is true if and only if snow is white.

Here, as Tarski has urged, is the significant residue of the correspondence theory of truth. To attribute truth to the sentence is to attribute whiteness to the snow. Attribution of truth to 'Snow is white' just cancels the quotation marks and says that snow is white. Truth is disquotation. An ignominious end, one may feel, to the correspondence theory of truth. But we shall see later that it is more gnominious than it looks.

A place remains also for something like the coherence theory. The significant contrast between the correspondence theory and the coherence theory, when we set the untenable details aside, is that correspondence looks to the relation of the true sentence to what it is about, such as the white snow, while coherence looks to the relations of the true sentence to other sentences. Some sentences, to begin with, we accept as true directly on the strength of observation; the essential mechanism here is a conditioning of strings of words to sensory stimulations. Further sentences are rated as true on the strength of systematic connections with the observation sentences. We work out the neatest world system we can that conforms to the record of observations, and we tighten the squeeze by multiplying the observations. (See ATOMS; PREDICTION; THINGS.) Here is the reasonable place to appeal to coherence, in a vaguer but richer sense than logical consistency.

Coherence and correspondence, properly considered, are not rival theories of truth, but complementary aspects. The coherence aspect has to do with how to arrive at truth, by the best of our lights. The correspondence aspect has to do with the relation of truths to what they are about.

We saw the correspondence theory dwindle to disquotation. The attribution of truth to a statement is equated to the statement itself. This has been called the disappearance theory of truth, but unjustly; the quotation marks are not to be taken lightly. What can justly be said is that the adjective 'true' is dispensable when attributed to sentences that are explicitly before us. Where it is not thus dispensable is in saying that all or some sentences of such and such a specified form are or are not true, or that someone's statement unavailable for quotation was or was not true, or that the libel laws do not apply to true statements, or that you will tell the truth, the whole truth, and nothing but the truth, so help you God. In such contexts, when paraphrased to fit PREDICATE LOGIC, what stands as subject of the truth predicate is not a quotation but a VARIABLE. It is there that the truth predicate is not to be lightly dismissed.

The disquotational account may be said still, in a sense, to *define* truth. It intelligibly demarcates all our intelligible truths, by rendering the truth of each sentence as intelligible as the sentence itself. But in a stricter sense it does not define truth. It does not tell us how to eliminate the adjective 'true', by paraphrase, from every context in which it can grammatically occur. It only tells us how to eliminate it when it is attached to a quotation. Definition in the strict sense is elimination, and this is not wholly forthcoming. We can be thankful, for we know at least one context where its definability would involve us in self-contradiction. See the final formulation of the Liar Paradox in the piece on PARADOXES. It is remarkable how nearly definable we just now found truth to be, and how trivially, and yet how lethal its genuine definability would be.

Tarski undertook to press the definition of truth. The "object language," whose truths were to be covered, comprised the notation of PREDICATE LOGIC with an unspecified lexicon of predicates. His strategy was RECURSION: start by defining the concept in application to atomic sentences, and then show how the definition, when achieved for sentences of any given degree of complexity, can be extended to the next. But he could not define truth in this way, because of the variables. Atomic sentences are neither true nor false; 'Fxy', say 'x inhabits y', is true *of* certain pairs of objects as values of the free variables 'x' and 'y', and false of others. It is only when all the variables in a sentence have been bound by quantifiers that we have a *closed* sentence, true or false.

What Tarski does define recursively is *satisfaction* of a sentence *by* an object or sequence of objects as values of its free variables. Truth falls out afterward, trivially; a closed sentence is true if it is satisfied by the sequence of length zero, so to speak.

It is a masterly construction when seen in detail, and it goes through. Why then does it not saddle us with the Liar Paradox after all? The answer emerges when we try to write the paradoxical sentence in the object language, using symbolic logic and whatever elementary devices go into talking about appending expressions to quotations (see end of PARADOXES). The word 'true' figures in the paradoxical sentence in such a way that in the explicit reconstruction it has the context 'x is true' where 'x' is subject to a quantifier. But the recursive definition of satisfaction and truth does not show how to eliminate 'satisfies x', or 'x is true'; it eliminates 'satisfies' and 'is true' only when these are predicated of explicitly given open or closed sentences. We are emphatically reminded of the gulf between recursive and direct definition.

We know how to turn a recursive definition into a direct one (see RECURSION), but the method draws on resources of set theory which, in the present instance, the object language must be presumed incapable of supplying. Add them and you do get a language in which truth and satisfaction for the old object language can be directly and fully defined; but still further set-theoretic resources would then be needed for direct definition of truth and satisfaction with respect to this strengthened language. We are headed up the hierarchy of levels of truth and denotation that was glimpsed under PARADOXES.

I must end on a somber note by reporting that all is perhaps not well in the hierarchy. What if two men say of each other on a given day that everything he said that day was true? Each of these two statements, then, would have to rank higher in the hierarchy than the other. Saul Kripke argues★ that quite casual and useful ascriptions of truth can get lodged crosswise in the hierarchy in similar but more complicated ways. He devises an alternative concept of truth that is univocal, rather than hierarchical, and yet can consistently be expressed within the language to which it applies. It avoids paradox by neither holding nor failing of certain sensitive sentences. Thus it suspends the law of EXCLUDED MIDDLE. Also it is discouragingly complex. Let me just say again that all is not well.

Type versus Token

ES IST DER GEIST DER SICH DEN KÖRPER BAUT: such is the nine-word inscription on a Harvard museum. The count is nine

---

★ *Journal of Philosophy,* 1974.

because we count *der* both times; we are counting concrete physical objects, nine in a row. When on the other hand statistics are compiled regarding students' vocabularies, a firm line is drawn at repetitions; no cheating. Such are two contrasting senses in which we use the word *word*. A word in the second sense is not a physical object, not a dribble of ink or an incision in granite, but an abstract object. In this second sense of the word *word* it is not two words *der* that turn up in the inscription, but one word *der* that gets inscribed twice. Words in the first sense have come to be called *tokens*; words in the second sense are called *types*.

A still further distinction can be drawn if we consult grammatical refinements. The word *der* figures as an article in its first occurrence and as a relative pronoun in its second. On this score it might be reckoned as two words, not one, even as types. My present purposes are better served, however, by abstracting from grammatical and semantical distinctions and addressing just the sheer forms of words.

The type, one is prepared to say, is the class of all its tokens. The type *der* has two of its members on the museum at Harvard and a host of others in books throughout Germany. This account fits *der* and other words well enough, but it breaks down when we press it to strings of words. What about two little lines of pentameter that are fated never to get thought up? Taken as classes of their tokens, each of the lines is identically the empty class; so there is but one. This we find unacceptable. We do not want to say that every possible line of pentameter, save one, is destined someday to be uttered or written.

When sharp formulations are offered for concepts that had been vague, they sometimes result in bizarre rulings along the edges, bizarre but harmless. Computer engineers call them don't-cares. Our present case, however, is quite the contrary: decidedly a care. Fruitful work in the mathematical theory of proof, stemming from FORMALISM and issuing in GÖDEL'S THEOREM and computer theory, hinges on the existence and distinctness of strings of signs of all finite lengths.

The postulate can be put thus: *If* a *and* b *are different strings, then the string consisting of* a *followed by* c *differs from* b *followed by* c. If types were the mere classes of their tokens, this would be false. For, if the strings *a* and *b* have actually been written but are destined never to get written with *c* appended, then the two strings with *c* appended would both be the empty class, if construed as the classes of their tokens, and would thus be identical, contrary to the postulate.

Classes are abstract objects (see CLASSES VERSUS PROPERTIES), but classes of tokens are not in general abstract enough for types. They do well enough for types of single words or signs, we saw, for we can assure the existence of tokens at that level, and thus avert emptiness of the classes. So far, so good; let us then construe the types of single signs as the classes of their tokens. Types of strings of signs thereupon call for a different logical tack: we can construe them as finite *sequences* of the types of the component signs, taking 'sequence' not in its physical, spatial, or temporal sense but in its abstract mathematical sense, where failure of existence is no longer to be apprehended.

And just what is that mathematical sense? A finite sequence is a FUNCTION, *q.v.*, that assigns things to the positive integers up to some point. Where f is the function, the nth thing in the sequence is f of n.

Type and token nicely span the abstract and concrete, from lexicon to inscription. It is seldom appreciated that *occurrence* is a third thing: not token, but something between. The word *der* has two occurrences in the sentence *Es ist der Geist der sich den Körper baut*; and I speak now of types, not tokens. Tokens occur in tokens, types in types.

Just what sort of thing, then, is an occurrence? In 1940 I had to take an explicit stand on the matter, in writing about GÖDEL'S THEOREM.* I found that I could construe an occurrence of a

* *Mathematical Logic* (1940; Harvard, 1951), last chapter.

word or sign in an expression as the initial segment of the expression up to and including that word or sign. Thus the first of the two occurrences of *der* in question is the type *Es ist der,* and the second is *Es ist der Geist der.* This version is artificial but adequate; whatever needs to be said by reference to occurrences of words or signs can be said by reference to these segments, thanks to a one-to-one correspondence.

Units

We can visualize a square yard and a square mile, but what of a square hour? Well, I can say what to do with it. Multiply it by an acceleration and you get a length, as we shall see in a moment.

Consider velocity, to begin with. Sixty miles an hour. We also say, with a slight touch of the technical, sixty miles *per* hour; succinctly, 60 mi/hr. Here *per* is the 'by' of 'divided by', as in 8 percent, or *per centum,* which is eight divided by a hundred, or .08. So much for Lesson 1.

Acceleration, next, is velocity divided by time. It is how much the velocity increases each hour, or each second; choose your unit. The velocity of a falling body, in feet per second, increases by about 32 each second; so the acceleration is about 32-feet-per-second *per second,* or (32 ft/sec)/sec, or, clearing fractions somewhat, 32 ft/sec^2. Acceleration is thus length divided by square time. Multiply the falling body's acceleration by a square second and you get a length: 32 feet. Multiply the falling body's acceleration by a square hour, instead, and you get a length too: 414,720,000 feet, actually, or 78,545 miles, nearly enough.

This does *not* mean that the body would fall that far in an hour. It would fall only half that far according to our figure of 32, which, anyway, does not apply at such distances from the earth. It does not apply near the earth either, for that matter, because of air resistance. My figures, for all their undeniable fascination, are studiously useless.

The number of square seconds in a square minute is the square of the number of seconds in a minute, hence 3,600. Thus there are just as many square seconds in a square minute as there are seconds in an hour. On the other hand there are 12,960,000 square seconds in a square hour.

Multiplication of dissimilar units is a familiar matter. Work is measured in foot-pounds. Money divided by work, then—dollars per foot-pound—gives a measure of earning facility; and its inverse, foot-pounds per dollar, measures earning difficulty. Pure number divided by money—one per dollar—measures bracket creep: the increase of tax rate with increase of income. Bracket creep is the reciprocal of money.

The foot-acre is unfamiliar but self-explanatory: a measure of volume, like the liter. It is enough water to cover an acre to a depth of a foot. The liter-hour is unheard of but eminently worthy of notice, for it is a unit for measuring the spatio-temporal lifetime bulk of a human being or other creature. (See SPACE-TIME.) Someone whose average bulk over his lifetime is sixty liters racks up a whacking lifetime bulk of nearly 37 million liter-hours in the course of his three score years and ten.

Measures of length, squared, give us measures of area: square yards, hectares, acres. The square root of an acre is about seventy yards. And what, in turn, is the square root of a yard? It defies imagination. Better: it *is* an imaginary unit, just as the square root of −1 is an imaginary number.

Next question: What is a square acre? Is it the volume of a cube each of whose faces is an acre? Here indeed is an imposing vision, but it is not the answer; a square acre has to have four dimensions. This puts it in a class with the liter-hour, except that its fourth dimension is not pinned down to time. If we take it to be time, then a square acre is the spatio-temporal bulk of a cube, an acre on a face, over a period the temporal equivalent of about seventy yards, whatever that is (see SPACE-TIME).

Acres and square hours find a niche in the energy concept if we look to the sweatshirt logo of relativity, "$E = mc^2$." Here c is a velocity, namely that of light, hence distance divided by time; so c^2 is squared distance divided by squared time, or acres per square hour. Finally m is mass; so the sweatshirt logo equates energy with acre tons per square hour. Let me say in extenuation that clarity of conception is not my present objective.

The scales of temperature lend themselves to less frivolous thoughts. Degrees Fahrenheit and degrees Celsius are proportional in size, five to nine, but they count up and down from different zero points. The bottomless negatives in these scales make no sense below $-273°$ C, or $-459.4°$ F, because at that point there is no heat at all: no movement of molecules. The Kelvin scale takes that point as zero and counts upward only, in Celsius degrees; thus $0°$ C = $273°$ K.

What I find interesting, then, is that we can nevertheless devise bottomless scales of temperature that do make full sense at all points. Thus we might take our zero as the old $0°$ C, and our 1 as the old $1°$ C, but then we might take our upward degrees as progressively larger than the Celsius degrees, and our descending ones as progressively smaller. Specifically, having taken our first degree above zero as $1°$ C, we might inflate our next higher degree by the slight factor of 1/273, and the next by that factor twice over, and so on up, while correspondingly shrinking all degrees from zero downward. The general formula is this: n degrees on the new scale, positive or negative, is equal to $274^n/273^{n-1}$ in degrees Kelvin.

What is interesting about this is that it shows the existence or nonexistence of a bottom temperature to be a question not of physics but merely of conventional measurement, even though the presence or absence of heat is a matter of physical fact. Our novel scale squeezes infinitely many degrees in between 0° C and 0° K. It is a logarithmic scale. Or, we could retort, the usual scales are logarithmic relative to it.

A similar trick can be played on the measurement of time, for the comfort of people (not you, not me) who puzzle about what could have been going on before the Big Bang (see CRE-ATION). By switching to a logarithmic scale, we can push the Big Bang back infinitely far, thereby declaring that there was always a world and never the Bang. Steven Weinberg's first three minutes expand to half an eternity. Scientific theory carries over intact, translated into the new units. But the translation calls for a compensatory rescaling of spatial measures, with the unwelcome result that past sizes are inflated and future ones are deflated. Atoms of the remote past take on cosmic proportions.

Universal Library

There is a melancholy fantasy, propounded a century and more ago by the psychologist Theodor Fechner and taken up by Kurt Lasswitz, Theodor Wolff, Jorge Luís Borges, George Gamow, and Willy Ley, of a complete library. The library is strictly complete, boasting as it does all possible books within certain rather reasonable limits. It admits no books in alien alphabets, nor any beyond the reasonable length say of the one you are now reading, but within those restrictions it boasts all possible books. There are books in all languages, transliterated where necessary. There are coherent books and incoherent, predominantly the latter. The principle of accession is simple, if uneconomical: every combinatorially possible sequence of letters, punctuation, and spaces, up to the prescribed book length, uniformly bound in half calf.

Other writers have sufficiently belabored the numbing combinatorial statistics. At 2,000 characters to the page we get 500,000 to the 250-page volume, so with say eighty capitals and smalls and other marks to choose from we arrive at the

500,000th power of eighty as the number of books in the library. I gather that there is not room in the present phase of our expanding universe, on present estimates, for more than a negligible fraction of the collection. Numbers are cheap.

It is interesting, still, that the collection is finite. The entire and ultimate truth about everything is printed in full in that library, after all, insofar as it can be put in words at all. The limited size of each volume is no restriction, for there is always another volume that takes up the tale—any tale, true or false— where any other volume leaves off. In seeking the truth we have no way of knowing which volume to pick up nor which to follow it with, but it is all right there.

We could narrow down the choice by weeding out the gib- berish, which makes up the bulk of the library. We could insist on English, and we could program a computer with English syntax and lexicon to do the scanning and discarding. The residue would be an infinitesimal fraction of the original, but still hyperastronomic.

There is an easier and cheaper way of cutting down. Some of us first learned from Samuel Finley Breese Morse what others of more mathematical bent knew before his time: that a font of two characters, dot and dash, can do all the work of our font of eighty. Morse actually used three characters, namely dot, dash, and space; but two will suffice. We could use two dots for the space and then admit no initial or consecutive dots in encoding any of the other old characters.

If we retain the old format and page count for our volumes, this move reduces the size of the library's collection to the 500,000th power of two. It is still a big number. Written out it would fill a hundred pages in standard digits, or two volumes in dots and dashes. The volumes are skimpier in thought con- tent than before, taken one by one, because our new Morse is more than six times as long-winded as our old eighty-character font of type; but there is no loss in content over all, since for each cliff-hanging volume there is still every conceivable sequel on some shelf or other.

This last reflection—that a diminution in the coverage of each single volume does not affect the cosmic completeness of the collection—points the way to the ultimate economy: a cutback in the size of the volumes. Instead of admitting 500,000 occurrences of characters to each volume, we might settle for say seventeen. We have no longer to do with volumes, but with two-inch strips of text, and no call for half-calf bindings. In our two-character code the number of strips is 2^{17}, or 131,072. The totality of truth is now reduced to a manageable compass. Getting a substantial account of anything will require extensive concatenation of our two-inch strips, and a re-use of strips here and there. But we have everything to work with.

The ultimate absurdity is now staring us in the face: a universal library of two volumes, one containing a single dot and the other a dash. Persistent repetition and alternation of the two is sufficient, we well know, for spelling out any and every truth. The miracle of the finite but universal library is a mere inflation of the miracle of binary notation: everything worth saying, and everything else as well, can be said with two characters. It is a letdown befitting the Wizard of Oz, but it has been a boon to computers.

Universals

If called upon to think of an object, just any object at all, we come up with some middle-sized body. Such are our objects first and foremost. In their image, scientists have gone on to postulate further bodies and quasi-bodies smaller and sketchier than meet the eye. Early and late there has been recognition also of abstract objects, or *universals*—thus properties, numbers, functions, classes. But the nominalists, philosophers of the stripe of William of Ockham, drew the line there. They repudiated universals as mere *flatus vocis*, which is to say voice blowing, or yackety-yack.

One spontaneously sympathizes with these no-nonsense

hardheads who make short shrift of intangible objects and suchlike moonshine. Seeing them persist in using predicates such as 'house' or 'human' and abstract nouns such as 'size' or 'humanity' as freely as the rest of us, however, we get to wondering: Just what are they in their hardheadedness really claiming or disclaiming? "Yes, we use those general and abstract words, but there are no correspondingly general or abstract objects." We agree that there are no such correspondents among the physical objects, but what does it mean to go on and say that there are or are not corresponding abstract ones? The moonshine, one begins to suspect, is on the other foot. Well, scratch 'foot'.

In some cases the nominalist can indeed defend his repudiation of universals by showing how to eliminate the suspect word. Belief that Gaul is divided into three parts commits us to the three parts but not, he claims, to a fourth object which is the number 3; and his defense is that there being three parts means only that there are parts x, y, and z such that $x \neq y$, $y \neq z$, and $x \neq z$. He has eliminated mention of the number 3. He shows similarly that belief in twelve Apostles and nine planets does not entail belief in numbers 12 and 9.

But he does not come off so easily when the reference is to numbers generally rather than specifically to just 3 or 12 or 9. Thus consider gravitation between two bodies. It is said to vary inversely with the square of their distance apart. This means that the attraction between them when they are a mile apart is x^2 times what it would be if they were x miles apart— for *all* numbers x. On the face of it our sentence is about bodies and numbers, the latter as irreducibly as the former.

At this point th'embattled nominalist might face the challenge of eliminating also the general reference to numbers, perhaps by trying to devise some scheme of paraphrase involving general reference to concrete numerical inscriptions instead. It would have to be an artificial and intricate scheme, certainly, to allow for the scattered multiplicity of inscriptions that express the same number. And it is surely hopeless for an opposite reason, the lack of inscriptions for most numbers. Actually this chance failure to have been written down is not all; there are countless REAL NUMBERS (*q.v.*) that we have no *way* of designating. Yet serious science is utterly dependent on unstinting appeal to numbers, as in the gravitation example. Science subsists on measurement, quantitative method, concomitant variation. See PREDICTION.

What now about other universals—properties, classes? Blithe spirits who are prodigal with their ontologies are prepared to recognize a property for any predicate. Whatever is said about a thing is felt to ascribe a property to it—or, equivalently, to assign the thing to a class. Actually even the blithe spirits have to stop somewhere, on pain of contradicting themselves. A moment's reflection or a peek into the entry on PARADOXES suffices to show that when we say of some class that it is not a member of itself we do not thereby assign it to a class of all non-self-members; for that class, if it existed, would have to be a member of itself if and only if it was not. Similarly when we say of some property that it is not a property of itself we do not thereby ascribe a property to it.

The nominalist, shunning properties and classes from the start, holds that they simply are not invoked by his bandying of general terms or predicates. His term 'dog' or 'fierce' or 'bark' denotes or is true of each concrete object that is a dog or is fierce or barks; such alone is its business, and no supplementary reference to an abstract class or property. Insofar I find the nominalist quite within his rights.

'Dog', 'fierce', and 'bark' are concrete general terms. Abstract singular terms are another thing: 'caninity', 'ferocity'. These do purport to designate universals, properties. The nominalist's strategy with them, as with the numerals '3', '12', and '9' earlier, would be to show how to avoid or eliminate them by paraphrase in each specific case, or anyway each useful case. Here again he may be expected to give a pretty good account of himself.

His nemesis, in the example of gravitation, lay rather in the generalized reference to individually unspecified numbers. So likewise with classes, or properties: reference to them *en masse* is what is irreducible. Nor is it to be dismissed as idle and dispensable. It is a powerful device for deriving one concept from another, even in domains not concerned with classes or properties as such. A neat example, considered at length under RECURSION, is Frege's definition of a man's ancestor as anyone who belongs to every class that contains the man's parents and the parents of all its own members. Mathematics, in particular, depends heavily on generalized appeal to classes—more heavily than meets the eye until we delve into the logical substructure. And generalized appeal to classes is familiar elsewhere in science, as when we are told that there are so many thousand species of beetles.

We imagined a desperate and ill-starred project, on the nominalist's part, of paraphrasing general reference to numbers into general reference to inscriptions. A similar project for classes or properties would be equally hopeless, for parallel reasons. We even find under INFINITE NUMBERS that classes, like numbers, outrun not only actual inscriptions but all possible modes of specification.

It is borne in on us by our various examples that a serious commitment to objects of one or another sort is to be looked for, not in the apparent references to single instances, but in the blanket references to instances in general. The term 'dog' passes innocently over the single abstract class or property that is dogkind or caninity, but makes blanket reference to concrete dogs in general. For universals, correspondingly, the decisive passages were the blanket references 'thousands of species' in the beetle example, 'every class that contains' in the ancestor example, and 'for all numbers x' in the gravitation example. Once science has been accommodated in the Procrustean bed of PREDICATE LOGIC, the ontologically pertinent turns of phrase are the quantifiers: 'everything x is such that', 'something x is such that'. To be is to be the value of a VARIABLE.

If to the nominalists' sorrow science is saddled with abstract objects, still there is some forlorn interest in noting that all these abstract needs, numbers and the rest, can be neatly subsumed under one: classes. If we admit all concrete objects, all classes of them, all classes of concrete objects *and* their classes, and so on up in a cumulative way, then we can indeed meet all the ontological needs of natural science. See NATURAL NUMBERS; REAL NUMBERS; COMPLEX NUMBERS; FUNCTIONS; CLASSES VERSUS PROPERTIES. But the abstract ontology is no less exorbitant for all that, and far from congenial to nominalist tastes. All that can be said by way of consolation is that some hope is held out, under CONSTRUCTIVISM, of a middle ground.

Usage and Abusage

We read that *abdómen* and *anchóvy* are the correct pronunciations, and thereafter we tend to avoid the words, despite even our taste for anchovies, disliking as we do to speak incorrectly on the one hand and to sound incorrect, even vulgar, on the other. We learn that *forte,* said of someone's strong point, is to be pronounced not in the elegantly disyllabic fashion of the Italian musical annotation, but as the French monosyllable; and thereafter we avoid the word, as we so easily can, disliking, again, to err on the one hand and to sound ignorant to unschooled ears on the other.

Fools, however, rush in. I overheard a woman, not of my acquaintance, saying: "He wants me to learn the computer, but it's not my for*tay*." I know something else that isn't her for*tay*.

Fortuitous for 'fortunate', *precipitous* for 'precipitate', and *luxurious* for 'luxuriant' are widely enough recognized as malapropisms to present no problem, rife though they are in virtually literate circles. Literates are divided more nearly haff and hahf in their awareness that our verb *eke,* cognate with the German adverb *auch,* means only supplementation and has nothing to do with the skin of one's teeth. I even heard a seemingly cultivated newscaster go so far as to speak of *eking through*.

Even the best of us, very nearly, are unaware that the meaning of *hectic* was 'chronic'. I say 'was' because the shift has been so massive. Not to be a party to the shift, I happily eschew the word. I still have 'chronic' for its old sense and 'frantic' for the new.

Which reminds me: what can possess anyone to say 'phrenetic' or 'ferocious' when he can say 'frantic' and 'fierce'?

It is heartwarming to hear *transpire* used correctly, and not an everyday occurrence. Similarly for *flair*. People picture a flaring flame of enthusiasm where they would do better to picture a great snout with flaring nostrils, sniffing out the bouquet. Actually even this good usage was the outcome of an earlier SEMANTIC SWITCH. The word is related to the Latin *fragrare,* which meant emitting the fragrance rather than detecting it. That shift, however, is beyond redemption.

Charisma lingered in the theological backwaters down the centuries. It meant 'gift', first in the literal sense and then in the sense of a talent. The different sense that it has taken on in recent years as a fad word in intellectual circles is due surely to its resemblance to *charm*. The word itself is evidently endowed with the same mysterious and exotic charm that it has come to be regarded as denoting.

Other fad words are *format* and *obverse*. They are straightforward and even indispensable on home ground in typography and numismatics, but in their increasingly indiscriminate use elsewhere they contribute at best a spurious air of professionalism, and error into the bargain. *Format* is seldom heard outside typography to mean anything but 'form', and *obverse* gets ignorantly applied to the back side instead of the front where it belongs.

I recall a time when *definitively* could be heard in the sense not of 'definitively' but of 'definitely'; but this ornament has mercifully subsided.

My fellow Americans in seemingly increasing numbers have

taken to saying *brochures* for what are called leaflets in English and *feuillets* in French. But perhaps they also say *brochures* for what are called pamphlets in English and *brochures* in French.

If I were intent on touching all bases, I would touch also on *hopefully*.

If fads are needed, why not content oneself with *No way, basically, No problem, Enjoy,* and *Have a nice day,* which bore without corrupting? Even in *being into* (jogging, ceramics, you name it), however solecistic, there is a trace of playfulness that is hygienic as far as it goes. You know what I mean?

We cannot stem linguistic change, but we can drag our feet. If each of us were to defy Alexander Pope and be the last to lay the old aside, it might not be a better world, but it would be a lovelier language. Readers who feel moved to join forces in this quixotic crusade are referred further to PLURALS.

Use versus Mention

Christian Morgenstern's werewolf betrayed intellectual limitations when he asked the schoolmaster to decline him. We do not decline people, or even werewolves; we decline words. Confusion of things with their names, signs with their objects, is confusion of use and mention.

To mention something we use its name, or some description. In saying that Boston has thirteen councilmen we use the name of the city and thereby mention the city, as I have just done. Little mystery thus far, thanks to the happy circumstance that there is little less like a city than a name. Mentioning cities and other concrete objects is child's play; just use their names.

Caution begins to be in order, however, when we take to mentioning names. To mention a name, like anything else, you use a name of it. Boston is not disyllabic, but 'Boston' is; the quotation serves as a name of the name. A quotation names its insides. It is a name of its own guts.

Nor let it be supposed that 'Boston' is a quotation. 'Boston' is just a six-letter word, and contains no quotation marks. To mention the quotation we use *its* name, a quotation of the quotation. ' 'Boston' ' contains one pair of quotation marks.

In mathematical writings, where there are no concrete objects such as cities to cleave to, confusion of use and mention is rife. The following passage, from a widely used textbook on the differential calculus, is fairly typical:

The expression $D_x y \Delta x$ is called the *differential* of the function and is denoted by *dy*:

$$dy = D_x y \Delta x.$$

The third line of this passage, an equation, is apparently supposed to reproduce the sense of the first two lines. But actually, whereas the equation says that the entities *dy* and $D_x y \Delta x$ (whatever these may be) are the same, the preceding two lines say rather that the one is a name of the other. And the first line of the passage involves further difficulties; taken literally it implies that the exhibited expression '$D_x y \Delta x$' constitutes a name of some other, unexhibited *expression* which is known as a differential. But all these difficulties can be removed by a slight rephrasing of the passage: drop the first two words and put the first occurrence of '*dy*' in quotation marks.★

Mathematicians' carelessness over use and mention has led to philosophical confusions about *identity*. Thus Leibniz explained identity as a relation between the signs, rather than between the named object and itself: "*Eadem sunt quorum unum potest substitui alteri, salva veritate.*" Various mathematicians, including Whitehead at one point (in *Universal Algebra,* 1898), were led to look upon equations as relating numbers that are equal but distinct. Count Alfred Korzybski, in *Science and Sanity,* went so far as to propound a doctrine of nonidentity:

★ Here I have transcribed a paragraph from my *Mathematical Logic* (1940; Harvard, 1951), p. 25.

identities are always false. Even '1 = 1' is false, he wrote, because the two numerals are unlike at least in position. He confused the ink spots with the number, abstract and invisible.

Granted, a robust nominalist will have no truck with abstract objects such as numbers. That still does not reduce '1 = 1' to an identification of ink spots; it rates it as not identifying anything.

Strict observance of the distinction between use and mention of expressions is essential to clear thinking, no matter what one's philosophical position may be regarding the reality of abstract objects that those expressions may purport to name. Clarity of the distinction is indispensable, in particular, to an understanding of the proof of GÖDEL'S THEOREM, and of Tarski's work on TRUTH.

Some philosophical diffidence regarding the existence of UNIVERSALS such as numbers has perhaps been a factor in mathematicians' mishandling of use and mention. The difference between a number and the numeral that names it does not vividly obtrude if there is no number, but it should. There being a numeral but no number should surely be difference enough.

Anyway the metaphysics of abstract objects is quite beside the point of use versus mention. Be there numbers or be there none, the point is to distinguish between the use of the numeral, '5' say, and the mention of *it*. We mention '5' when we contrast it with its modern Arabic counterpart, which looks more like '0', or when we explain that the curved lower part of '5' derived from three strokes, making for a five-stroke character. We use '5' when we say there are 5 fingers on a hand, or 5 New England states other than one's own.

Confusion of use and mention can surface in subtle ways also beyond the bounds of mathematics, as this dialogue illustrates: "Well, pătronage, pātronage, as you please." "You seldom get one without the other."

Quotation is one of two usual ways of naming an expression. The other way, customary in linguistic studies, is putting the expression itself in italics. This way is impractical in treating of mathematical and logical formulas, which are largely in italics to begin with, or in alien alphabets, or in none. This book deals largely with matters where it is usual to name expressions by italics, and largely also with matters where it is usual to name them by quotation. I have wanted to conform to custom on both sides, and yet to maintain some semblance of consistent usage. I have found I can reconcile these three desiderata to some degree by using italics when the main interest lies in the form or history of the expression, and quotation otherwise.

There is another use of quotation marks, called sneer quotes or scare quotes, that is not meant to switch use to mention. It serves rather to mark the expression as one that the writer is using without recommending. It has the force of use without prejudice, or, in Yiddish, *soll mir nicht schuldigen*. Italics also of course have uses other than the naming of expressions—notably, as just now, for foreign languages.

The naming of expressions by quotation proves inadequate when we rise to generalities. Thus the logician wants to say that the sentence 'Tufa floats or tufa does not float', and all sentences like it, are true. *Like* it? Well, where ϕ is any sentence, 'ϕ or not ϕ' is true. No, this will not do. If the letter 'ϕ' is being used as a variable ranging over sentences (see VARIABLES), or in effect as a name of an unspecified sentence, then it is grammatically a noun, and 'ϕ or not ϕ' is not a sentence at all, much less true. What we want to say is rather that 'ϕ or not ϕ' *becomes* true when the letter 'ϕ' is supplanted in it by the sentence ϕ. In 1940 I introduced a notation of *quasi-quotation* for the purpose: $\ulcorner\phi$ or not $\phi\urcorner$ is to be understood as the result of supplanting 'ϕ' by ϕ in 'ϕ or not ϕ'. The general convention is that the quasi-quotation designates what its insides would become if all its Greek letters were supplanted by the expressions they designate. The device has been taken up, for it is needed in some logical studies. I have avoided it in this book;

I would simply say, if occasion arose, that 'p or not p' is true where 'p' stands in place of any sentence. I have gone into the matter now only to illustrate that there is more to quotation and its like than at first meets the eye. For still more in that vein see TYPE VERSUS TOKEN.

Variables

If the amount of some substance available for packaging at one time is different from the amount available at another, it is fairly usual and highly professional to speak of the amount as variable. It is as if there were those various amounts at the various times, 837 gallons for example, and then, over and above all those amounts, some further amount that is simply called *the* amount and is said, unlike them, to vary from time to time. Of course this doesn't fool anybody.

The idiom is pressed farther. It has long been customary to use a letter, first and foremost the proverbial '*x*', as if it were a name of that phantom number, on a par with numerals like '837' that are names of genuine numbers.

A somewhat different and more celebrated role of that same letter is as an *unknown:* something to solve for in high-school algebra. Variation is not the idea there; *x* is some fixed number, and the problem is to find out which one. It varies only from problem to problem. In both of these roles, however, and in further uses as well, '*x*' and its fellow letters are called variables. We must acquiesce in the word, which is well entrenched, and let its etymology go. But the word is to be seen as referring to the letters themselves, in their pertinent uses, and not to some strangely unstable sort of number. Every number is simply what it is, as Bishop Butler might have said, and not another thing.

Numbers, indeed, are the least of it; variables in their various uses can range over objects of any sort. As for those various uses, they are not so various after all when we probe their inner nature. Variables are essentially pronouns. I shall make the connection by turning to pronouns and building out from that side.

Pronouns are so called because they sometimes stand for a repetition of a singular noun as in 'John took off *his* hat and hung *it* up', which is to say 'John took off *John's* hat and hung *John's hat* up'. Such are the pronouns of laziness, as Peter Geach calls them. They are of no logical or philosophical interest and of little interest even to linguistics. On the other hand 'Sadie stole something and sold it' tells us more than that Sadie stole something and sold something. The 'it' here is not a pronoun of laziness; it is serious business. Pronouns in their serious use are even a more serious business than the singular nouns themselves, as may be sensed in reading the pieces on PREDICATE LOGIC and UNIVERSALS. Charles Sanders Peirce quipped that nouns might more justly have been called pro-pronouns.

The true genius of the pronoun is manifested in the relative clause. This is a device for packaging what a sentence says about something. What the sentence 'I bought Fido from a man who found him' says about Fido can be packaged in the relative clause 'that I bought from a man who found him'. In the relative pronoun 'that' here, and the pronoun 'him' that refers back to it, we see the logically fundamental role of pronouns. Our relative clause here can be thought of as an adjective phrase, and in effect our original sentence about Fido predicates this adjective phrase of Fido. A more succinct adjective phrase to the same effect is 'bought from finder', but the importance of the relative clause is that it is a uniform device for abstracting what any sentence says about anything.

The uniformity in the construction of relative clauses can be heightened and contortions in word order can be avoided, at some cost in stylistic elegance, by switching to the 'such that' idiom. We get 'such that I bought him from a man who found him'. The recipe for constructing such a clause from a sentence is simple: just prefix 'such that' to the sentence and substitute a pronoun for the noun from which you are abstracting. The 'such that' idiom is helpful in coping with intricate contexts; hence its popularity in mathematical writing.

Our present example actually shows one relative clause nested within another. Converting the inner one likewise into the 'such that' idiom, we get 'such that I bought him from a man such that he found him'. At this point a latent ambiguity is activated: who found whom?

The mathematician settles matters by putting distinctive letters for his ambiguous pronouns and then labeling each 'such that' with its appropriate letter, thus: 'x such that I bought x from a man y such that y found x'.

Here, I say, is the birth of the variable: in the disambiguation of nested 'such that' clauses, which is to say nested relative clauses. This is not true historically, but it could have been. It is a myth of origins that reveals the basic role and ultimate utility of the variable. The variable is a device for marking and linking up various positions in a sentence so as to encapsulate, in an adjective phrase, what a sentence says about something. Its business is linking and permuting.

This is not just an example of the use of variables; it is the whole story. All use of variables is reducible to their use as the pronouns of 'such that' clauses. When we solve the equation '$x + 5 = 9$' the unknown x we are finding is the number x *such that* $x + 5 = 9$. Most uses of variables, when written out explicitly, already exhibit the 'such that' construction in so many words: thus 'the class of all objects x such that . . .', 'everything x is such that . . .', 'something x is such that . . .'. Incidentally the last two contexts listed, known as quantifiers, can be shown to suffice; all others can be paraphrased in terms of these. Indeed either of the two quantifiers suffices alone; the other can be paraphrased in terms of it.

Z

Zero

The word derives from the Arabic and is the same in origin as *cipher,* for all their dissimilarity. The number itself, for all its self-effacement, is an incalculable boon to the human calculator, as is borne in on anyone who tries to do sums and products in Roman numerals. Our Arabic numeration owes its efficacy to its use of the successive positions in a string of digits to indicate successive powers of, as it happens, ten (see DECIMALS AND DIMIDIALS). Zero is what enables us to hold open any unused intervening places.

A primitive and clumsy forerunner of what we call Arabic numeration seeped into Arab lands from India around 775, lacking zero. Addition of zero is said to change nothing, but what a change it wrought! It was added by 875, both in Hindu and Moslem circles. Arabic numerals in some form entered Christian Europe from Moslem Spain in 972, but without zero. By 1020 a Hindu mathematician was fully articulate on zero, enunciating the laws '$a \pm 0 = a$' and '$a \cdot 0 = 0$'. Zero flourished in China by 1250, thanks to India, and was known to Fibonacci in Pisa by 1220. Such is the testimony of my sundry secondary sources.

We know how accountants in ancient Rome were able to cope with their clumsy numerals: they had the abacus. Since it operates on the same principle as our Arabic positional notation, one may wonder why zero was so slow in surfacing. The answer must lie in perennial confusions over nothingness. A bemused Plato reasoned that nonbeing must in some sense be, otherwise what is it that there is not? In our own day Martin Heidegger ventured that *das Nichts nichtet*—"the nothing nothings"—evidently still sensing a problem. Anomalies of nothingness have lent themselves readily to tired humor, as in Gershwin's "I got plenty o' nothin'" and in Lewis Carroll's atypically uninspired bit about the Anglo-Saxon messenger passing nobody on the road.

Related perplexities lingered in logic into modern times. 'Nothing' is a false substantive, along with 'something', 'everything', 'everyone', and the like. Grammatically these behave like nouns, but logically they do not. Where 'x' stands for a genuine noun, 'x is red' and 'x is not red' are incompatible; yet 'Something is red' and 'Something is not red' are both true. Again 'x is red and not red' is self-contradictory, but 'Nothing is red and not red' is logically true. As late as 1900 some symbolic logicians were trying to handle these false nouns somewhat similarly to real ones, and were having their troubles. They did not know that Frege with his quantifiers had had such matters under control by 1879. (See PREDICATE LOGIC.)

Perplexity more like Plato's lingered in modern logic over the empty class, Λ. The perplexity may have been aggravated by the notion that a class consists of its members, and so cannot exist without members. When this misconception is corrected (see CLASSES VERSUS PROPERTIES), there is no bar to Λ. Once Λ is recognized, 0 can be clearly identified too: either as the singleton $\{\Lambda\}$, as by Frege (see NATURAL NUMBERS), or as Λ itself, as by von Neumann.

Even when understood, 0 has its awkward side. It is the one number, as we so well know, that we cannot divide by. And even if we accommodate $n/0$ after all by admitting ∞ to the number system, our troubles are not over. We would have $1/0 = \infty = 2/0$, and hence seemingly $1 = 0 \cdot \infty = 2$. Having admitted ∞ for the sake of $n/0$, we would have to forbid multiplication of ∞ by 0.

A lesser oddity of 0 emerges when we look to $n!$, read 'n factorial'. It is the product of all integers from 1 to n. Clearly we have to dodge 0 here; the product of all integers from 0 to n is 0. Evidently then 0! is inadmissible. Actually it can be accommodated, by an amusingly devious course. Since in general $(n + 1)!$ is $n + 1$ times $n!$, just take n as 0 and you have $1! = 1 \cdot 0!$. But $1! = 1$. So $0! = 1$.

Index